Panda3D 1.6 Game Eng

Beginner's Guide

Create your own computer game with this 3D rendering and game development framework

David Brian Mathews

PUBLISHING

BIRMINGHAM - MUMBAI

Panda3D 1.6 Game Engine
Beginner's Guide

Copyright © 2011 Packt Publishing

First published: February 2011

Production Reference: 1040211

Published by Packt Publishing Ltd.
32 Lincoln Road
Olton
Birmingham, B27 6PA, UK.

ISBN 978-1-849512-72-5

www.packtpub.com

Cover Image by Charwak A (charwak86@gmail.com)

Credits

Author
David Brian Mathews

Reviewers
Paulo Barbeiro Ferreira

Joni Hariyanto

Acquisition Editor
Usha Iyer

Development Editor
Reshma Sundaresan

Technical Editors
Arun Nadar

Manasi Poonthottam

Indexer
Hemangini Bari

Editorial Team Leader
Mithun Sehgal

Project Team Leader
Ashwin Shetty

Project Coordinators
Zainab Bagasrawala

Joel Goveya

Proofreaders
Aaron Nash

Jonathan Todd

Graphics
Nilesh R. Mohite

Production Coordinator
Kruthika Bangera

Cover Work
Kruthika Bangera

About the Author

David Brian Mathews is a graduate in Electronic Visualization program from the University of Illinois at Chicago. He began programming in the fifth grade with QBASIC and has been designing games of various kinds, from table-top board games to computer games, since childhood. Prior to entering higher education, he served for two years in the United States Navy as a nuclear engineer before being honorably discharged for medical reasons, where he learned discipline, advanced mathematics, and nuclear theory, as well as teamwork and leadership skills. During his years in school, Mathews earned valuable experience with professional game development methods working both by himself and with teams. He is skilled at programming, 3D modeling and animation, drawing, and 2D compositing.

I'd like to thank my friends and family, who have been immensely supportive of me throughout the writing of this book. In particular, I'd like to thank my mother, Carol Malley, and my friends Jeff Fuja and William Hebert for all their efforts and sacrifices on my behalf.

About the Reviewers

Paulo Barbeiro Ferreira is Brazilian, from São Paulo, and graduated in Graphic Design in 2004 at Belas Artes SP college. He is a postgraduate in Game Development at SENAC SP. Paulo started his professional career in 1999 as a web developer.

Today, besides the web and mobile application development work, Paulo is involved in experimental educational projects in technology and cyber culture at SESC SP, where he leads activities about creative code and art software, such as interactive environments, games, and entertainment media.

Joni Hariyanto graduated from the Engineering Faculty of Brawijaya University a few years ago. Now, he works as a freelance architect.

Actually, he's just a hobbyist in the computer science world. He has been programming since first grade junior high in languages including Pascal, Python, and C++.

Bored with the never changing architectural visualization teaching materials at uni, he wandered on the Internet searching for a way to get unlimited control over visualization, for the sake of design clarity and without sacrificing too much time in the "post-design" phase; that is, rendering the gazillion frames.

He stumbled upon Panda3D in 2005, a free 3D game engine, which makes perfect balance of power, flexibility, and handling (from programmer's point of view). Liked it, melted with it in no time, thanks to Python.

www.PacktPub.com

Support files, eBooks, discount offers, and more

You might want to visit www.PacktPub.com for support files and downloads related to your book.

Did you know that Packt offers eBook versions of every book published, with PDF and ePub files available? You can upgrade to the eBook version at www.PacktPub.com and as a print book customer, you are entitled to a discount on the eBook copy. Get in touch with us at service@packtpub.com for more details.

At www.PacktPub.com, you can also read a collection of free technical articles, sign up for a range of free newsletters and receive exclusive discounts and offers on Packt books and eBooks.

http://PacktLib.PacktPub.com

Do you need instant solutions to your IT questions? PacktLib is Packt's online digital book library. Here, you can access, read and search across Packt's entire library of books.

Why Subscribe?

- Fully searchable across every book published by Packt
- Copy and paste, print, and bookmark content
- On demand and accessible via web browser

Free Access for Packt account holders

If you have an account with Packt at www.PacktPub.com, you can use this to access PacktLib today and view nine entirely free books. Simply use your login credentials for immediate access.

Table of Contents

Preface

Panda3D is a game engine, a framework for 3D rendering and game development for Python and C++ programs. It includes graphics, audio, I/O, collision detection, and other abilities relevant to the creation of 3D games. Also, Panda3D is Open Source and free for any purpose, including commercial ventures. This book will enable you to create finished, marketable computer games using Panda3D and other entirely open source tools, and then sell those games without paying a cent for licensing.

Panda3D 1.6 Game Engine Beginner's Guide follows a logical progression from a zero start through the game development process all the way to a finished, packaged installer. Packed with examples and detailed tutorials in every section, it teaches the reader through first-hand experience. These tutorials are followed by explanations that describe what happened in the tutorial and why.

You will start by setting up a workspace, and then move on to the basics of starting up Panda3D. From there, you will begin adding objects such as a level and a character to the world inside Panda3D. Then, the book will teach you to put the game's player in control by adding changes over time and responses to user input. Then, you will learn how to make it possible for objects in the world to interact with each other by using collision detection and beautify your game with Panda3D's built-in filters, shaders, and texturing. Finally, you will add an interface, audio, and package it all up for the customer.

This is a simple but detailed guide to using Panda3D, which will take you from a blank text file all the way through the Python programming process to a finished game with a single level, including such topics as handling tasks over time, event handling and response, collision set up and detection, audio, and more.

Who this book is for

This book is targeted at independent developers who are interested in creating their own video games or other 3D applications for personal or commercial distribution at minimal expense. A basic understanding of general programming, such as knowing what a variable is, is necessary. Some familiarity with object-oriented programming and the Python language is expected, but not required.

Development teams who are interested in using Panda3D for production of 3D applications or video games would also find this book useful for training team members in the use of Panda3D.

This book does not cover the creation of three-dimensional models or similar art assets, nor does it cover the creation of two-dimensional art assets or audio assets.

What this book covers

Chapter 1, Installing Panda3D and Preparing a Workspace guides the reader through downloading and installing Panda3D and Notepad++ (an open source text editor) as well as acquiring assets provided with the book (from CD or website) and setting up the file structure for that content using Windows Explorer.

Chapter 2, Creating the Universe: Loading Terrain is the reader's first opportunity to get their hands dirty with some coding. It will take them from a blank file to a simple program that will load up a terrain model and introduce related basic concepts.

Chapter 3, Managing Tasks Over Time introduces the reader with tasks, the task manager, and controlling processes that need to occur over time or in an ongoing manner.

Chapter 4, Taking Control: Events and User Input focuses on creating user controls for the game. Keyboard, mouse click, and mouse movement response will be covered. Camera control will be integrated with handling mouse input.

Chapter 5, Handling Large Programs with Custom Classes; as the game has grown larger, the time has come to show the reader how to break it apart into custom classes.

Chapter 6, The World in Action: Handling Collisions will focus on making the reader comfortable with collision detection and the different collision event handlers. Collisions are vital to a working game and their use is one of the hottest topics on the Panda3D forums.

Chapter 7, Making it Fancy: Lighting, Textures, Filters, and Shaders will explain textures and the built-in shaders available in Panda3D while allowing the reader to apply lighting, textures, filters, and shaders to the world and the characters in it.

Chapter 8, GUI Goodness: All About the Graphic User Interface takes the reader through the production of the game's GUI, including the HUD that displays during game play, the start menu, and other bits and pieces.

Chapter 9, Animating in Panda3D; here the reader will replace the static models of hover cycles with actors and learn all about actor animation and joint manipulation.

Chapter 10, Creating Weaponry: Mouse Picking and Intervals focuses on using intervals to create weapons and their controls and describes how sequences and parallels can be used to create interval scripts.

Chapter 11, What's that Noise? Using Sound; here with the game nearly complete, it's time to introduce some sound effects and background music to bring the game to life. This chapter also introduces editing the `config.prc` file to change the audio library Panda3D uses.

Chapter 12, Finishing Touches: Getting the Game Ready for the Customer is the final chapter of the guide and focuses on some important functions for Panda3D-based games, including saving and loading files, garbage collection, and packing the game into a standalone package ready for shipping.

Appendix A, Creating a Sky Sphere with Spacescape teaches the reader how to use the freely available software Spacescape to create engaging backdrops for Panda3D applications.

Appendix B, Using Egg-Texture-Cards and ExploTexGen; here the reader learns how to create explosion animations with the freely available software ExploTexGen and learns to turn them into Panda3D assets with the Egg-Texture-Cards command-line utility.

What you need for this book

Panda3D 1.6, Notepad++, and Python.

Conventions

In this book, you will find several headings appearing frequently.

To give clear instructions of how to complete a procedure or task, we use:

Time for action – heading

1. Action 1

2. Action 2

3. Action 3

Instructions often need some extra explanation so that they make sense, so they are followed with:

What just happened?

This heading explains the working of tasks or instructions that you have just completed.

You will also find some other learning aids in the book, including:

Pop quiz – heading

These are short multiple choice questions intended to help you test your own understanding.

Have a go hero – heading

These set practical challenges and give you ideas for experimenting with what you have learned.

You will also find a number of styles of text that distinguish between different kinds of information. Here are some examples of these styles, and explanations of their meanings.

Code words in text are shown as follows: "The event name we give to the `accept()` method is a string that serves as an identifier for the unique event we want to respond to."

A block of code is set as follows:

```
if(self.keyMap["d"] == True):
    self.turn("r", dt)
elif(self.keyMap["a"] == True):
    self.turn("l", dt)
```

When we wish to draw your attention to a particular part of a code block, the relevant lines or items are set in bold:

```
self.menuGraphics = loader.loadModel(
    "../Models/MenuGraphics.egg")
self.fonts = {
    "silver" : loader.loadFont("../Fonts/LuconSilver.egg"),
    "blue" : loader.loadFont("../Fonts/LuconBlue.egg"),
    "orange" : loader.loadFont("../Fonts/LuconOrange.egg")}
```

New terms and **important words** are shown in bold. Words that you see on the screen, in menus or dialog boxes for example, appear in the text like this: "Now we see an entry for the **Cycle Move** task in the **sleep** column".

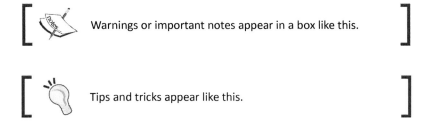

Warnings or important notes appear in a box like this.

Tips and tricks appear like this.

Reader feedback

Feedback from our readers is always welcome. Let us know what you think about this book—what you liked or may have disliked. Reader feedback is important for us to develop titles that you really get the most out of.

To send us general feedback, simply send an e-mail to feedback@packtpub.com, and mention the book title via the subject of your message.

If there is a book that you need and would like to see us publish, please send us a note in the **SUGGEST A TITLE** form on www.packtpub.com or e-mail suggest@packtpub.com.

If there is a topic that you have expertise in and you are interested in either writing or contributing to a book, see our author guide on www.packtpub.com/authors.

Customer support

Now that you are the proud owner of a Packt book, we have a number of things to help you to get the most from your purchase.

Downloading the example code for this book

You can download the example code files for all Packt books you have purchased from your account at http://www.PacktPub.com. If you purchased this book elsewhere, you can visit http://www.PacktPub.com/support and register to have the files e-mailed directly to you.

Downloading the color images of this book

We also provide you a PDF file that has color images of the screenshots used in this book. The color images will help you better understand the changes in the output. You can download this file from https://www.packtpub.com/sites/default/files/2725_images.pdf

Errata

Although we have taken every care to ensure the accuracy of our content, mistakes do happen. If you find a mistake in one of our books—maybe a mistake in the text or the code—we would be grateful if you would report this to us. By doing so, you can save other readers from frustration and help us improve subsequent versions of this book. If you find any errata, please report them by visiting `http,//www.packtpub.com/support`, selecting your book, clicking on the **errata submission form** link, and entering the details of your errata. Once your errata are verified, your submission will be accepted and the errata will be uploaded on our website, or added to any list of existing errata, under the Errata section of that title. Any existing errata can be viewed by selecting your title from `http,//www.packtpub.com/support`.

Piracy

Piracy of copyright material on the Internet is an ongoing problem across all media. At Packt Publishing, we take the protection of our copyright and licenses very seriously. If you come across any illegal copies of our works, in any form, on the Internet, please provide us with the location address or website name immediately so that we can pursue a remedy.

Please contact us at `copyright@packtpub.com` with a link to the suspected pirated material.

We appreciate your help in protecting our authors, and our ability to bring you valuable content.

Questions

You can contact us at `questions@packtpub.com` if you are having a problem with any aspect of the book, and we will do our best to address it.

1

Installing Panda3D and Preparing a Workspace

It's time to take the first big step. In this chapter we're going to acquire Panda3D and get our work environment set up. Once we have all that done, we're going to take a look at the game we'll be creating over the course of this book.

In this chapter we shall:

- ◆ Download and install Panda3D
- ◆ Download and install Notepad++
- ◆ Install all of the content necessary for the game
- ◆ Demo the game we'll be creating
- ◆ Install any optional tools desired
  - ❑ Blender and Chicken
  - ❑ Spacescape
  - ❑ Explosion Texture Generator

There's no time to waste, so let's get cracking!

Getting started with Panda3D installation packages

The kind folks who produce Panda3D have made it very easy to get Panda3D up and working. You don't need to worry about any compiling, library linking, or other difficult, multi-step processes. The Panda3D website provides executable files that take care of all the work for you. These files even install the version of Python they need to operate correctly, so you don't need to go elsewhere for it.

Time for action – downloading and installing Panda3D

I know what you're thinking: "Less talk, more action!" Here are the step-by-step instructions for installing Panda3D:

1. Navigate your web browser to `www.Panda3D.org`.

2. Under the **Downloads** option, you'll see a link labeled **SDK**. Click it.

3. If you are using Windows, scroll down this page you'll find a section titled **Download other versions**. This book is written for Panda3D version 1.6.2, which is the most current stable version at the time of writing. Find the link to **Panda3D SDK 1.6.2** and click it. If you aren't using Windows, click on the platform you are using (Mac, Linux, or any other OS.). That will take you to a page that has the downloads for that platform. Scroll down to the **Download other versions** section and find the link to **Panda3D SDK 1.6.2**, as before.

Panda3D SDK 1.7.0
The latest unstable, experimental release.

Panda3D SDK 1.6.2
The latest stable release.

4. When the download is complete, run the file and this screen will pop up:

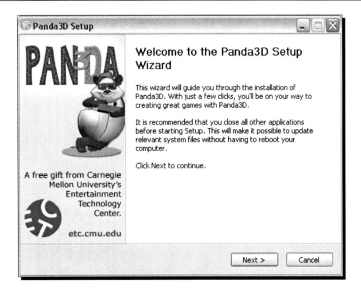

5. Click **Next** to continue and then accept the terms. After that, you'll be prompted about where you want to install Panda3D.

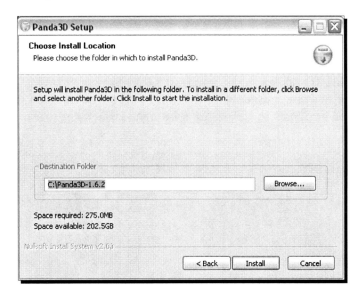

6. The default location is just fine. Click the **Install** button to continue. Wait for the progress bar to fill up. When it's done, you'll see another prompt.

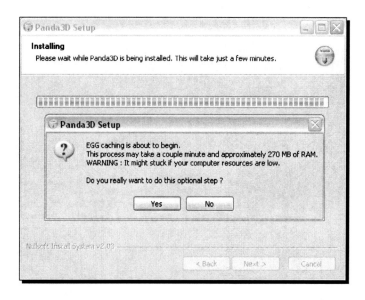

7. This step really isn't necessary. Just click **No** and move on.

8. When you have finished the installation, you can verify that it's working by going to **Start Menu | All Programs | Panda3D 1.6.2 | Sample Programs | Ball in Maze | Run Ball in Maze**. A window will open, showing the Ball in Maze sample game, where you tilt a maze to make a ball roll around while trying to avoid the holes.

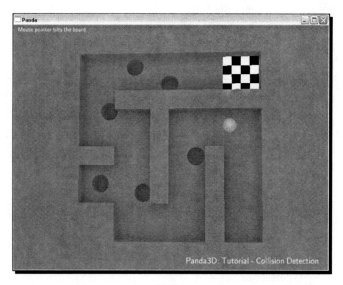

What just happened?

You may be wondering why we skipped a part of the installation during step 7. That step of the process caches some of the assets, like 3D models and such that come with Panda3D. Essentially, by spending a few minutes caching these files now, the sample programs that come with Panda3d will load a few seconds faster the first time we run them, that's all.

Now that we've got Panda3D up and running let's get ourselves an advanced text editor to do our coding in.

Switching to an advanced text editor

The next thing we need is Notepad++. Why, you ask? Well, to code with Python all you really need is a text editor, like the notepad that comes with Windows XP. After typing your code you just have to save the file with `.py` extension. Notepad itself is kind of dull, though, and it doesn't have many features to make coding easier.

Notepad++ is a text editor very similar to Notepad. It can open pretty much any text file and it comes with a pile of features to make coding easier. To highlight some fan favorites, it provides language mark-up, a Find and Replace feature, and file tabs to organize multiple open files. The language mark-up will change the color and fonts of specific parts of your code to help you visually understand and organize it. With Find and Replace you can easily change a large number of variable names and also quickly and easily update code. File tabbing keeps all of your open code files in one window and makes it easy to switch back and forth between them.

Time for action – downloading and installing Notepad++

Now that you're convinced, let's get Notepad++ up and running. If you aren't convinced or want to use some other software to code with, that's fine. Just skip to the next section.

1. Navigate your web browser to `http://notepad-plus-plus.org`. Click on the **Download** tab on the page.

2. Click the link to **Download Current Version**.

3. Click the link that ends with **Installer.exe**.

4. When your download is finished run the file and you'll see this screen pop up:

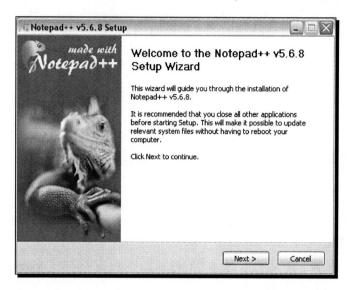

5. Click **Next** to get the installation started and accept the terms. You'll be prompted again about where you want to install.

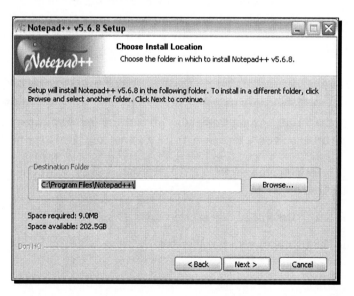

6. Again, the default directory is just fine. Click **Next** and you'll find yourself prompted once more, this time about the components you want to install.

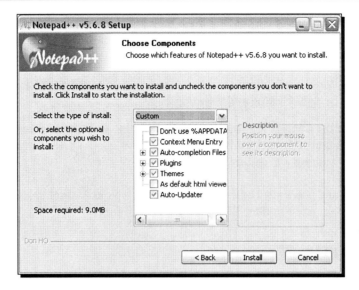

7. The default configuration contains everything you'll need, so just click **Install**. When it's done go ahead and open Notepad++ so it can update itself if necessary.

What just happened?

That does it for Notepad++. Next we need to install all the game content we'll be using as we go through the tutorials in this book.

Installing the game content

To get all the content for the game that will be used over the course of the book, head to the Packt website and download the code file . Unzip the file, and place the folder BGP3D in an easy-to-get-to place on the system. For Windows users, the C: drive is recommended.

Time for action – demoing Suicide Jockeys

The last thing we'll cover in this chapter is how to load a Panda3D game from the command prompt. Until the game is packaged and ready for shipping, this is how we'll run it. Don't worry, it's easy.

1. Open a command prompt by going to the **Start menu | All Programs| Accessories** and choosing **Command Prompt**.

2. Open Windows Explorer the same way.

3. In Windows Explorer click on the **View** menu at the top, highlight toolbars, and if Address Bar does not have a check before it, click on it. This will show your current directory in the window.

4. Navigate Windows Explorer to `BGP3D/Demo` and copy the entire address bar with *Ctrl+C* or by right-clicking and selecting **Copy**.

5. Return to the Command Prompt window and type in `cd` followed by a space. Then right-click on the Command Prompt window and select **Paste**. This will insert the directory address you copied from Windows Explorer.

6. Hit *Enter* and you'll see the directory in the Command Prompt change. Next, type in `python main.py` and hit *Enter*. The game will launch.

What just happened?

Not bad, right? We just learned how to run a Python file from the command prompt, something we'll be doing quite a bit. The `python` command we used tells the system to use the Python interpreter to run the file we supply.

`main.py` is the name of the file that starts Panda3D and the game components. We'll go into more depth about how that works in the next chapter, so get ready!

Installing optional tools

There are a couple of optional tools that you can get for free and are worth pointing out. These tools are great for specific things, but none of them are strictly necessary for this book since all of the content they create is provided with the book. Nevertheless, we'll mention them here and provide tutorials on using some of them in the appendices for later projects when you've finished this book and need to create your own content for your own games. Since these tools are optional we won't go step-by-step through their installations, but we will tell you where you can find them.

Blender and Chicken

Blender is an open source, free to use, 3D modeling and animation package based in Python. It's a full service package that's quite powerful and even used in some professional studios. Furthermore, it has an active community and lots of tutorials available on the web to help get new users up to speed with the program. A significant portion of the Panda3D community uses Blender to create their 3D content as well.

Another feather in Blender's cap isn't part of the core package but bears mentioning. That is Chicken, a plug-in for Blender that exports models and animations in .egg files, one of the formats that Panda3D uses. Chicken let's you directly export from Blender to Panda3D without any intermediate conversions, and if you have experience with game development you know how nice that sort of simple pipeline from content creation to implementation really is. If you don't have that experience, then take our word for it. **It's really nice.**

You can find Blender, and some Blender tutorials, at www.blender.org. Blender v2.5 introduces some major changes that Chicken is not currently compatible with, so it may be wise to get an older version. Blender is available in executable installers, and all the default options work just fine. Do note that Blender doesn't come with Python like Panda3D does. To get the most out of Blender, install the version of Python it requires. For example, Blender v2.49 requires Python v2.6. The version of Python that comes with Panda3D is v2.5, so that won't work. Also, the latest version of Python at the time of this writing, v2.7, also won't work. Python does offer older versions on their website, and version 2.6.6 will work with Blender v2.49. Python also comes in executable installers, and again the default options are fine. Having both versions of Python on one computer won't cause any conflicts either. The Blender installer will direct us to the Python website when it fails to detect a Python version that it can use, but that website is at www.python.org if needed. Python documentation can also be found there.

You can find Chicken at http://chicken-export.sourceforge.net/. Chicken doesn't provide an executable installer, but the zip file that it does come in has a text file with installation instructions for various platforms in it. Note that in order for Chicken to work with Blender, the appropriate version of Python must be installed as noted in the previous paragraph.

Spacescape

The next optional tool was created by Alex Peterson and is used for creating sky boxes. If that's a new term to you, a sky box is basically a very large cube placed around an outdoor environment in a game that provides a backdrop. Spacescape in particular is designed for creating space environments, full of stars and nebulas. The nice thing about spacescape is that it exports all six of the images you need for a sky box, one for each face, and they are all seamless and virtually ready to use. For Panda3D, all you need to do is rename the files. Here are a few example of images you can make in Spacescape:

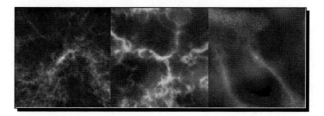

You can find Spacescape by searching for it on `sourceforge.net` or by going to Alex Peterson's blog at `http://alexcpeterson.com/spacescape`. Spacescape doesn't require any sort of installation, per se. All that's needed is to extract the zip file it comes in and place the folder that is contained in it somewhere on the computer. Once that's done, the program will run.

Explosion Texture Generator

This is another tool created by a single author, a gentleman by the name of Sascha Willems. Explosions are pretty common in video games but creating a series of images to turn into an animated "movie" of an explosion can be a real pain. This tool makes it much easier. All that's needed is to input a couple of values for the explosions before and the tool will produce a palette image with every frame of the animation you need. There's a good deal of customization available so you can create gobs of different explosion types. Also, the tool outputs `.png` files with the alpha already embedded in them, so you don't have to worry about what parts of the image need to be transparent. It's handled for you. Explosion Texture Generator can be found on Sascha Willems's web page at `http://www.saschawillems.de/?page_id=253`. Here's an example of the output this tool creates:

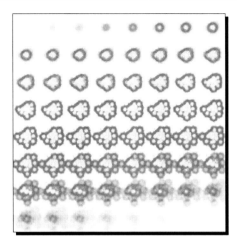

Like Spacescape, ExploTexGen doesn't require an installation. Just unzip the file and put the contents in a folder, then it will run as intended.

Summary

We spent most of the chapter installing the tools we need to use Panda3D.

We talked about and installed:

- Panda3D 1.6.2
- Notepad++

We also talked about some helpful optional tools that can be useful for creating game content. Oh, and let's not forget that we took a look at the demo for the game we'll be making over the course of this book!

We've got everything prepared now; it's time to move on to the real deal.

2
Creating the Universe: Loading Terrain

It's time to really get our feet wet. This chapter will lay out the foundation we need to start programming in Panda3D and take us into our first program. We'll talk about some basic concepts and then we'll see those concepts in action as we put together the beginnings of our game.

Here's what we're going to cover:

- Setting up a new file in Notepad++
- Importing Panda3D components
- Creating a World Object
- Loading the terrain
- Loading files into Panda3D
- NodePaths and nodes
- The Scene Graph
- Render attributes

Each of these points is very important in understanding how Panda3D operates. With that in mind, let's move on.

Notepad++

As we go through these points, we'll talk about Notepad++ as well. Notepad++ is user friendly and easy to get accustomed to, so these little interruptions will be short and sweet.

Setting up a new file in Notepad++

The first thing we need to do is create a new file and tell Notepad++ which mark-up language we want it to use. The mark-up will make reading our code much easier and can point out when we are using important keywords as well. It will also allow us to use Notepad++'s block sorting, which we'll talk about a little later in this chapter.

Time for action – setting up a new file in Notepad++

Now we know why we need to set up a new file properly, so let's do it.

1. Open Notepad++ by going to your **Start** menu | **All Programs** | **Notepad++** | **Notepad++**.

2. We already have a blank document to start with, so we just need to set the mark-up language. Click on the **Language** menu at the top of the screen, scroll down to **P**, and select **Python** from the pop-up menu.

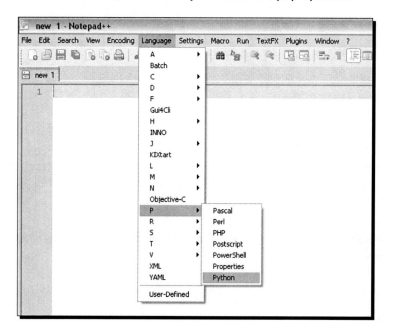

What just happened?

Now the document is set for Python and Notepad++ will mark-up our code for us.

So let's start coding.

Importing Panda3D components

In order to use Panda3D we need to start by importing the core components of the engine in our Python file. Fortunately, Panda3D is very accommodating. To get it running, we only need to import `DirectStart`.

Time for action – importing DirectStart

1. In your blank document type the following. Don't worry about the color and font of the word "**import**", that's Notepad++'s mark-up and it will be applied automatically.

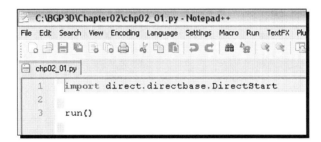

2. Save the file as `"chp02_01.py"` in the directory `"BGP3D/Chapter02"` in the file tree we set up last chapter.

3. Open up Windows Explorer and navigate to `"BGP3D/Chapter02"` in the file tree we set up last chapter. Then right-click on the address bar and copy the entire address. If you don't have an address bar, click on the **View** menu | **Toolbars** | **Address Bar** to display it.

4. Open a windows command prompt and type `"cd "`. Note the space at the end. Then right-click on the command prompt window and select **paste** to insert the address we copied. Hit *Enter*, and the command prompt will navigate to that folder.

5. Type `"python chp02_01.py"` into the command prompt and hit *Enter*.

```
C:\>cd C:\BGP3D\Chapter02
C:\BGP3D\Chapter02>python chp02_01.py_
```

What just happened?

The import command tells Python that you want to add to the file you're working on from another file.

```
import direct.directbase.DirectStart
```

Usually, when you import one of Panda3D's components it becomes available but it doesn't do anything more than that. `DirectStart` is a special import in that it executes immediately when it's imported.

`DirectStart` takes care of everything needed to start up Panda3D by creating the architecture that is necessary for Panda3D to run. This includes creating a default Panda3D window, the graphics pipe for the window, the renderer, the task manager, and more. To put it simply, `DirectStart` makes Panda3D go. The other statement is also very important:

```
run()
```

This call starts up the components created by `DirectStart` so that the game can operate. Without `run()`, the utility that controls all of Panda3D's actions, each frame wouldn't start. The game would be completely static. Panda3D relies on a main loop that performs several important operations, including processing graphics and rendering frames. Each time this main loop executes, it performs these functions, renders a frame, and then repeats. It can also call pieces of code we create, called **Tasks**, which we'll talk about in the next chapter. The call to `run()` starts this main loop.

As we go through more tutorials throughout this book we'll run into more objects that `DirectStart` creates for us, including the one that `run()` initiates. For now, we'll move on to the next step.

Creating a World Object

Let's take a moment to talk about object-oriented programming. OOP, as object-oriented programming is often abbreviated, is a design idea for organizing a program's code. Instead of creating a long list of line after line of code that defines the entire program all at once, we break it into pieces. For example, one of these code pieces might be all of the code that controls the player character in the game. Another might be the code for a menu. Because we break the program apart along these logical lines that pertain to objects within the program we refer to them as objects as well. That's where object-oriented programming gets its name.

We break the program apart by using classes. A class is a grouping of code that defines a type of object in the program, and it can be reused multiple times. Within a class we put the code that stores the values for the object and the code that makes the object perform whatever duties it needs to perform. A character class may contain variables for remaining health, instructions on how to attack, and so on.

When we define a class we are creating a type of object for our program to use, but to create an actual object of that type, we need to create an instance of the class. An instance is just what its name implies, a single object of the type defined by the class.

To understand this better, think about toy building blocks. They come in several shapes, sizes, and colors. We can think of each type of block, like the red 1x1 type of block, or the yellow 2x1 type of block, as a class. Each individual block is an instance of the class that describes its type. If we had four red 1x1 blocks, then we would have four instances of the red 1x1 class.

Just like building something from blocks we combine instances of classes to build a program in Panda3D. Keep in mind that our classes define the code for the building blocks that we will use to construct our game, and that each time we use one of those blocks, we're using an instance of a class.

We'll create our first type of building block now by defining a World class. We don't have to name it World; it could be named Core, MyGame, or whatever, but all the sample programs that come with Panda3D use the name World, so we will too.

In order for us to see our `World` in action, we'll need to make it do something. To keep it simple, we'll just change the color of the background.

Time for action – creating a World Object

1. Edit your .py file to look like this:

```
import direct.directbase.DirectStart

class World:
    def __init__(self):
        base.setBackgroundColor(0, 0, 0)

w = World()
run()
```

2. Save the file as "chp02_02.py" in the same directory.

3. Run this python file the same way you ran chp02_01.py.

What just happened?

A number of things are going on there, so we'll take a moment and talk about them.

First, we used the `class` command to create a new class called `World`.

```
class World:
```

In Python, code is grouped by using indentation. In order to tell Python we're starting a new group of indented code we end the line with a colon. We can't just throw colons where ever we want, though. They need to follow specific commands. We'll see more uses of colons as we continue coding.

Next, we defined a method with the `def` command and called it `__init__`.

```
def __init__(self):
```

A method is a function that belongs to a class. To better understand what a method is, we need to talk about functions.

Essentially, a function is just a block of code that is given a name. Later on, we can call the function by name and all the code in it will be executed. The call we made to `run()` earlier is a perfect example; run is the name of the function that starts the main loop in Panda3D. Functions are really handy both for organizing code and for reusing code in different places.

The difference between a method and a function, as we said earlier, is that a method belongs to a class. What this really means is that while a function can be called by itself, a method must be called on an instance of a class. For example, if we created a class called `MyClass` and gave it a method called `MyMethod`, we couldn't just call `MyMethod` by itself. We would need to make an instance of the class, `MyClassInstance` let's say, and then call `MyMethod` on that instance by typing `MyClassInstance.MyMethod()`. The period that follows `MyClassInstance` tells Python that we are accessing an attribute of the class. So, in plain speech, `MyClassInstance.MyMethod()` means "run the `MyMethod` method of the `MyClassInstance` instance of the `MyClass` class."

We can use the class name followed by a period to access both methods and variables that we've given to a class. That brings us to another important topic, called variable scope.

Variable scope refers to what can access a variable that we have created, and when that variable will be deleted from the computer's memory. We use three different kinds of variable scope in Panda3D. The first is called global. A variable with a global scope, simply called a global variable, can be accessed by everything, everywhere in our program. The variable base that we used is an example with this. It's tempting to use global variables for everything in a program, so that we don't have to worry about what has access to what, but it really isn't such a good idea. There's a bunch of different reasons why, and the following are just a few:

- Because global variables can be accessed by the entire program it's easy to forget when and where they are being used. This can cause unexpected data to creep up in them.

- Global variables make testing and debugging more complicated. If a set of code uses a global variable, and isn't producing the expected result, the debugger has to go through all of the code that uses the global variable to make sure the expected values are coming through.

- Code that relies on global variables is harder to read. If we're looking at a small piece of code in the program and we suddenly run into a global variable that we haven't seen before, we have to go digging through other parts of the program to find out what that variable is.

We will use some global variables that Panda3D creates for us, but we won't be making any new ones.

The second variable scope we'll use is called local. A variable with a local scope only exists within the function or method where it is defined. Once the function or method finishes, the variable is removed from memory. Local variables are used for temporary values.

The last type of variable scope is a sort of combination of global and variable. It's a class attribute. A class attribute is a variable that belongs to a class. They can be accessed through class instances, just like methods, and when a class instance is removed from memory all of its attributes are removed as well. This is the most common type of variable we'll use.

Getting back to our code, we called our method `__init__` with the four underscores because that is one of several keyword method names that are automatically called when something happens. `__init__` is called when an instance of the class is created, `__del__` is called when an instance is garbage collected, and there are others, but we'll only be using `__init__` and, later on, `__del__`.

Let's take another short break to talk about passing variables to functions and methods. When a function or a method is called, we always put parenthesis at the end of the method or function name. This serves two purposes. First, it tells Python that we want to run the function or method. Second, we can put variables or data into those parentheses to pass them into the function or method.

A function or method can only take in variables or data it's been told to accept. We tell a function or method to accept an input by putting a variable name into the parentheses in the `def` statement. For example:

```
def myFunc(variable1, variable2):
```

The order of the variable names in the parenthesis is important. Whatever is passed into the method or function when it's called will be entered into the variables in left-to-right order. Note that the variables are separated by commas. The different pieces of data that are passed in when the function or method is called should be separated by commas as well.

If a function or method is passed the wrong number of inputs, it will generate an error and the program will crash. It's also possible to give a variable a default value in the function or method's definition.

```
def myFunc(variable1, variable2 = 0):
```

Variables with default values have to be last in the definition. There can be more than one variable with a default value, but all variables without default values must be listed before any variables that do have default values.

Getting back to our code again, we told the __init__ method to accept a variable, which we called `self`. The reason for this has to do with another aspect of Python. Every method of every class is always passed a reference to the class instance the method was called on. This is always the first variable given to the method. The reason for this has to do with the variable scope we mentioned earlier. By receiving this reference to the class instance, the method gains the ability to access the class's attributes and methods. It wouldn't be able to otherwise. To change the background color we made a call to `base.setBackgroundColor`.

```
base.setBackgroundColor(0,0,0)
```

`base` is one of the objects that `DirectStart` creates for us and it is an instance of the `ShowBase` class. Through `base` we can access a wide variety of useful things, such as the properties of the default window, the default camera through which we see the game world, and more. That said, we won't be running to `base` for every little thing. We'll probably use it less than you think.

The method `setBackgroundColor` is pretty self-explanatory. It sets the background color of the window to the RGB value it's given. Panda3D uses a 0-1 range for RGB values, so 0,0,0 is black and 1,1,1 is white. These values can be over driven, so 10,10,10 wouldn't produce an error but if you expected a 0-255 scale, having 10,10,10 be bright then white might be a bit confusing. Take a moment to enter different values into the call to `base.setBackgroundColor` and rerun the program to see the results. When finished, change the values back to 0,0,0.

The last line of code creates an instance of the `World` class, which causes the __init__ method to run.

```
w = World()
```

Any additional variables that the __init__ method of the class needs to accept, beyond `self`, would be put in the parentheses.

Before we move on, direct your attention to the following little boxes in Notepad++:

These boxes are there to help organize code by allowing blocks of code to be collapsed. They'll appear beside every indented block we make, whether it's for an `if` statement, a loop, a method, or whatever. If you click on one of those boxes it will change to a plus and the indented block will be replaced with a line to indicate that there is some collapsed code there. When you click the box again, the code reappears. Handy!

Loading the terrain

An empty window is pretty boring. We need to fill that window with something to really start getting into Panda3D, and that means loading a 3D model. To do that, we're going to use another one of the objects created by `DirectStart`, the `loader`.

Time for action – loading the terrain

1. Add these two lines to the World class __init__ method:

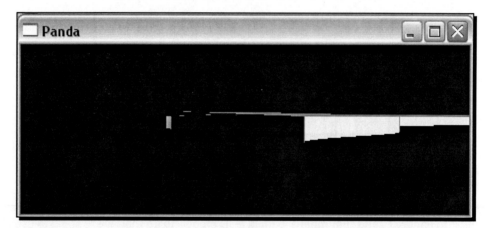

2. Save this as chp02_03.py and run it. This window will pop up:

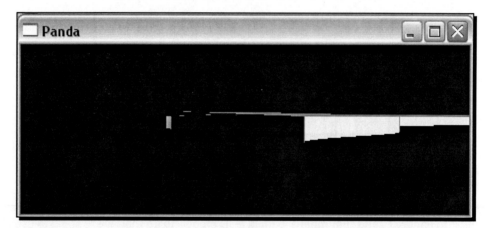

3. This doesn't look quite right, does it? Move the mouse over the Panda3D window, hold down the left mouse button, and drag down. The view will change to something like the following:

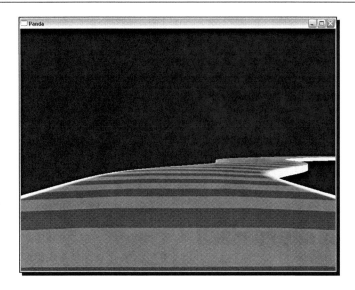

What just happened?

Congratulations! We're looking at our first 3D model loaded into Panda3D.

Let's talk a bit about the code we used to do this, starting with the following line:

```
self.track = loader.loadModel("../Models/Track.egg")
```

We have a couple of things going on here. First, we are creating a new variable, called "track". By creating it as "self.track" we are making it an attribute of the World class. Remember back to earlier when we made the World class and we told the __init__ method to accept a variable called "self", and how we mentioned that would let us interact with the instance of the World class from within the __init__ method? That's exactly what we're doing. We are creating a new attribute for the instance called "track". Why do we create the variable as an attribute of the instance? Good question. If we had done this instead:

```
track = loader.loadModel("../Models/Track.egg")
```

The "track" variable would have been a local variable. That means the variable only exists within that method. When the method finished executing, the "track" variable would get garbage collected and cease to exist. We want the variable to persist, so we use "self.track" so that as long as the instance of the World class exists, so will the variable.

The call to loader.loadModel pretty much does what it says. The loader finds the file using the path we gave it and creates a model object from that file. It returns that model object, and that is what we're storing in "self.track". Note that Panda3D uses Unix style file paths, with forward slashes.

The next line of code is used to insert the model into the Scene Graph:

```
self.track.reparentTo(render)
```

This is necessary to tell Panda3D that the model is in the scene and needs to be rendered. If we skipped this step, the model wouldn't appear.

So what did dragging the left mouse button on the window do, besides fix it? By default, Panda3D has some rudimentary mouse controls for the camera through which we view the scene. Left-clicking and dragging down moves the camera up. The reason the view was strange to begin with was because the camera was inside of the track. When we moved the camera up above the track, we fixed that problem.

Loading files into Panda3D

Loading files into a game is pretty easy with Panda3D, but there are some things to talk about now that we've seen it happen. We'll start by going over the path that Panda3D searches for files, and then we'll talk about a few file types we'll be using.

The model path

Panda3D searches a few different places for files when they are loaded, and these locations are controlled by the configuration file. There are a couple default folders in the Panda3D installation directory that are searched, but using them isn't really recommended. The best path to make use of is the most dynamic one, the path to the python file that's being run.

That means that when loading a file, it's best to use a relative path from the file that is launching the Panda3D application. Right now, that file is `chp02_03.py`. In that file, we used the path "`../Models/Track.egg`" to point to our model file. Our `chp02_03.py` file is located in "`/BGP3D/Chapter02`" and our model is located in "`/BGP3D/Models`". Thus, the "`../`" at the start of the path takes us out of the `Chapter02` folder and puts us in the `BGP3D` folder. Then we enter the `Models` folder, and that's where we find `Track.egg`.

A final note to remember, in Panda3D all paths are case-sensitive. So while "`../Models/Track.egg`" works "`../models/Track.egg`" won't, and neither will "`../Models/track.egg`".

Eggs

The egg format is designed for two purposes. First, it contains all the model data needed by Panda3D, from vertices and faces to textures and their settings. It can also hold animation data. The second purpose is to be human readable. If we open `Track.egg` in Notepad++ we see this:

```
C:\BGP3D\Chapter02\chp02_03.py - Notepad++
File  Edit  Search  View  Encoding  Language  Settings  Macro  Run  TextFX  Plugins  Wind

 chp02_03.py   Track.egg

  1   <CoordinateSystem> { Y-Up }
  2
  3   <Texture> "Track:Track" {
  4     "../Images/Basic.png"
  5     <Scalar> format { rgb }
  6     <Scalar> wrapu { repeat }
  7     <Scalar> wrapv { repeat }
  8     <Scalar> minfilter { linear_mipmap_linear }
  9     <Scalar> magfilter { linear }
 10   }
 11   <Texture> "Track:FinishLine" {
 12     "../Images/Finishline.png"
 13     <Scalar> format { rgb }
 14     <Scalar> wrapu { repeat }
 15     <Scalar> wrapv { repeat }
 16     <Scalar> minfilter { linear_mipmap_linear }
 17     <Scalar> magfilter { linear }
 18   }
 19   <Group> groundPlane_transform {
 20   }
 21   <Group> "Track:default1" {
 22     <VertexPool> "Track:defaultShape.verts" {
 23       <Vertex> 0 {
 24         20.0275 -2.5 -20.25
 25         <UV> { 1 0.5 }
 26         <Normal> { 0.999995 0 -0.00331354 }
 27         <RGBA> { 1 1 1 1 }
 28       }
 29       <Vertex> 1 {
 30         20.0275 0 -20.25
 31         <UV> { 0.975 0.5 }
 32         <Normal> { 0.720209 0.693753 -0.0024115 }
 33         <RGBA> { 1 1 1 1 }
```

It's a bit longer than just that, but the point is that we can open an egg file and see all of the data in a legible format. We can edit it too.

The Panda3D installer comes with command line utilities for making eggs out of the files used by some of the major 3D modeling packages. They can be found in Panda3D-1.6.2/bin. Chicken, which we talked about in the last chapter, will export eggs from the open source 3D modeling package Blender.

Bams

The second file format Panda3D uses for models is the bam file. This format can store everything an egg can store, but it's built for speed. Bam files are optimized to load quickly, and a finished game should be shipped to the consumer with bams, not eggs. On the other hand, bams can't be read or edited with a text editor, like eggs can. Opening a bam file in Notepad++ will show garbage and possibly a few readable file paths.

Panda3D includes a utility for converting eggs to bams. It can be found in the Panda3D-1.6.2/bin as well. Additionally, bam files can be written out directly from a Panda3D application, while egg files cannot.

Pop Quiz – starting Panda3D and loading models

It's time to test our understanding of what we've done so far. If we can answer these questions, we're ready to move on:

1. What line of code is required to initiate Panda3D and open a Panda window?
2. Why did the __init__ method accept a variable and call it `self`?
3. Why was the __init__ method given that name?
4. We used the `loader` object's `loadModel` method to load the track model. What created that `loader` object?
5. How did our program locate the file for the model we loaded? Where did it search for that file?
6. What kind of information is stored in egg and bam files?
7. What is the difference between egg and bam files?

NodePaths and nodes

Panda3D implements a superclass called `PandaNode`, from which many other classes inherit. Collectively, all of these classes are referred to as nodes. Some examples include `ModelRoots`, which are the root of models (surprise!), `GeomNodes`, which store vertex data and other information for geometry, `CameraNodes`, which serve as the windows through which we see the world within Panda3D, `CollisionNodes`, which allow items in that world to interact with one another, and there are many more. Each of these node types have methods specific to them for setting attributes that only node type require. `ModelRoots` don't have methods for setting lens attributes, but `CameraNodes` do.

There are also attributes that every kind of node needs, such as the node's position and orientation in the world. These attributes are not stored in the nodes themselves. Instead, they are kept in a handler class, called a `NodePath`. We will often interact with the `NodePath` instead of the node itself because so many important attributes common to all nodes are handled by the `NodePath`.

Earlier, we talked about how the call to `loader.loadModel` returned a model object and we stored it in `self.track`. That isn't entirely true. When a model is loaded, the object returned is actually a `NodePath`. The `NodePath` is the handler for the `ModelRoot` that serves as a parent for all the other nodes that make up the model. By using this structure, even the most complex models can be handled by a single `NodePath`. This means that `self.track` doesn't point directly to the model itself, but to a `NodePath` that handles the model.

`NodePaths` also serve as the medium for nodes to be placed in the Scene Graph. We'll talk about the Scene Graph in detail in just a moment, but for now it's important to understand that in order for nodes to be rendered in the Panda window, the `NodePath` that handles them must be part of the Scene Graph. When we called `reparentTo(render)` on `self.track`, we inserted the `NodePath` into Scene Graph so that it would appear in the Panda Window.

Let's do a little exercise to show this. First we'll print out the `NodePath`, which will show us the location of the `NodePath` within the Scene Graph. After that, we'll print out the node that the `NodePath` points to.

Time for action – introducing NodePaths and nodes

To better understand `NodePaths`, let's go ahead and use the print statement to take a closer look at what's going on.

1. At the end of the `__init__` method in our world class, add this line:

```
print(self.track)
```

2. Make sure it's part of the indented block that makes up the method.

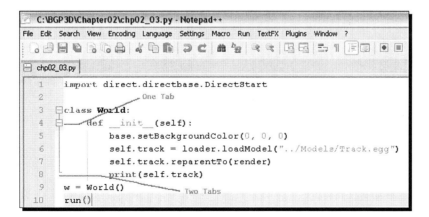

3. Save the file as "chp02_04.py" and run it. Look at the command prompt window to see the output of the print statement.

```
DirectStart: Starting the game.
Known pipe types:
   wglGraphicsPipe
(all display modules loaded.)
render/Track.egg
```

4. Note that at the bottom it says "**render/Track.egg**" in a format that looks just like a file path. That's because "**render/Track.egg**" is the model's location in the Scene Graph. Whenever we print out a NodePath, we'll get a result like this.

5. Next, change the print statement to look like this:

```
                                    C:\BGP 3D\Chapter02\chp02_05.py - Notepad++

File  Edit  Search  View  Encoding  Language  Settings  Macro  Run  TextFX  Plugins  Window  ?

chp02_05.py

1    import direct.directbase.DirectStart
2
3    class World:
4        def __init__(self):
5            base.setBackgroundColor(0, 0, 0)
6            self.track = loader.loadModel("../Models/Track.egg")
7            self.track.reparentTo(render)
8            print(self.track.node())
9    w = World()
10   run()
```

6. Save the file as "chp02_05.py" and run it.

```
DirectStart: Starting the game.
Known pipe types:
   wglGraphicsPipe
(all display modules loaded.)
ModelRoot Track.egg
```

7. Now the output says "**ModelRoot Track.egg**". The ModelRoot is the node that the self.track NodePath **points to**.

What just happened?

The purpose of this exercise was to better understand the difference between a NodePath and a node. When we printed self.track:

```
print(self.track)
```

We printed out the NodePath that the call to the loader returned to us. We know it was a NodePath because the output was similar to a file path and showed the location of the NodePath in the Scene Graph. Next we used a call to the NodePath method node():

```
print(self.track.node())
```

This printed out the node itself, a ModelRoot named Track.egg.

Manipulating NodePaths

Locked within NodePaths are the most common tools we'll use to manipulate the virtual world inside Panda3D. It is through these tools that we will make our game dance and twirl. They are the tools that change the position, rotation, and scale of the node the NodePath handles. Each of these tools is made up of several methods, one to control changing all three axes at once, and three more methods to control each axis individually.

First we have the methods that control the position within the 3D world:

```
myNodePath.setPos([x],[y],[z])
myNodePath.setX([x])
myNodePath.setY([y])
myNodePath.setZ([z])
```

Panda3D uses a z-up coordinate system. That means that in the world of Panda3D, the x and y axis control horizontal positioning, and the z axis controls height. This is contrary to many modeling packages and can take some getting used to. Try to keep it in mind as we continue through the tutorials in this book.

Next are the methods that control the rotation of the node:

```
myNodePath.setHpr([h],[p],[r])
myNodePath.setH([h])
myNodePath.setP([p])
myNodePath.setR([r])
```

hpr stands for heading, pitch, and roll. If you imagine the node as a jet, facing down the positive y axis, heading will turn left and right, pitch will climb and dive, and roll will spin the jet and make you throw up. To put it in technical terms, heading rotates the model around its z axis, pitch rotates it around its x axis, and roll rotates it around its y axis.

Lastly we have the scalar methods:

```
myNodePath.setScale([sx],[sy],[sz])
myNodePath.setSx([sx])
myNodePath.setSy([sy])
myNodePath.setSz([sz])
```

The scale methods work relative to the original scale of the node, so setting a scale to 2 will double the size along that axis and setting it to 0.5 will halve the scale along that axis. We can also call `setScale` with only a single argument:

```
myNodePath.setScale([scale])
```

This will change the scale of the node uniformly along all axis.

Time for action – manipulating NodePaths

Let's try using the `setPos` method to move our model around.

1. Change your `.py` file to look like this:

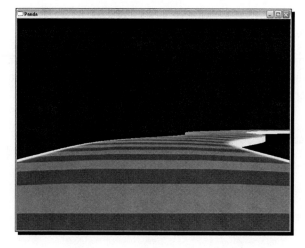

2. Save the file as "chp02_06.py" and run it.

What just happened?

The camera didn't start inside the track this time. That's because we moved the track 5 units down on the z axis. `NodePath` manipulation is pretty easy, but also very important. Let's do some more to get the hang of it.

Have a go hero – more NodePath manipulation

We should do some more manipulations with the `NodePath`. Try using the other methods we mentioned to reposition, rescale, and rotate the model.

The Scene Graph

Now it's time we talk about the Scene Graph. In most game engines, there is a list of what objects need to be rendered and in order for a model or some other element to appear they need to be added to the list. Panda3D uses a similar structure, but instead of a list, we have a tree.

At the root of the tree is `render`, which is created for us by `DirectStart`. In order for something to appear in the Panda3D window, it needs to be attached to `render`. It doesn't have to be directly attached to `render`, though. If you attach element A to `render`, and attach element B to element A, that's enough. That's why we refer Scene Graph as a tree.

`NodePaths` have a specific method used to move them around in the Scene Graph. We've already used it, once.

```
self.track.reparentTo(render)
```

The method `reparentTo()` makes the `NodePath` it's called on a child of the `NodePath` it's passed.

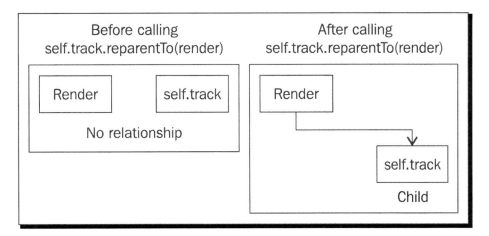

In this way we can build a tree of `NodePaths` using parent and child relationships. The tree can be as wide and shallow or as narrow and deep as we like, depending on our needs. Here's an example of a more complicated tree with several `NodePaths` in it.

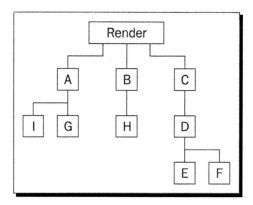

We need to carefully consider parent and child relationships, however. Many `NodePath` properties are passed down from parent to child.

Time for action – understanding parent child inheritance

To better understand how children inherit properties from their parents, we're going to add two more models to our scene and see how they mingle.

1. We need to add six more lines of code to our file in order to load two more models, add them to the Scene Graph, and position them in view:

```
C:\BGP3D\Chapter02\chp02_07.py - Notepad++
File  Edit  Search  View  Encoding  Language  Settings  Macro  Run  TextFX  Plugins  Window  ?

chp02_07.py
1    import direct.directbase.DirectStart
2
3    class World:
4        def __init__(self):
5            base.setBackgroundColor(0, 0, 0)
6            self.track = loader.loadModel("../Models/Track.egg")
7            self.track.reparentTo(render)
8            self.track.setPos(0,0,-5)
9            self.cycle1 = loader.loadModel("../Models/Cycle.bam")
10           self.cycle1.reparentTo(render)
11           self.cycle1.setPos(2,15,0)
12           self.cycle2 = loader.loadModel("../Models/Cycle.bam")
13           self.cycle2.reparentTo(render)
14           self.cycle2.setPos(-2,15,0)
15   w = World()
16   run()
```

2. Save the file as "chp02_07.py" and run it.

3. The cycles look like white blobs because they are untextured and unlit. We don't need to worry about that right now. Next, let's parent the second cycle to the first, instead of to render. Change line 13 to

```
self.cycle2.reparentTo(self.cycle1).
```

4. Save the file as "chp02_08.py" and run it.

What just happened?

Notice how the left cycle changed position. This is because child `NodePaths` inherit the coordinate system of their parent. That means that originally, when it was a child of `render`, the left cycle was positioned at (-2,15,0), relative to `render`. When we changed the parent, the left cycle moved to (-2,15,0) relative to the right cycle. Another way to think of it is that the child's origin is the origin of the parent. That means if you position the left cycle at (0,0,0) it would be on top of its parent, the right cycle.

Time for action – explaining relative coordinate systems

It's also possible to use the coordinate system of other `NodePaths` when calling any of the position, rotation, or scale methods. Let's take a look at how.

1. Change line 13 back to:

   ```
   self.track.reparentTo(render)
   ```

2. Change line 11 to:

   ```
   self.cycle1.setPos(self.track,2,15,0)
   ```

3. Save the file as "chp02_09.py" and run it.

What just happened?

The cycle on the right is much lower now. That's because we set it to (2,15,0) in the coordinate system of `self.track`, and `self.track` has been lowered 5 units. Lowering `self.track` also lowers the coordinate system of `self.track`. This is another very useful concept to remember. The coordinate system of a `NodePath` moves, rotates, and scales with the `NodePath`.

Have a go hero – parenting and relative coordinate systems

Take some time and play around with different parenting settings and using relative coordinate systems. To use a different coordinate system for a position, rotation, or scale method we just need to pass the `NodePath` whose coordinate system we want to use as the first argument of the method. Let's make sure we fully understand the use of parenting and relative coordinate systems before we move on.

Loading a file multiple times

In the recent Time for Actions we loaded the cycle model twice. It wouldn't be unusual for us to assume that the cycle model has been loaded into memory twice now, but that isn't the case. Having all the information generated from the bam file in memory multiple times would be a waste, because we could instead just tell the program to use the information twice. Panda3D does this for us automatically when we load a file more than once. The second call to `loader` detects that `cycle.bam` has already been loaded once and uses the information already in memory to create the components for the new model. This only applies to the information that exists in the file. Panda3D also does this with other file types as well.

Render attributes

Size, rotation, and scale aren't the only things we can do with `NodePaths`. Render attributes are also set on `NodePaths`. Controls that change how a model is handled by the renderer are called render attributes, and they can do a number of different things. They can change the color of a model, they can make it render as a wireframe instead of a solid, they can make it render as two-sided, and more. Let's take a look at the list of render attributes to get a feel for what they are:

- `AlphaTestAttrib`: Hides part of the model, based on the texture's alpha channel.
- `AntialiasAttrib`: Controls full-screen antialiasing and polygon-edge antialiasing.
- `AudioVolumeAttrib`: Applies a scale to audio volume for positional sounds.
- `AuxBitplaneAttrib`: Causes shader generator to produce extra data.
- `ClipPlaneAttrib`: Slices off a piece of the model, using a clipping plane.

- ◆ `ColorAttrib`: Tints the model. Only works if the model is not illuminated.
- ◆ `ColorBlendAttrib`: This specifies how colors are blended into the frame buffer, for special effects.
- ◆ `ColorScaleAttrib`: Modulates vertex colors with a flat color.
- ◆ `ColorWriteAttrib`: Causes the model to not affect the R, G, B, or A channel of the framebuffer.
- ◆ `CullBinAttrib`: Controls the order in which Panda renders geometry.
- ◆ `CullFaceAttrib`: Causes backfaces or frontfaces of the model to be visible.
- ◆ `DepthOffsetAttrib`: Causes the Z-buffer to treat the object as if it were closer or farther.
- ◆ `DepthTestAttrib`: Alters the way the Z-buffer affects the model.
- ◆ `DepthWriteAttrib`: Controls whether or not the model affects the Z-buffer.
- ◆ `DrawMaskAttrib`: Controls which cameras can see which objects.
- ◆ `FogAttrib`: Causes the model to be obscured by fog if it is far from the camera.
- ◆ `LightAttrib`: Causes the model to be illuminated by certain lights.
- ◆ `LightRampAttrib`: Enables HDR tone mapping or cartoon shading.
- ◆ `MaterialAttrib`: Changes the way the model reflects light.
- ◆ `RenderModeAttrib`: Used to enable wireframe rendering.
- ◆ `RescaleNormalAttrib`: Can disable the automatic correction of non-unit normals.
- ◆ `ShadeModelAttrib`: Can cause the model to appear faceted instead of smooth.
- ◆ `ShaderAttrib`: Gives almost unlimited control, but is difficult to use.
- ◆ `StencilAttrib`: Causes the model to affect the stencil buffer, or be affected by the stencil buffer.
- ◆ `TexGenAttrib`: Causes the system to synthesize texture coordinates for the model.
- ◆ `TexMatrixAttrib`: Alters the existing texture coordinates.
- ◆ `TextureAttrib`: Applies a texture map to the model.
- ◆ `TransparencyAttrib`: Causes the model to be partially transparent.

There's no small number of them, but only a few are commonly used. Also, they typically aren't accessed by these direct names, but with methods of the `NodePath` class. For instance:

```
myNodePath.setColor([r],[g],[b])
myNodePath.setRenderModeWireframe()
```

Some render attributes are really easy to use. The two we just mentioned are straight forward, where as others get pretty complicated. For example, `TransparencyAttrib` requires certain objects as the arguments we pass to its method. `ShaderAttrib` is for use with custom shaders, and custom shaders are complicated enough to deserve their own book.

Time for action – demonstrating render attributes

Let's try changing render attributes and see what that does for our scene.

1. Make sure that all of your model `NodePaths` are reparented to render instead of each other.

2. Remove any scale or rotation adjustments made to the NodePaths.

3. Set the track position to (0,0,-5) again and set the cycles' positions back to (2,15,0) and (-2,15, 0).

4. Add this line after line 14 so that the file looks like figure 23:

```
self.cycle2.setRenderModeWireframe()
```

5. Save the file as "chp02_10.py" and run it.

6. Now the cycle on the left is rendered in wireframe mode. Let's try one more thing before we move on. Change line 13 to:

```
self.cycle2.reparentTo(self.cycle1)
```

7. Change line 15 so that it affects cycle1 instead of cycle2:

```
self.cycle1.setRenderModeWireframe()
```

8. Save the file again, this time as "chp02_11.py" and run it.

What just happened?

Like position, rotation, and scale, render attributes are also inherited from parent to child! That's why both cycles are now rendered in wireframe mode. This, in particular, is something to be very careful with. It can be very helpful, and also very dangerous.

Pop Quiz – using NodePaths and understanding Scene Graph inheritance

We just covered so many important concepts that we better take a moment to make sure we fully understand them. If we don't, we'll have serious problems trying to move on from here!

1. What is the difference between a `NodePath` and a node?
2. Where did the `NodePaths` we used to manipulate our scene come from?
3. What does the `reparentTo()` method do?
4. If model B is a child of model A, and you set model A to a new position, what will happen to model B?
5. If model B is a child of model A, and you set model B to render in wireframe mode, what will happen to model A?

Have a go hero – render attributes

Try changing the color of our three `NodePaths` using the `setColor([r],[g],[b])` method. Remember that Panda3D uses values between 0 and 1 for RGB values.

Summary

The main focus of this chapter was learning about `NodePaths`, where they come from, and what we can do with them.

Specifically, we covered:

- First we learned how to get Panda3D started so we could begin exploring how it works. We did that by importing `DirectStart`.
- After that, we learned how to load models into the scene, which gave us our first `NodePaths` to play around with. We used `loader.loadModel` to bring our track and, later, two cycles into the scene.
- Next we learned about transforming `NodePaths` with the position, rotation, and scale methods. We also learned about how each `NodePath` has its own coordinate system, and how parent child relationships affect that.
- Finally, we learned about render attributes, their basic uses, and how parent child relationships affect them as well.

We also talked about the Scene Graph, how it controls what is rendered and what isn't, and how `NodePaths` can be moved around in it.

Now that we've learned about `NodePaths` we're ready to make them move around on their own over time using tasks—which is the topic of the next chapter.

3
Managing Tasks Over Time

A video game is composed of three primary components. The first is a visual element; we've already started working on that part. The second is user interaction and that is what we'll cover in the next chapter. Right now, we're going to start work on the third element—dynamism. Video games change over time, whether it's the movement of objects on the screen, the rise or fall of statistics like health or ammo, or any number of other dynamic elements. Some of these changes occur at irregular times, but others require ongoing management. That ongoing management is the focus of this chapter.

This is what we'll talk about:

- The task manager
- Understanding delta time
- Over viewing task return options
- Prioritizing tasks
- Removing tasks from the task manager
- Dissecting task objects

Tasks are used extensively in Panda3D applications and are a very important in controlling what happens in our game, so let's learn all about them together.

The task manager

We can't talk about tasks without talking about the task manager. DirectStart creates the task manager for us when it's imported, just like the loader. The purpose of the task manager is to act as a keeper for all the tasks that have been created. Every frame the task manager executes each of the tasks; it's been given in sequential order. Once one task is finished, the task manager moves on to the next.

Time for action – printing the task list from the task manager

The task manager starts with some important tasks already assigned to it. Let's go ahead and print the list of tasks so we can see what the task manager is up to.

1. Let's start where we left off last chapter. Open up chp02_11.py and resave it in the Chapter03 folder as chp03_01.py.

2. We only need to add one line of code to the __init__ method to accomplish our goal here. At the end of the method add the following line:

    ```
    print(taskMgr)
    ```

3. We can also remove the Render Attribute changes we have made, and we should make sure that all of our model NodePaths are reparented to render instead of anything else.

    ```
    class World:
      def __init__(self):
        base.setBackgroundColor(0, 0, 0)
        self.track = loader.loadModel("../Models/Track.egg")
        self.track.reparentTo(render)
        self.track.setPos(0,0,-5)
        self.cycle1 = loader.loadModel("../Models/Cycle.bam")
        self.cycle1.reparentTo(render)
        self.cycle1.setPos(2,15,0)
        self.cycle2 = loader.loadModel("../Models/Cycle.bam")
        self.cycle2.reparentTo(render)
        self.cycle2.setPos(-2,15,0)
        print(taskMgr)
    ```

4. Hit *Ctrl+S* on the keyboard to resave the file and then run it. Remember that we have to change the folder our Windows command prompt is at. We're working in the Chapter03 folder now.

```
C:\BGP3D\Chapter03>python chp03_01.py
DirectStart: Starting the game.
Known pipe types:
  wglGraphicsPipe
(all display modules loaded.)
AsyncTaskManager TaskManager

  Task chain "default"
  Task                           sleep(s)   dt(ms)     avg     max    sort
  -----------------------------------------------------------------------
  resetPrevTransform                                                    -51
  dataLoop                                                              -50
  eventManager                                                           0
  ivalLoop                                                              20
  collisionLoop                                                         30
  igLoop                                                                50
  audioLoop                                                             60

C:\BGP3D\Chapter03>
```

What just happened?

The output we see is a table that shows us what tasks are in the task manager and some statistics related to them. The tasks we see are the default tasks that are set up for us. The reason we don't see any stats for them is because we are printing the taskMgr before our game is starting. Note that our print statement is in the __init__ method for the World class, and our instance of the World class is being created before we call run. We can only see stats for our tasks after Panda3D has generated at least one frame for the game.

Avoiding multiple task managers

Right now we have one task manager, the default one, which is called taskMgr. It is possible to create new task managers that will run concurrently with taskMgr, but in most cases that really isn't necessary or even wise. When using only one task manager we know that each task is executed from start to finish before the next task.

> If we start using multiple task managers, we can run into the problem of multiple tasks trying to use the same variables at the same time and run into some real trouble.

One of the primary reasons to have different task managers is to employ threading, but that is a complicated programming challenge that we won't be covering in this book. One task manager is plenty for our game, so we'll stick to just using taskMgr.

Adding tasks to the task manager

In order to take advantage of the task manager, we need to add tasks to it. To do that, we need to have a method to add. The methods we add to the task manager need to have a few special features in them to interact with the task manager—a variable the method must accept and a return statement that returns a particular value. We'll go into more detail about these features in just a moment, but before we do, we need to create a method and add it to the task manager.

Time for action – creating a task and adding it to the task manager

1. To create the method we'll add to the task manager we need to add a few more lines to the `World` class in our program. Create a blank line at the end of the __ init__ method with only one *tab* at the start of it. Then add this code block there:

```
def cycleMove(self, task):
    self.cycle1.setY(self.cycle1, .1)
    return task.cont
```

2. This won't do the job on its own, though. We need to add our new method to the task manager. Add a new line right above `print(taskMgr)`:

```
taskMgr.add(self.cycleMove, "Cycle Move")
```

3. Our code should look like this now:

```
class World:
    def __init__(self):
        base.setBackgroundColor(0, 0, 0)
        self.track = loader.loadModel("../Models/Track.egg")
        self.track.reparentTo(render)
        self.track.setPos(0,0,-5)
        self.cycle1 = loader.loadModel("../Models/Cycle.bam")
        self.cycle1.reparentTo(render)
        self.cycle1.setPos(2,15,0)
        self.cycle2 = loader.loadModel("../Models/Cycle.bam")
        self.cycle2.reparentTo(render)
        self.cycle2.setPos(-2,15,0)
        taskMgr.add(self.cycleMove, "Cycle Move")
        print(taskMgr)
    def cycleMove(self, task):
        self.cycle1.setY(self.cycle1, .1)
        return task.cont
```

4. Save the file as `chp03_02.py` and then run it. You'll see something like the following when the cycle on the right moves forward.

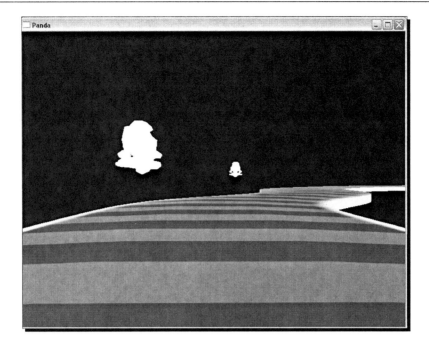

What just happened?

When we run this file, we see the cycle on the right slowly advancing forward, but that's not all. If we look at the output in our command prompt, we can see that a new task has been added to the list.

```
C:\BGP3D\Chapter03>python chp03_02.py
DirectStart: Starting the game.
Known pipe types:
  wglGraphicsPipe
(all display modules loaded.)
AsyncTaskManager TaskManager

  Task chain "default"
  Task                          sleep(s)   dt(ms)     avg     max    sort

  resetPrevTransform                                                  -51
  dataLoop                                                            -50
  Cycle Move                                                            0
  eventManager                                                          0
  ivalLoop                                                             20
  collisionLoop                                                        30
  igLoop                                                               50
  audioLoop                                                            60
```

To make this happen, we first used the `def` statement to create a new method called `cycleMove`. We fed two variables into that method, `self` and `task`.

Remember that whenever a class method is called, the instance of the class is passed to it first and we need the self variable to accept that.

When the task manager runs a method it also passes in a task object, so we need the `task` variable to accept that.

Our `cycleMove` method only performed one action. Using `self.cycle1.setY(self.cycle1, .1)` we told `self.cycle1` to reposition itself **relative to itself**. Therefore, each time that line is executed, the cycle moves 0.1 units forward.

The last line of our method, `return task.cont`, is necessary to keep the task running frame after frame. We'll talk about this in detail when we go over the different task return options later in this chapter, in the *Over viewing task return options* section.

After we set up the method we used the `add` method of `taskMgr` to add our method to the list of tasks that need to be executed. We passed two inputs into `add`; the first was the name of the method we wanted to be executed as a task.

Note that we didn't put any parenthesis at the end of the method name. That's because we wanted to pass the method without calling it.

If we had put the parenthesis in, the method would have been called and its return would have been passed into `add` instead of the method itself.

The next input we passed was a string to use for the task's name. Every task needs a name, but the names don't need to be unique. The task name can be used for some task manager operations, such as removing the task from the task manager.

Time for action – looking at task statistics

We still don't see any stats for our tasks because we are still printing the task manager before the first frame is being generated. Let's change that next.

1. To see the statistics on our tasks we just need to move the `print(taskMgr)` command to a place where it will be executed after the first frame has been generated. The simplest solution to that is to move that line into our task method so that it's called every frame. Highlight that line and hit *Ctrl+X* to cut it. Then paste it into the `cycleMove` method just above the `return` statement.

```
class World:
    def __init__(self):
        base.setBackgroundColor(0, 0, 0)
```

```
self.track = loader.loadModel("../Models/Track.egg")
self.track.reparentTo(render)
self.track.setPos(0,0,-5)
self.cycle1 = loader.loadModel("../Models/Cycle.bam")
self.cycle1.reparentTo(render)
self.cycle1.setPos(2,15,0)
self.cycle2 = loader.loadModel("../Models/Cycle.bam")
self.cycle2.reparentTo(render)
self.cycle2.setPos(-2,15,0)
taskMgr.add(self.cycleMove, "Cycle Move")
def cycleMove(self, task):
self.cycle1.setY(self.cycle1, .1)
print(taskMgr)
return task.cont
```

2. Save your file as `chp03_03.py` and run it. Check the command prompt for output; it should look something like this:

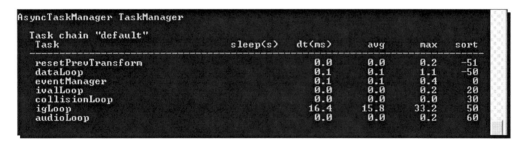

What just happened?

Our output from the task manager is showing us some stats on the tasks it's running now. The first column, **sleep**, is empty because it displays the remaining delay time for a task and none of our tasks are on a delay. Next up is **dt**, which shows how many milliseconds it took to run the task this frame. After **dt** is the **avg** column where we can see the task's average completion time for all the frames so far. Following that we have **max**, the largest completion time for the task so far. The last column, **sort**, shows us the priorities that have been assigned to the tasks.

Notice that our task method, `cycleMove`, doesn't show up in the list anymore. This is because we're printing the task manager from within `cycleMove`.

When we print `taskMgr` from within a task method, we won't see that task method in the list.

Adding a delay to tasks

When adding tasks to the task manager we don't always have to make them execute immediately. We can tell them to wait a certain amount of time before their first execution. This requires using another method of `taskMgr`, the `doMethodLater` method.

Time for action – using doMethodLater

1. Change the line where we add our task to `taskMgr` so it matches the following:

   ```
   taskMgr.doMethodLater(5, self.cycleMove, "Cycle Move")
   ```

2. Save this as `chp03_04.py` and run it. Wait 5 seconds for the task to startup. All of the output stays the same, but now there is a 5 second delay before the task beings.

3. Let's create a new task to really see this in action. Add a new method to the `World` class with this code:

   ```
   def debugTask(self, task):
     print(taskMgr)
     return task.cont
   ```

4. We don't need to print the `taskMgr` in two places, so remove the `print(taskMgr)` line from the `cycleMove` method. Also, we need to add the new task to the `taskMgr`. Add the following line below the `taskMgr.doMethodLater` method call:

   ```
   taskMgr.add(self.debugTask, "Debug Task")
   ```

5. Once we've done that, our code should look like this:

   ```
   class World:
     def __init__(self):
       base.setBackgroundColor(0, 0, 0)
       self.track = loader.loadModel("../Models/Track.egg")
       self.track.reparentTo(render)
       self.track.setPos(0,0,-5)
       self.cycle1 = loader.loadModel("../Models/Cycle.bam")
       self.cycle1.reparentTo(render)
       self.cycle1.setPos(2,15,0)
       self.cycle2 = loader.loadModel("../Models/Cycle.bam")
       self.cycle2.reparentTo(render)
       self.cycle2.setPos(-2,15,0)
       taskMgr.doMethodLater(5, self.cycleMove, "Cycle Move")
       taskMgr.add(self.debugTask, "Debug Task")
     def cycleMove(self, task):
   ```

```
        self.cycle1.setY(self.cycle1, .1)
        return task.cont
    def debugTask(self, task):
        print(taskMgr)
        return task.cont
```

6. Save the file as chp03_05.py and run it.

```
AsyncTaskManager TaskManager

 Task chain "default"
   Task                         sleep(s)   dt(ms)      avg       max      sort
--------------------------------------------------------------------------------
   resetPrevTransform                        0.0       0.0       0.0       -51
   dataLoop                                  0.1       0.1       0.5       -50
   eventManager                              0.1       0.1       0.5         0
   ivalLoop                                  0.0       0.0       0.0        20
   collisionLoop                             0.0       0.0       0.1        30
   igLoop                                   15.8      15.8      28.7        50
   audioLoop                                 0.0       0.0       0.2        60
   Cycle Move                      2.0                                      0
```

What just happened?

Now we see an entry for the **Cycle Move** task in the **sleep** column. This number counts down to when the task will execute. Note that the **sleep** column is the only column that uses full seconds for its units.

Pop quiz – the task manager

1. What object does DirectStart create for the purposes of managing tasks?

2. What method of the object from question 1 do we use if we want a task to be executed immediately? What method do we use if we want the task to have a delay?

3. How do we view a list of the tasks currently being run by the task manager?

Using delta time

Within video games, it's rarely a good idea to have continuous actions, such as movement, use a static value every frame. For instance, we have our cycle moving 0.1 units per frame, so if our frame rate is 60, the cycle will move 6 units per second. If our frame rate is 30, our cycle will move 3 units per second. What we want is to have our cycle move at a constant speed, regardless of the frame rate. We can achieve that by using delta time.

Delta time means change in time. In our case, delta time will be the change in time from the last frame to the current frame. We can get delta time from the globalClock object using the method getDt. Fortunately, DirectStart creates the globalClock object for us, so we don't need to worry about that step.

Time for action – using delta time

We're going to employ delta time to make our cycle move at a constant speed instead of a speed based on frame rate. Once we have that done, we'll learn how to use delta time to protect against hiccups in the game—moments when the time between frames is abnormally large, and could cause the action to skip forward.

1. We need to make two changes to use delta time for our cycle's movement. This first is to add this line at the beginning of our `cycleMove` method:

   ```
   dt = globalClock.getDt()
   ```

2. This will create a temporary variable and fill it with the delta time from `globalClock` in one go. The delta time we get will be in full seconds, so if we want our cycle to move at 10 units per second, we need to change our call to `setY` in `cycleMove` to the following:

   ```
       self.cycle1.setY(self.cycle1, 10 * dt)
   def cycleMove(self, task):
       dt = globalClock.getDt()
       self.cycle1.setY(self.cycle1, 10 * dt)
       return task.cont
   ```

3. Save the file as `chp03_06.py` and run it.

4. If our frame rate has been fluctuating, we'll notice the cycle moving more smoothly than it did before. If not, we won't really see much of a difference. Let's move on to protecting against hiccups. Add two more lines to our file, right after we get our delta time and store it in `dt`.

   ```
   if( dt > .20):
       return task.cont
   ```

5. Before we save the file and run it, let's add one more line to get some better output from the program. Right after the lines we just added, put in the following:

   ```
   print(dt)
   ```

6. Our `cycleMove` method should look like this now:

   ```
   def cycleMove(self, task):
       dt = globalClock.getDt()
       if( dt > .20):
           return task.cont
       print(dt)
       self.cycle1.setY(self.cycle1, 10 * dt)
       return task.cont
   ```

7. Save the file as `chp03_07.py` and run it to see the following output:

```
Task chain "default"
Task                      sleep(s)    dt(ms)       avg      max     sort
────────────────────────────────────────────────────────────────────────
resetPrevTransform                     0.0         0.0      0.1      -51
dataLoop                               0.1         0.1      0.4      -50
eventManager                           0.1         0.1      1.1        0
Cycle Move                             0.1         0.1      2.2        0
ivalLoop                               0.0         0.0      0.2       20
collisionLoop                          0.0         0.0      0.1       30
igLoop                                15.9        15.8     25.1       50
audioLoop                              0.0         0.0      0.2       60

0.0166675755013
```

What just happened?

Once `cycleMove` starts we begin to see a number in between our `taskMgr` prints. That's the delta time value we're getting from `globalClock.getDt`. Other than that, we didn't see much of a difference in our outputs. Despite that, we made a very important change. By getting the delta time and changing the `cycleMove` method so that the cycle moves based on time passed instead of using a static amount every frame, we've made certain that the cycle maintains a constant speed regardless of computer performance.

We also put in some protection against irregular frame rates:

```
if( dt > .20):
    return task.cont
```

The first line of this little code block checks if the delta time has risen too high. If it has, we execute the second line of code which exits the task immediately. This way, if we get an unusually high delta time for one frame we won't move the cycle on that frame, because we tell the task to quit and execute again next frame, when the delta time will (hopefully) have fallen back to a reasonable value. On the next frame, the task will continue as normal unless the delta time is too high again.

Pop quiz – delta time

1. What is delta time?
2. Why do we use delta time?

Over viewing task return options

So far, all of our tasks have used the same `return` statement, `return task.cont`. This isn't our only option, though. In reality, we have three options to choose from:

♦ `task.cont` is our first option. Using this return value tells the task to execute again next frame. This option is intended for tasks that continue without interruption.

- ◆ `task.again` is our second option. This option is meant for use with `doMethodLater`. If we use this return value, the task will execute again after the delay that's provided to `doMethodLater`. This means that if we have a one second delay in `doMethodLater` and we use `return task.again`, the task will execute once every second.

- ◆ `task.done` is the last return value. This tells the task to remove itself from the task manager and stop executing. We can use `task.done` with a `doMethodLater` to perform an action once after a delay, or we could use `task.done` to stop a task that is no longer needed. Returning `task.done` is the same as returning nothing or `None`.

In Python, all methods and functions automatically return `None` when they finish, unless they are told otherwise. That means if we don't need to return any specific values, we can just omit the `return` statement altogether. However, it helps with keeping code organized and easy to read if we put in a return statement, so it's good programming practice to do so.

About the None type object

There is a special object in Python called `None`, which represents nothing. In Python, when we want to set a variable to equal nothing at all, not even the value `0`, we set it equal to `None`. Python is built to understand that a reference to `None` is a reference to nothing at all.

Time for action – exploring task return options

We're going to modify our two tasks to take advantage of some of these other task return options. To start with, we're going to change `cycleMove` so that it stops after the cycle has moved a set distance. After that, we'll change `debugTask` to only print once every second.

1. The first thing to do is create a variable that will store the distance the cycle has travelled, so we can make it stop once that distance is greater than a certain amount. In our `__init__` method, we need to add a line to declare the variable. Put this line just before our call to `taskMgr.doMethodLater` in the `__init__` method.

    ```
    self.cycle2.setPos(-2,15,0)
    self.distTrav = 0
    ```

2. `taskMgr.doMethodLater(5, self.cycleMove, "Cycle Move")` Now we need to increment that variable, and tell the task to stop after `self.distTrav` increases past a value. Add this block of code to `cycleMove`, above the return statement we currently have.

    ```
    self.distTrav += 10 * dt
    if(self.distTrav >= 40): return task.done
    ```

3. Now we need to change the line where we add the `debugTask` to `taskMgr` so that we add `debugTask` with a `doMethodLater`, like so:

```
taskMgr.doMethodLater(1, self.debugTask, "Debug Task")
```

4. We also need to change the `return` statement for `debugTask` from a `task.cont` to a `task.again`. Once we've finished all of that, our code should look like this:

```
class World:
  def __init__(self):
    base.setBackgroundColor(0, 0, 0)
    self.track = loader.loadModel("../Models/Track.egg")
    self.track.reparentTo(render)
    self.track.setPos(0,0,-5)
    self.cycle1 = loader.loadModel("../Models/Cycle.bam")
    self.cycle1.reparentTo(render)
    self.cycle1.setPos(2,15,0)
    self.cycle2 = loader.loadModel("../Models/Cycle.bam")
    self.cycle2.reparentTo(render)
    self.cycle2.setPos(-2,15,0)
    self.distTrav = 0
    taskMgr.doMethodLater(5, self.cycleMove, "Cycle Move")
    taskMgr.doMethodLater(1, self.debugTask, "Debug Task")
  def cycleMove(self, task):
    dt = globalClock.getDt()
    if( dt > .20):
      return task.cont
    print(dt)
    self.cycle1.setY(self.cycle1, 10 * dt)
    self.distTrav += 10 * dt
    if(self.distTrav >= 40): return task.done
    return task.cont
  def debugTask(self, task):
    print(taskMgr)
    return task.again
```

5. Go ahead and save this file as `chp03_08.py` and run it to see the following output:

What just happened?

This time we have two big changes in our output. The first is that the cycle stops moving after a while. Each time `cycleMove` is executed, the variable `self.distTrav` is incremented. When it reaches 40 or more it triggers the following line of code:

```
if(self.distTrav >= 40): return task.done
```

Which ends the task. `taskMgr` is also being printed less frequently now, because we gave the `debugTask` a one second delay and we are using `task.again` to re-queue it with the same delay each time it's executed.

Pop quiz – task return options

1. What options for task return values are available to us?

2. Which return option should we use if we want the task to stop executing?

3. If we want a task to execute again after the delay it was originally given passes, which return option should we use?

Have a go hero – creating more tasks

Try creating some more tasks on your own. Make a task that slowly changes the color of a cycle, or slowly rotates it. Create a task that launches another task after a certain amount of time or when it reaches a certain value. Get used to using tasks in combination with each other as well as individually.

Prioritizing tasks

When a task is added to the task manager, it may be given an optional priority. We've actually seen these priorities already; remember the sort column of the `print(taskMgr)` output? That column shows the priorities assigned to the tasks in the task manager. Tasks with a lower priority are executed before tasks with a higher priority. That may seem a little backwards, but that's the way it is.

The default priority of a new task is `0`. To assign a different priority, just add a priority number to the end of the `add` or `doMethodLater` call.

```
taskMgr.add(self.myTask, "My Task Name", 5)
taskMgr.doMethodLater(10, self.myTask, "My Task Name", 129)
```

Tasks with the same priority number are executed in no particular order, and that order may change from frame to frame. However, if two tasks have priority 1 and two tasks have priority 5, both of the tasks with priority 1 will execute before either task with priority 5.

Prioritizing tasks this way can be helpful, but generally it isn't needed.

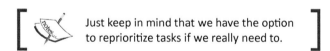

Just keep in mind that we have the option to reprioritize tasks if we really need to.

Removing tasks from the task manager

We've already talked about one method for removing tasks that we don't want running anymore. We can return `task.done` to end a task permanently. There are other methods we can use as well, so let's talk about them now.

There may come a time when we need to remove a task from outside the task in question. In this case, `task.done` doesn't help us at all. The task manager comes equipped with two methods, called `remove` and `removeTasksMatching` to help us out with this. Both of these methods operate on task names. `remove` requires the exact name of the task we wish to remove, but `removeTasksMatching` can use a partial task name with wild cards to remove a group of tasks. Both methods remove all tasks that match the given name, so if multiple tasks have the exact same name either method can remove all of them at once. Here is what the calls look like:

```
taskMgr.remove("My Task Name")
taskMgr.removeTasksMatching("My Task *")
```

Time for action – removing tasks by name

For this lesson, we're going to make a second task to move `self.cycle2`. Then we're going to remove both of the cycles' movement tasks at the same time. We'll use `remove` first, and then we'll do it again with `removeTasksMatching`.

1. First off, we don't want the cycle tasks removing themselves prematurely, so we need to delete the `return task.done` from `cycleMove`. Take out the `if` statement that triggers it as well, we don't need that anymore either. While we're at it, we should remove the lines that reference `self.distTrav` as well.

2. To keep our command prompt from getting too cluttered, we should delete the line in `cycleMove` that prints delta time, `print(dt)`. After that, copy the entire `cycleMove` method and paste a copy in beneath the original. Rename the original to `cycleMove1` and rename the copy to `cycleMove2`. Finally, in `cycleMove2`, change all the references to `self.cycle1` to `self.cycle2`. We can use Notepad++'s Find and Replace dialogue to do this. Bring it up by hitting *Ctrl+F*. Click over to the **Replace** tab and type `self.cycle1` into the **Find What** box. Type `self.cycle2` into the **Replace** box. Click on **Find Next** until the `self.cycle1` you want to replace is highlighted, and click the **Replace** button.

3. The next step is to duplicate the line where we add `cycleMove` to the task manager. Paste a copy of that line right beneath it, and change both lines so that they reference `cycleMove1` and `cycleMove2` respectively. Don't change the name we're giving either of them: we want them both to be named "Cycle Move". Once all these edits are done, our code should look like this:

```
class World:
  def __init__(self):
    base.setBackgroundColor(0, 0, 0)
    self.track = loader.loadModel("../Models/Track.egg")
    self.track.reparentTo(render)
```

```
        self.track.setPos(0,0,-5)
        self.cycle1 = loader.loadModel("../Models/Cycle.bam")
        self.cycle1.reparentTo(render)
        self.cycle1.setPos(2,15,0)
        self.cycle2 = loader.loadModel("../Models/Cycle.bam")
        self.cycle2.reparentTo(render)
        self.cycle2.setPos(-2,15,0)
        taskMgr.doMethodLater(5, self.cycleMove1, "Cycle Move")
        taskMgr.doMethodLater(5, self.cycleMove2, "Cycle Move")
        taskMgr.doMethodLater(10, self.debugTask, "Debug Task")
    def cycleMove1(self, task):
        dt = globalClock.getDt()
        if( dt > .20):
            return task.cont
        self.cycle1.setY(self.cycle1, 10 * dt)
        return task.cont
    def cycleMove2(self, task):
        dt = globalClock.getDt()
        if( dt > .20):
            return task.cont
        self.cycle2.setY(self.cycle2, 10 * dt)
        return task.cont
    def debugTask(self, task):
        print(taskMgr)
        taskMgr.remove("Cycle Move")
        return task.again
```

4. Now that we have our two tasks setup, we just need a way to tell them to stop. Change the delay we're giving to debugTask to 10.

5. In debugTask, add the following line:

```
        taskMgr.remove("Cycle Move")
```

6. Save the file as chp03_09.py and run it.

7. Both cycles get stopped 10 seconds into the program, just as intended.

8. Next, change the names we're giving cycleMove1 and cycleMove2 from "Cycle Move" to "Cycle Move 1" and "Cycle Move 2". Also change the line where we remove the tasks to use the removeTasksMatching method instead of the remove method, as shown here:

```
        taskMgr.removeTasksMatching("Cycle Move *")
```

9. Save the file as chp03_10.py and run it to see the following output:

What just happened?

When we ran chp03_09.py we used the remove method to remove any and all tasks named "Cycle Move", so the tasks moving each of the cycles were stopped and taken out of the task manager. In chp03_10.py we used removeTasksMatching instead. That time we gave it the string "Cycle Move *". The * in that string acted as a wild card, so any task that started with "Cycle Move " (including the spaces) was stopped and removed from the task manager. We can use the * wild card at the beginning of the string we give to removeTasksMatching, too!

Dissecting task objects

There is one more subject to cover before we're finished with our exploration of tasks, and that is the task object itself. Every method we created as a task so far was set to accept a variable called task. The task manager passes a task object into that variable.

Honestly, we don't need to interact with the task object very often. For the most part, it just supplies us with extra information about the task. We access that information by using the following attributes of the `task` object:

- `task.time` returns a float that tells us how much time has passed since the first time the task was executed. This float continues to increase even when the task isn't being executed.

- `task.frame` returns an integer that tells us how many frames have passed since the task was added to the task manager. This count may start from 0 or 1.

- `task.id` returns a unique id number for the task. The task manager assigns this id number when the task is added.

- `task.name` returns the name given to the task.

Again, these aren't used very often, but they might help with debugging.

Summary

In this chapter we learned all about using and managing tasks.

Here are some of the things we covered:

- We talked about the task manager and how to add and remove tasks from it
- We talked about how to design methods for use as tasks
- After that we went over the different return options that influence how a task behaves in the future

We also covered how task priorities influence the order they are executed in, and we talked about the task objects that are passed to task methods.

Next chapter we're going to talk about another method for adding dynamism to our game: events and input handling. We're going to set up one of our cycles so that we can use keyboard controls to steer our way around the track, so get ready!

4
Taking Control: Events and User Input

In addition to tasks, we have one more system in Panda3D that we can use to control dynamic elements in our game: events. In this chapter, we're going to use events and tasks to set up our cycle so that the player can move it around the track. We're also going to set up some important rules for our cycle's movement, such as acceleration and simulating drift.

This is what we'll talk about:

◆   Working with events

◆   Using keyboard events

◆   Implementing advanced cycle controls

◆   Utilizing mouse input and creating camera control

◆   Ending event response

The event system is vital to making our game respond to anything other than the passage of time. It's not too complicated, but we still need to pay attention and make sure we don't miss anything!

Working with events

Events are basically messages that are handled by the `messenger` object created by `DirectStart`. When an event occurs, all of the objects that have been told to respond to that event will call a specified function. It's really a pretty simple system. Most of the set up of events is handled for us when the `messenger` is created, which makes them very easy to use.

The first step to using events is to register an event response. To do this, we need to use the `accept()` method. By default, our `World` class doesn't have an `accept()` method, so to give it one, we need to inherit that method from a built-in class called `DirectObject`.

Once we have the `accept()` method, we can use it like this:

```
self.accept([eventName], [function])
```

The event name we give to the `accept()` method is a string that serves as an identifier for the unique event we want to respond to. The function we pass in will be called when the event occurs.

Let's set up a simple event-response system in our program to see how this works.

Time for action – registering and responding to events

We need to make several changes to our code to make this work. We should be extra careful when following these directions to avoid making a mistake:

1. Start by opening up `chp03_10.py` and resave it in the `Chapter04` folder as `chp04_01.py`.

2. The first thing we need to do is import `DirectObject` so that we can inherit from it. Add the following line to your program below the very first line. This is case sensitive, so make sure to type it correctly.

```
from direct.showbase.DirectObject import DirectObject
```

3. Once we have that, we need to change the way we're creating our `World` class. Change the class definition line to the following:

```
class World(DirectObject):
```

4. We have some extra lines in our program that aren't really necessary for what we're doing now. We should clean those up so we can focus on what's important. To start with, we should remove the second cycle from our game. Delete the following lines:

```
self.cycle2 = loader.loadModel("../Models/Cycle.bam")
self.cycle2.reparentTo(render)
self.cycle2.setPos(-2,15,0)
```

5. Also remove the entire `cycleMove2()` function, and the call to `taskMgr.doMethodLater` which initiates it.

6. Next, highlight the words `self.cycle1` on any of the lines where we see it. Press *Ctrl+F* to bring up the **find and replace** window, go to the **replace** tab, and notice that the text we highlighted is in the **find** field. Change the **replace** field to `self.cycle` and click the **replace all** button.

7. When all of that is finished, our code will look like the following block of code:

```
import direct.directbase.DirectStart
from direct.showbase.DirectObject import DirectObject

class World(DirectObject):
  def __init__(self):
    base.setBackgroundColor(0, 0, 0)
    self.track = loader.loadModel("../Models/Track.egg")
    self.track.reparentTo(render)
    self.track.setPos(0,0,-5)
    self.cycle = loader.loadModel("../Models/Cycle.bam")
    self.cycle.reparentTo(render)
    self.cycle.setPos(2,15,0)
    taskMgr.doMethodLater(5, self.cycleMove1, "Cycle Move 1")
    taskMgr.doMethodLater(10, self.debugTask, "Debug Task")
  def cycleMove1(self, task):
    dt = globalClock.getDt()
    if( dt > .20):
      return task.cont
    self.cycle.setY(self.cycle, 10 * dt)
    return task.cont
  def debugTask(self, task):
    print(taskMgr)
    taskMgr.removeTasksMatching("Cycle Move *")
    return task.again
w = World()
run()
```

8. Add the following line to the __init__ method just before the def cycleMove1 statement:

```
self.accept("h", self.setKey)
```

9. Right below that addition, add the following block of code:

```
def setKey(self):
  print("Hello!")
```

10. Use *Ctrl+S* to save the file and then run it. When the window opens, press the *H* key on the keyboard and look at the command prompt window.

What just happened?

The first thing we accomplished was to import the `DirectObject` class and change our `World` class to inherit from it. That allowed us to use the `accept()` method. We then used `self.accept` to register an event called `"h"` and tie it to the function called `setKey()`. We told the `setKey()` function to print out a little bit of text so that we could see when the function was called.

The program responded to pressing the *H* key because that activates the `"h"` event. When the `"h"` event occurred, the `setKey()` function was called and our message got printed to the command prompt window. This is an example of a keyboard event, which we're going to talk about in the next section.

Pop quiz – working with events

1. Why did we change the `World` class to inherit from `DirectObject`?

2. What does the `accept()` method do?

Using keyboard events

By default, Panda3D ties events to every key on the standard keyboard. In fact, it ties two events to each key. The first event occurs whenever the key is pressed down, and the second happens when the key is released. Each of these events is named after the key it corresponds to. For all the keys that type characters, the event is named after that character. These are always lowercase, even when *Shift* is involved. Here are some examples:

`"a", "b", "c", " [", "5"`

The following event names won't work:

`"A", "B", "C", "{", "%"`

The event for releasing the key adds up to the end of the event name. For example:

`"a-up", " [-up", "5-up"`

There is also an event for the auto-repeat that occurs when a key is held down on the keyboard. This uses `repeat`.

`"a-repeat", " [-repeat", "5-repeat"`

Keys that don't type a character are labelled as follows:

`"escape", "f1", "f2", "f12", "print_screen", "scroll_lock", "num_lock"`

`"backspace", "insert", "home", "page_up", "delete", "end", "page_down"`

```
"caps_lock", "enter", "space", "tab", "pause"

"arrow_left", "arrow_up", "arrow_down", "arrow_right"

"shift", "lshift", "rshift"

"control", "alt", "lcontrol", "lalt", "ralt", "rcontrol"
```

Note that some keys will initiate multiple events. For example, the right shift key will initiate the `"shift"` event and the `"rshift"` event.

Modifier keys pressed with other keys will initiate a unique combined event in addition to individual events for the keys. The order for multiple modifier keys is always *shift*, then *control*, then *alt*. For example:

```
"shift-a", "control-a", "shift-control-a", "shift-control-alt-a"
```

It's possible to tell the `messenger` to display these events by calling `messenger.toggleVerbose()`

Using a key map

When programming video games, it isn't very helpful to have controls activating only when an event is triggered. Usually, we want to have the controls working continuously for as long as the key is held down and to stop when the key is let up. To get this kind of utility, we'll use a key map.

A key map is just a python dictionary with entries for each key we're using. The value stored in that entry is `False` when the button is up, and `True` when the button is down. This is easy enough to set up, but to do it, we need to pass extra arguments to the `setKey()` function when the key events are triggered. The `accept()` method gives us that option.

```
self.accept([eventName], [function], [[extraArg1, extraArg2, ...]])
```

Note the double brackets around the extra arguments. The extra arguments need to be passed enclosed in square brackets of their own. Here's an example to clarify:

```
self.accept("h", self.setKey, ["h", True])
```

For the key down events, the value in the key map is set to `True`, and for key up events the value in the key map is set to `False`.

Putting the key map to use requires a task that checks the key map values for every frame and performs actions or calls functions in response to those key map values. This way we can use events to control what actions a task performs each frame.

Time for action – creating and using a key map

1. The first step to using a key map is to actually create the dictionary that serves the purpose. Right after the line that calls `self.cycle.setPos()` method in the `__init__` method, insert the following block of code to create the dictionary:

```
self.keyMap = {"w" : False,
               "s" : False,
               "a" : False,
               "d" : False}
```

2. Now we need to register events for the four keys in our key map. Replace the current `self.accept()` call, with the following code:

```
self.accept("w", self.setKey, ["w", True])
self.accept("s", self.setKey, ["s", True])
self.accept("a", self.setKey, ["a", True])
self.accept("d", self.setKey, ["d", True])
self.accept("w-up", self.setKey, ["w", False])
self.accept("s-up", self.setKey, ["s", False])
self.accept("a-up", self.setKey, ["a", False])
self.accept("d-up", self.setKey, ["d", False])
```

3. Next, we need to change our `setKey()` method to look like this:

```
def setKey(self, key, value):
    self.keyMap[key] = value
```

4. The key map is ready to go but we won't get any results at this point because we aren't using the key map for anything. To fix that, change the line where we add the `cycleMove1()` method to the task manager from a `taskMgr.doMethodLater()` call to a `taskMgr.add()` call and rename the method it uses.

```
taskMgr.add(self.cycleControl, "Cycle Control"
```

5. Scroll down to the `cycleMove1()` method and change its name to `cycleControl`. We'll also add an `if` statement to this method.

```
if(self.keyMap["w"] == True):
    self.cycle.setY(self.cycle, 10 * dt)
```

6. Our code should look like the following one when we're done:

```
import direct.directbase.DirectStart
from direct.showbase.DirectObject import DirectObject

class World(DirectObject):
    def __init__(self):
        base.setBackgroundColor(0, 0, 0)
```

```
        self.track = loader.loadModel("../Models/Track.egg")
        self.track.reparentTo(render)
        self.track.setPos(0,0,-5)
        self.cycle = loader.loadModel("../Models/Cycle.bam")
        self.cycle.reparentTo(render)
        self.cycle.setPos(2,15,0)
        self.keyMap = {"w" : False,
            "s" : False,
            "a" : False,
            "d" : False}
        taskMgr.add(self.cycleControl, "Cycle Control")
        taskMgr.doMethodLater(10, self.debugTask, "Debug Task")
        self.accept("w", self.setKey, ["w", True])
        self.accept("s", self.setKey, ["s", True])
        self.accept("a", self.setKey, ["a", True])
        self.accept("d", self.setKey, ["d", True])
        self.accept("w-up", self.setKey, ["w", False])
        self.accept("s-up", self.setKey, ["s", False])
        self.accept("a-up", self.setKey, ["a", False])
        self.accept("d-up", self.setKey, ["d", False])
    def setKey(self, key, value):
        self.keyMap[key] = value
    def cycleControl(self, task):
        dt = globalClock.getDt()
        if( dt > .20):
            return task.cont
        if(self.keyMap["w"] == True):
            self.cycle.setY(self.cycle, 10 * dt)
        return task.cont
    def debugTask(self, task):
        print(taskMgr)
        taskMgr.removeTasksMatching("Cycle Move *")
        return task.again
w = World()
run()
```

7. After doing all that, save the file as chp04_02.py and run it. While it's running press the *W* key and hold it for a second or two. Note that the Panda3D window needs to have focus to respond to keyboard input. If you click on another window or *Alt+Tab* for another window, the game won't respond to the keyboard anymore.

What just happened?

Now the cycle moves only when the *W* key is held down. That's because when the *W* key is pressed, the value for "w" in the key map changes to True, and when the key is released, the value changes back to False. The cycleControl task only moves the cycle forward when the value for "w" equals True.

Pop quiz – using keyboard input

1. What Python object type do we use for a key map?
2. What would the event name string generated by holding *shift* and *alt* and pressing the *Q* key be?

Implementing advanced cycle controls

Now it's time to get serious about our cycle controls. We need acceleration, throttle, and turning, if we want our cycle to behave the way it should. We've covered all the topics we need to implement these advanced controls, so let's get down to it.

Time for action – implementing acceleration

Our cycle needs to accelerate at a constant rate until it reaches the throttle setting, or decelerate to the throttle, if necessary. This will take two things to make happen, some new variables and two new methods.

1. To start with, we're going to add some variable declarations at the beginning of our __init__ method. Place this code right below the line where we define the __init__ method.

   ```
   self.speed = 0
   self.throttle = 0
   self.maxSpeed = 200
   self.accel = 25
   ```

2. We also want to add a new method to our World class. Add this code to the end of the World class, right above the line that sets w = World()

   ```
   def speedCheck(self, dt):
       tSetting = (self.maxSpeed * self.throttle)
       if(self.speed < tSetting):
         if((self.speed + (self.accel * dt)) > tSetting):
           self.speed = tSetting
         else:
           self.speed += (self.accel * dt)
       elif(self.speed > tSetting):
         if((self.speed - (self.accel * dt)) < tSetting):
           self.speed = tSetting
         else:
           self.speed -= (self.accel * dt)
   ```

3. Some changes to our cycleControl task method are needed as well. Replace this line:

   ```
   self.cycle.setY(self.cycle, 10 * dt)
   ```

   With the following code block:

   ```
   self.throttle = 1
   elif(self.keyMap["s"] == True):
   ```

```
        self.throttle = -1
    else:
        self.throttle = 0
```

4. At the end of the `cycleControl()` method, just above `return task.cont`, add the following lines of code:

    ```
    self.speedCheck(dt)
    self.move(dt)
    ```

5. Finally, we need to add the `move()` method we just made a call to. Place this code right at the end of the `speedCheck()` method:

    ```
    def move(self, dt):
        mps = self.speed * 1000 / 3600
        self.cycle.setY(self.cycle, mps * dt)
    ```

6. Our program has gotten too big now to fit into a simple screenshot, but don't forget that we can look at the example code provided with this book to check and make sure we did everything right. The file for this code is `chp04_03.py` and you can find it in the `Chapter04/Examples` folder.

7. Save the file as `chp04_03.py` and run it. Press the *W* and *S* keys to make the cycle move forward and backward.

What just happened?

We just made some major changes to the way our cycle moves. Let's break the changes down and go over them step by step.

First we added some variables to the program:

- `self.speed`—Represents the current speed of the cycle, in kilometres per hour.
- `self.maxSpeed`—Stores the maximum speed of the cycle, also in kilometres per hour.
- `self.throttle`—Contains the current setting for the throttle. This is expressed as a decimal that can range from -1 to 1. We use it like a percentage. For example, .5 would tell the cycle to move forward at 50% of the max speed, and -.2 would tell the cycle to move backward at 20% of the max speed.
- `self.accel` is the rate of acceleration for the cycle, in kilometres per hour. Since our cycle is a hovering vehicle, it can't use friction to stop. Instead, it can only accelerate in reverse. This means we can use `self.accel` for our deceleration as well.

Our speed variables are expressed in kilometres per hour, but our game is scaled such that one unit in Panda3D is equal to one meter. For that reason, we have to convert kilometres per hour to meters per second in order to move our cycle the correct amount. We do this in the `move()` method we created.

```
def move(self, dt):
  mps = self.speed * 1000 / 3600
  self.cycle.setY(self.cycle, mps * dt)
```

We also created a method called `speedCheck()`. The purpose of this method is to compare the current speed of the cycle with the throttle setting and check whether the cycle needs to accelerate or decelerate in order to match its speed to the throttle. Let's take a look at this method to see how it works.

```
def speedCheck(self, dt):
```

This line defines the method name and tells it to accept `self` and `dt`. Since we want the changes in the cycle's speed to happen based on time and not on frames, we need to use `dt`. Instead of acquiring the `dt` again, we pass in the `dt` from `cycleControl`. That saves us a little bit of work.

```
tSetting = (self.maxSpeed * self.throttle)
```

This line creates a temporary variable to store the throttle setting. Remember that `self.throttle` is a decimal that represents the percentage of maximum speed the throttle is set to, so we need to multiply `self.throttle` and `self.maxSpeed` to get the actual kilometres per hour the throttle is set for.

```
if(self.speed < tSetting):
  if((self.speed + (self.accel * dt)) > tSetting):
    self.speed = tSetting
  else:
    self.speed += (self.accel * dt)
```

The first line checks if the current speed is lower than the throttle setting. If so, we proceed to the next line. Here, we perform a limit check. We add (self.accel * dt) to self.speed to find out what our speed would be if we accelerate this frame. If it would put our speed above the throttle setting, then we would accelerate too much. In this case, we proceed to the next line and simply set self.speed equal to the throttle setting. If accelerating would not exceed our throttle setting, then we proceed to the last line and increase the speed based on our acceleration rating and delta time.

```
elif(self.speed > tSetting):
  if((self.speed - (self.accel * dt)) < tSetting):
    self.speed = tSetting
  else:
    self.speed -= (self.accel * dt)
```

This code performs the same operations as the block we just went over, except it handles deceleration instead of acceleration. We start this block with an else-if because self.speed can only be greater than tSetting if it isn't less than tSetting, which we already checked.

Then we made some changes to cycleControl. We had two goals here. The first was to read the key map and set the throttle to maximum if *w* was pressed, to maximum reverse if *s* was pressed, and to 0 if nothing was pressed. We use elif and else for the latter two conditions because we want forward to take priority over backward, and backward to take priority over stopping.

This alone would accomplish nothing, so we also added two method calls, one for speedCheck() and one for move(). We call these methods from cycleControl instead of making them separate tasks because it's easier that way. Either way would work, but making them separate tasks would require more code, and we would have to set priorities to make sure they execute in the correct order.

Time for action – implementing throttle control

We already have rudimentary throttle control, in that we can set the throttle to maximum forward or maximum reverse, but we need finer control than that for our game. We'll create a new method for this:

1. Just below the end of the cycleControl() method, add a new method that looks like the following code:

```
def adjustThrottle(self, dir, dt):
  if(dir == "up"):
    self.throttle += .25 * dt
    if(self.throttle > 1 ): self.throttle = 1
  else:
    self.throttle -= .25 * dt
    if(self.throttle < -1 ): self.throttle = -1
```

2. Next, we can simply delete these lines from the `cycleControl()` method:

```
else:
  self.throttle = 0
```

3. Now we need to change the lines where we set our throttle to use the new `adjustThrottle()` method. Change the line that sets `self.throttle = 1` to:

```
self.adjustThrottle("up", dt)
```

4. Change the line that sets `self.throttle = -1` to:

```
self.adjustThrottle("down", dt)
```

5. Check `chp04_04.py` in the `Chapter04/Examples` folder, if you need to see the code.

6. Save the file as `chp04_04.py` and run it.

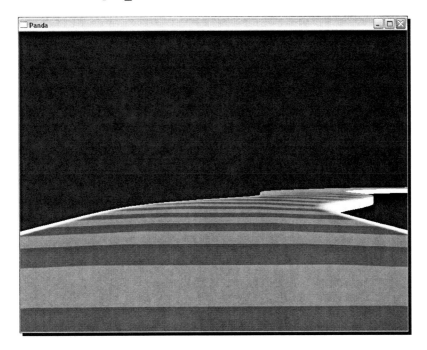

What just happened?

This time the cycle didn't stop when we released the keyboard keys. That's because the position of the throttle is being saved. Let's take a look at the `adjustThrottle()` method to see how it works:

```
def adjustThrottle(self, dir, dt):
  if(dir == "up"):
    self.throttle += .25 * dt
    if(self.throttle > 1 ): self.throttle = 1
  else:
    self.throttle -= .25 * dt
    if(self.throttle < -1 ): self.throttle = -1
```

First, we accept two variables other than `self`. `dt`. We should recognize that `dir` just tells the method whether we are adjusting the throttle up or down. We start the method with an `if` statement to determine the direction we're adjusting the throttle in, and then we adjust it by 0.25 per second. After the adjustments, we check to see if it has gone outside the limit of -1 to 1, and if so, we set it to the limit.

Time for action – implementing turning

Going only in straight lines is no fun. We can't have a racing game without turning so we need to get that put in as well.

1. First, we want to add a new variable. Place the following code just below the line where we create the `self.accel` variable:

   ```
   self.handling = 20
   ```

2. Next, we're going to write another method for turning. Add the following code just below the end of the `cycleControl()` method:

   ```
   def turn(self, dir, dt):
     turnRate = self.handling * (2 -
       (self.speed / self.maxSpeed))
     if(dir == "r"): turnRate = -turnRate
     self.cycle.setH(self.cycle, turnRate * dt)
   ```

3. Finally, add the following code above the line in the `cycleControl()` method that calls `self.speedCheck(dt)` to put the new method to use:

   ```
   if(self.keyMap["d"] == True):
     self.turn("r", dt)
   elif(self.keyMap["a"] == True):
     self.turn("l", dt)
   ```

4. Check the file `chp04_05.py` in the `Chapter04/Examples` folder to see the code, if necessary.

5. Save the file as `chp04_05.py` and run it.

What just happened?

Now we can turn our cycle left and right as well as move it forward and backward. We accomplished this in pretty much the same way we implemented the throttle control. One major difference is that we didn't limit how much the cycle could turn, we want it to be able to rotate as far as it likes, in either direction. We did limit the handling of the cycle based on its speed, however; therefore, the faster the cycle is moving, the harder it becomes to turn. We did that with the following lines:

```
turnRate = self.handling * (2 -
    (self.speed / self.maxSpeed))
```

This calculation limits the `turnRate` to between 1 and 2 times the variable, depending on the speed of the cycle. This way, the `turnRate` never drops too low.

Utilizing mouse input and creating camera control

The keyboard isn't the only piece of hardware we can get input from. Mouse-clicks also trigger events and we use the same methods to respond to them. The event names for the mouse buttons are:

- `"mouse1"`: Left mouse button
- `"mouse2"`: Middle mouse button
- `"mouse3"`: Right mouse button

Like keyboard keys, the mouse events also have versions that we can take advantage of.

In order to make use of the mouse, we first have to disable the default mouse camera control. For that, we turn back to our old friend `base`. The method `base.disableMouse()` has a deceptive name, because it doesn't actually turn off mouse input. Instead, it removes the camera control scheme that Panda3D uses by default, and allows us to use the mouse for other things, and to control the camera with our own code.

Once we've called the `base.disableMouse()` method, we can access the camera by manipulating the `NodePath` that points to it. For the default camera, that `NodePath` is `base.camera`.

Time for action – tying the camera to the cycle

It's difficult to move the cycle when the camera doesn't go with it, so we're going to make the camera move with the cycle and while we're at it we can set up some zoom in and zoom out controls using the mouse buttons.

1. For starters, we'll disable the default camera controls. Add this code just below our variable declarations in the __init__ method.

   ```
   base.disableMouse()
   ```

2. After that, put this code into the __init__ method right below the line that calls `self.cycle.setPos`.

   ```
   base.camera.reparentTo(self.cycle)
   base.camera.setY(base.camera, -5)
   ```

3. Now, we need to expand our key map to include the left and right mouse buttons. Change the key map definition to the following:

   ```
   self.keyMap = {"w" : False,
           "s" : False,
           "a" : False,
           "d" : False,
   ```

```
               "mouse1" : False,
               "mouse3" : False}
```

4. Naturally, we also need to register the mouse-click events. Add the following two lines at the very bottom of the __init__ method:

    ```
    self.accept("mouse1", self.setKey, ["mouse1", True])
    self.accept("mouse3", self.setKey, ["mouse3", True])
    self.accept("mouse1-up", self.setKey, ["mouse1", False])
    self.accept("mouse3-up", self.setKey, ["mouse3", False])
    ```

5. We'll need a new method to handle the camera's movement, so add this method below the cycleControl() method:

    ```
    def cameraZoom(self, dir, dt):
      if(dir == "in"): base.camera.setY(base.camera, 10 * dt)
      else: base.camera.setY(base.camera, -10 * dt)
    ```

6. Last but not least, we need to add some lines to the cycleControl() method to call the method we just made when the mouse buttons are held down. This code will go above the line that calls self.speedCheck:

    ```
    if(self.keyMap["mouse1"] == True):
      self.cameraZoom("in", dt)
    elif(self.keyMap["mouse3"] == True):
      self.cameraZoom("out", dt)
    ```

7. Take a glance at the example code in Chapter04/Examples/chp04_06.py to check the code we just wrote.

8. Save the file as chp04_06.py and run it.

What just happened?

Now, our camera is behaving much more appropriately. Aside from using base. disableMouse to turn off the default mouse camera controls, we didn't need to do much that we haven't done before. We just expanded our key map to include the left and right mouse buttons and created a new method to zoom the camera in or out when the buttons are held down.

Later on, we'll be making some changes to use the mouse for selecting, aiming, and firing the weapons of our cycle.

Reacting to mouse movement

The last kind of input we're going to cover in this chapter is reacting to mouse movement. To use mouse movement in Panda3D, we'll be tracking the mouse's position in the Panda3D window using a method called base.mouseWatcherNode.getMouse(). This method returns the 2D coordinates of the mouse's position in a decimal. The center of the window is (0,0), the top-right corner is (1,1), and the bottom-left corner is (-1,-1).

Using `base.mouseWatcherNode.getMouse()` carelessly will cause problems. If the mouse isn't within the Panda3D window when that call is made, the program will error out and crash. To avoid this issue we use `base.mouseWatcherNode.hasMouse()` to find out whether the mouse is in the window or not. If the mouse is in the window, the method will return `True`. Otherwise, it will return `False`.

Time for action – turning the camera with the mouse position

To see this in action, we're going to set the camera's heading and pitch based on where the mouse is in the window.

1. Add this code to the `cycleControl()` method right above the call to `self.speedCheck`:

```
if(base.mouseWatcherNode.hasMouse() == True):
    mpos = base.mouseWatcherNode.getMouse()
    base.camera.setP(mpos.getY() * 30)
    base.camera.setH(mpos.getX() * -30)
```

2. Save the file as `chp04_07.py` and run it.

What just happened?

Now, the camera snaps to a new rotation based on the position of the mouse in the window. To be specific, the new rotation is equal to a percentage of 30 degrees according to how far the mouse is from the center of the window.

Pop quiz – utilizing mouse input

1. What happens if we call `base.mouseWatcherNode.getMouse()` when the mouse isn't in the window?

2. What is `base.mouseWatcherNode.hasMouse()` commonly used for?

Have a go hero – creating more tasks

Take some time to play with setting up control schemes. Change the keys that are being used, add keys to change the colour or scale of things, and so on. Try different ideas, like changing the colour of the cycle based on the mouse position within the window, until you feel comfortable with handling user input. Make sure you save the files containing these changes with new names!

Ending event response

In order to tell an object which inherits from `DirectObject` to stop listening to events, we can use two methods. The first method, and the simplest, is `ignoreAll()`. A call to this method would look like the following:

```
self.ignoreAll()
```

This call turns off all event responses for the object. For instance, if we called this method within the `World` class, the `World` class would no longer respond to any of the events we have told it to listen to with `self.accept`.

The second method we can use is the `ignore()` method. We can provide `ignore()` with an event string name just like the `accept()` method to stop listening to that particular event. For example:

```
self.ignore("a")
```

That call would stop event response to the *A* key being pressed.

If we wanted to respond to an event only once, we could use the `acceptOnce()` method instead of the `accept()` method.

Summary

This chapter focused on user input.

Here are some of the things we covered:

- We started by talking about events—what they are, and how to use them.
- Then we talked about the keyboard and the events it triggers. We also went through how to create and use a key map to track the status of the keyboard and mouse buttons.
- We set up some controls for our cycle that use input from the keyboard.
- We used the mouse position in the Panda3D window and the mouse buttons to control the camera, after disabling the default mouse camera controls.
- Lastly, we covered the methods we can use to stop listening for events.

Now that the game is starting to get large, it's time to break it apart into separate classes instead of putting everything in the `World` class. Fortunately, custom classes are what the next chapter is all about!

5

Handling Large Programs with Custom Classes

Our program is really starting to develop now, and it's growing a bit too large to be easily manageable. That means it's time to start breaking it into smaller chunks to make it easier to handle. The topic of this chapter, custom classes, will let us do just that.

We're going to cover:

- ◆ Importing custom classes
- ◆ Adding `NodePath` functionality to a custom class
- ◆ Accessing classes from within another class

Once we have these topics under our belt, we'll be able to handle our program no matter how large it grows by breaking it down into bite-size pieces. So, what are we waiting for, right?

Importing custom classes

A class is a kind of definition. It allows us to describe a certain kind of object, and then later we can use that definition to create one, two, or even dozens of copies of that object, called instances, using the class definition.

We've already started diving into the realm of custom classes with our `World` class. We put the definition for that class into the same file we were running in the Windows command prompt, so we didn't need to import it to gain access to it. If it were in another file, for example `WorldClass.py`, we would need to use an `import` statement to gain access to it. That import statement would look like this:

```
from WorldClass import World
```

The `from` part of the statement tells Python what file to look in to find the definition of the `World` class we are telling it to import. For this to work, the file we're running and the file we're importing should be in the same directory. If they aren't, we would need to include a relative path from the file we're running to the file we want to import in the `from` portion of the `import` statement.

The `import` part of the statement tells Python what we want to bring in from the file. In this case, we're telling it to import something named `World`, so it finds the `World` class and brings it in for us. We have the option of using wild cards here, so we could have used the following code to import everything from the `WorldClass.py` file:

```
from WorldClass import *
```

Time for action – making and importing a custom class

To start with, we're going to make a simple class for the track in our game and import it into our main file.

1. Start by opening up the file `chp04_07.py` and resave it in the `Chapter05` folder as `WorldClass_01.py`.

2. Next, open a new blank document in Notepad++ and save it as `TrackClass_01.py`.

3. In the new file, add the following lines of code at the very top:
```
class Track:
    def __init__(self):
```

4. The next step is to copy a few lines from `WorldClass_01.py`, specifically the lines where we load our track, reparent it, and reposition it. Once you've copied the lines to the clipboard, you can delete them from the `WorldClass_01.py` file. These are the lines we're referring to:
```
self.track = loader.loadModel("../Models/Track.egg")
self.track.reparentTo(render)
self.track.setPos(0,0,-5)
```

5. Go back to the file `TrackCLass_01.py` and paste the three lines into the __init__ method, like so:

```
def __init__(self):
    self.track = loader.loadModel("../Models/Track.egg")
    self.track.reparentTo(render)
    self.track.setPos(0,0,-5)
```

6. Go ahead and save `TrackClass_01.py`. We won't be editing it anymore in this *Time for Action* section.

7. In `WorldClass_01.py`, we need to add a new `import` statement to bring in our new custom class. Add the following code right beneath our other `import` statements:

```
from TrackClass_01 import Track
```

8. Leave a blank line above and below the line we just typed to help keep things organized. Our imports should look like the following code now:

```
import direct.directbase.DirectStart
from direct.showbase.DirectObject import DirectObject

from TrackClass_01 import Track

class World(DirectObject):
```

9. Finally, we'll need to create an instance of the `Track` class in order to call its __init__ method and load the track model. Add the following line just below the line where we change the background colour of the window:

```
self.track = Track()
```

10. Because we've imported `Track` from `TrackClass_01`, our program will know that `Track()` means to create a new instance of the `Track` class.

```
def setKey(self):
  print("Hello!")
```

11. Use *Ctrl+s* to save `WorldClass_01.py` and then run it to see the following screenshot:

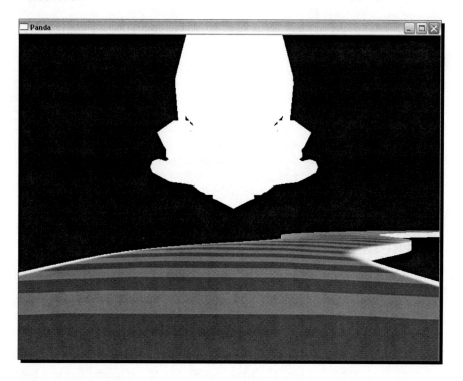

What just happened?

It doesn't look like much has changed since we last ran our program, but we've made a big step by moving the lines of code that handle loading and positioning the track into a new file and importing them from there. A very big step indeed!

Pop quiz – importing custom classes

Custom classes don't do any good unless we import them, so let's make sure we understand how importing works.

1. Where does our program look for files to import classes from?

2. If we want to import all of the objects in a Python file, how can we do that?

Adding NodePath functionality to a custom class

The next custom class we're going to make will be the `Cycle` class, which will represent our characters, the hover cycles for us. Later on, when we start to have these characters interact with one another, we'll want to be able to use `NodePath`-type operations such as `setPos` on them. That means we need to add `NodePath` functionality to the class.

Before we jump the gun and try to inherit from `NodePath` when we make the class, like how the `World` class inherits from `DirectObject`, there's something we need to understand about Panda3D. In order to make Panda3D run faster, many of its classes are written in C++, `NodePath` included among them. These C++ classes can't be directly inherited from by a class in Python. That crossover just doesn't work. Instead, we need to use a little workaround.

Instead of making our class itself a `NodePath`, we're going to create a proxy `NodePath` within our class to act as the root of the class instance. This `NodePath`, which we'll call `root` for convenience, will serve as the parent for all the other `NodePath` in the class. We'll also use it to determine the exact position of the class instance in the world. We can even add `setPos()` and `getPos()` methods to our class that will call `setPos()` and `getPos()` on our `root` so that the class behaves like we inherited from `NodePath`.

To get the proxy `NodePath`, we'll use a new method called `attachNewNode()` that all `NodePath` have, including `render`. This method creates a new `NodePath` that points to whatever node is passed to it, or if a string is passed in it creates a `NodePath` named after the string that doesn't point to any nodes at all. The `NodePath` is returned, so we need to place it into a variable to get a reference to it. For example:

```
self.root = render.attachNewNode("Root")
```

This statement will create a new `NodePath` that is a child of `render`, has the name `Root`, and can be accessed through the `self.root` variable.

Time for action – defining the Cycle class

This example will mostly involve taking code we've already written and moving it to a new file. Be sure to follow along carefully so we don't move any code we don't want to move.

1. First, create a blank file in Notepad++ and save it as `CycleClass_01.py`.

2. Add the following two lines to the new file:
```
class Cycle(DirectObject):
  def __init__(self):
```

3. Next, cut the following lines that declare the speed, acceleration, turning, and other cycle variables from `WorldClass_01.py`, and paste them into the `__init__` method of the `Cycle` class.

```
self.speed = 0
self.throttle = 0
self.maxSpeed = 200
self.accel = 25
self.handling = 20
```

4. Do the same to these lines, which load the cycle model, and reparent and reposition it. They also need to be in the `Cycle` class' `__init__` method.

```
self.cycle = loader.loadModel("../Models/Cycle.bam")
self.cycle.reparentTo(render)
self.cycle.setPos(2,15,0)
```

5. The line where the `cycleControl` task is added to the task manager is next. Place that in the `__init__` method of the `Cycle` class as well.

6. Our next target for cutting and pasting is the definition for the key map. Move that to the bottom of the `__init__` method in the `Cycle` class. Notepad++ will automatically indent pasted blocks from the initial indent when they are pasted. To get the key map to indent correctly, remove the indents from the line you paste on before pasting.

7. Most of the methods in the `World` class at this point are used for controlling the cycle, as are the events that we have registered with the `World` class. We're going to move all of this into the `Cycle` class. Cut the following methods from the `World` class and paste them into the `Cycle` class: `setKey`, `cycleControl()`, `cameraZoom()`, `turn()`, `adjustThrottle()`, `speedCheck()`, and `move()`. This will include everything from where we add the `debugTask()` to the task manager all the way down to right before the `debugTask()` method is actually defined.

8. Now, we need to tell our `World` class to make use of the new `Cycle` class we've moved all this code into. Just below the line where we import the `Track` class, add the following line of code:

```
from CycleClass_01 import Cycle
```

9. Below the line where we instantiate the track, add this to instantiate a cycle:

```
self.cycle = Cycle()
```

10. Save the file containing the `World` class as `WorldClass_02.py`, and save the changes to `CycleClass_01.py`. Check both files against the examples to make sure we did everything correctly, and then run `WorldClass_02.py`. You'll get this error in the Windows command prompt:

```
C:\BGP3D\Chapter05>python WorldClass_02.py
DirectStart: Starting the game.
Known pipe types:
  wglGraphicsPipe
(all display modules loaded.)
Traceback (most recent call last):
  File "WorldClass_02.py", line 21, in <module>
    w = World()
  File "WorldClass_02.py", line 13, in __init__
    base.camera.reparentTo(self.cycle)
TypeError: NodePath.reparentTo() argument 1 must be NodePath, not instance
```

11. Don't worry, we were expecting that error. Next, change `WorldClass_02.py` to import from `CycleClass_02` instead of `CycleClass_01`.

12. Now, go down to the line displayed in the error message, where the camera is reparented to `self.cycle`. Change that line to:

```
base.camera.reparentTo(self.cycle.root)
```

13. Resave `WorldClass_02.py` as `WorldClass_03.py`.

14. Move over to the tab for `CycleClass_01.py` and resave the file as `CycleClass_02.py`. Then, at the very beginning of the `__init__` method, add the following line:

```
self.root = render.attachNewNode("Root")
```

15. Since we're inheriting from `DirectObject` when we create the `Cycle` class, we need to import `DirectObject` or we'll get another error. Of course, we already imported `DirectObject` in our `WorldClass` file, but that doesn't help our `CycleClass` file. Don't worry about the duplication of the import; two copies of `DirectObject` won't be put in memory. The second `import` statement will automatically reference back to the earlier import. Add the following line at the very top of `CycleClass_02.py`:

```
from direct.showbase.DirectObject import DirectObject
```

16. Add a blank line beneath it as well to make it easier to see the division between the import and the creation of the class.

17. Save those changes, and then run `WorldClass_03.py` to see the following screenshot:

What just happened?

The camera doesn't follow the cycle anymore! Our first impression might be that it's because we moved all of the cycle controls over to a new class, but that's actually not the case. The real reason is because our camera is now parented to `self.cycle.root`. This reference points to the new `NodePath` we created with the line:

```
self.root = render.attachNewNode("Root")
```

This is an important concept to catch hold of. We can access the variables within a class instance by appending them to the instance name with a `.` operator. So, `self.cycle.root` in `World` class is the same as `self.root` in `Cycle` class. Since our cycle controls are moving `self.cycle` instead of `self.root`, the camera sits in place.

For now, we're going to leave it broken. In a moment, we're going to take advantage of the proxy `NodePath` we created in the `Cycle` class to start simulating drift when the cycle turns, and that will give us a new parent for the camera that is superior to both the proxy `NodePath` and the cycle model itself.

Simulating drift

The vehicles in our game hover, so it only makes sense that they would drift while turning. The actual physics of drift is kind of complicated and would require some intense vector math to employ in our game. We would need to calculate forces acting in multiple directions.

Instead of doing anything that is complicated, we're going to cheat and simulate drift with a much simpler system. The basic concept of drift is that when the vehicle turns, it takes a little while for the direction it's moving to catch up to and match the direction it's facing. We'll make a system that creates that effect.

To create the system, we're going to need a total of four `NodePaths`. The first is the `root` we created in the last *Time for Action*. In addition to that, we'll need another proxy `NodePath` that faces in the direction the cycle is moving. We'll need the `NodePath` that points to the cycle model, which we already have of course. Lastly, we'll need a third proxy `NodePath` that we can use for a reference to get vector information.

Along with the four `NodePaths`, we'll need the `Vec3` Panda3D class that we haven't seen before. The `Vec3` class is designed to hold a three-coordinate vector, and it has a very handy method for what we want to do.

Time for action – simulating drift

Instead of talking about it all day, let's get the system working and talk about the code once we've finished. Having the examples on hand will help clarify how it all works.

1. First off, let's import the `Vec3` Panda3D class that we'll be using. Add this below the first line of `CycleClass_02.py`:

    ```
    from pandac.PandaModules import Vec3
    ```

2. To keep our `Cycle` class's `__init__` method from getting too cluttered, we're going to create a new method to handle some of our set up. Right after the `setKey()` method, add a new definition that looks like the following line of code:

    ```
    def setupVarsNPs(self):
    ```

3. To give this new method some purpose right off, move these lines from the `__init__` method down into the new method we just defined:

    ```
    self.root = render.attachNewNode("Root")
    self.speed = 0
    self.throttle = 0
    self.maxSpeed = 200
    self.accel = 25
    self.handling = 20
    ```

```
self.cycle = loader.loadModel("../Models/Cycle.bam")
self.cycle.reparentTo(render)
self.cycle.setPos(2,15,0)
```

4. Before we forget, let's add a call to the new method to the very beginning of the
__init__ method.

```
self.setupVarsNPs()
```

5. Next, add the following block of code to the new method below the line where we
create the root NodePath:

```
self.dirNP = self.root.attachNewNode("DirNP")
self.refNP = self.root.attachNewNode("RefNP")
self.dirVec = Vec3(0,0,0)
self.cycleVec = Vec3(0,0,0)
self.refVec = Vec3(0,0,0)
```

6. Now, we want to change our code so our cycle model is parented to root, not to
render, and we need to set the position of the root, not the cycle model's position.

```
self.cycle.reparentTo(self.root)
self.root.setPos(2,15,0)
```

7. While we're here, let's fix our little camera problem. Switch over to
ClassWorld_03.py and cut these lines. Paste them into the bottom
of the setupVarsNPs() method of the Cycle class.

```
base.camera.reparentTo(self.cycle.root)
base.camera.setY(base.camera, -5)
```

8. Change the first line you just pasted to reparent the camera to self.dirNP instead
of to self.cycle.root.

9. Now, we need to add a new method to our Cycle class to actually create the drift
effect. We'll put this method right before the move() method.

```
def simDrift(self, dt):
  self.refNP.setPos(self.dirNP, 0, 1, 0)
  self.dirVec.set(self.refNP.getX(), self.refNP.getY(), 0)
  self.refNP.setPos(self.cycle, 0, 1, 0)
  self.cycleVec.set(self.refNP.getX(), self.refNP.getY(), 0)
  self.refVec.set(0,0,1)
  vecDiff = self.dirVec.signedAngleDeg(self.cycleVec,
    self.refVec)
  f(vecDiff < .1 and vecDiff > -.1):
    self.dirNP.setH(self.cycle.getH())
  else: self.dirNP.setH(self.dirNP, vecDiff * dt * 2.5)
```

```
self.dirNP.setP(self.cycle.getP())
self.dirNP.setR(0)
```

10. Our `cycleControl` task needs to call `simDrift()` before it calls `move()`, so let's add this line just above the call to `self.move(dt)`:

```
self.simDrift(dt)
```

11. Now, we need to make a change to our `move()` method so that it employs these changes when moving the cycle. Change the `move()` method to look like the following code:

```
def move(self, dt):
  mps = self.speed * 1000 / 3600
  self.refNP.setPos(self.dirNP, 0, 1, 0)
  self.dirVec.set(self.refNP.getX(), self.refNP.getY(),
    self.refNP.getZ())
  self.root.setPos(self.root,
    self.dirVec.getX() * dt * mps,
    self.dirVec.getY() * dt * mps,
    self.dirVec.getZ() * dt * mps)
```

12. Save the `Cycle` class file as `CycleClass_03.py`. Change the `World` class file to import from `CycleClass_03` instead of `CycleClass_02`, and save that file as `WorldClass_04.py`. Check both files against the examples to make sure everything looks right, and then run the game.

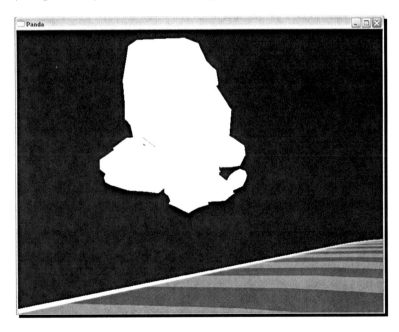

What just happened?

The first thing we should talk about is the import from `pandac.PandaModules`. This is a package of classes belonging to Panda3D where many of Panda3D's built-in components can be found. We'll come back to `pandac.PandaModules` for much more than just `Vec3` as we continue on.

Our next step was to build the `setupVarsNPs()` method. While doing that, we created two new proxy `NodePaths`: `dirNP` and `refNP`, as children of `root`. The fact that they are children of `root` is crucial to the function of our drift simulation system. Being children means they move along with `root` when its position changes, and they exist in the coordinate space of `root`. If that wasn't the case, this drift simulation wouldn't work.

Next, we created three `Vec3` objects: `dirVec`, `cycleVec`, and `refVec`. Technically, we don't need to keep these objects from frame to frame; we don't care about any data they retained from previous frames. The reason we make them permanent attributes of `Cycle` class instead of just temporary variables is to avoid constructing and deconstructing the object's every frame. That's unnecessary extra work for the program. We'll talk more about how we use these objects when we discuss the `simDrift()` method in a minute.

After that, we made the cycle model a child of the `root` `NodePath`. Again, we do this to ensure that the cycle moves along with `root` and that it exists in the coordinate space of `root`. The last thing we did in `setupVarsNPs()` was to parent the camera to `dirNP`. Since `dirNP` faces in the direction the cycle is moving, it makes sense for the camera to follow it. That's what the player will expect.

When we finished with `setupVarsNPs()`, we moved on to create `simDrift()`. This is the workhorse of the drift system, so we'll go over it line by line. Before we do, let's talk about what the method is trying to achieve.

When drifting, a vehicle is really described by two different directions. One is the direction the vehicle is moving in, and the other is the direction the vehicle is facing in. Drifting occurs when those two directions aren't the same, and it ends when they are the same. To create drift, what we need to do is generate a lag between when the cycle turns to a new direction and when its motion changes to match that direction. That's what `simDrift()` does. We move the cycle in the direction `dirNP` faces, and we force `dirNP` to take a little bit of time to turn and match the facing our cycle model has turned to, we'll have drift.

Now, let's look at the code:

```
def simDrift(self, dt):
```

Just like with other methods in the past, we want `simDrift()` to operate based on the amount of time that has passed, not the frame rate the game is running at. We need to pass in `dt` to make that happen.

```
self.refNP.setPos(self.dirNP, 0, 1, 0)
```

This line places `refNP` at one unit on the Y axis, relative to `dirNP`. That means that after this line, `refNP` is exactly one unit forward in the direction `dirNP` is facing. This will help us figure out what direction `dirNP` is facing in.

```
self.dirVec.set(self.refNP.getX(), self.refNP.getY(), 0)
```

If `refNP` is exactly one unit forward in the direction that `dirNP` is facing then that means that the position of `refNP` is a unit vector that shows the direction `dirNP` is facing. That's what we want because we need to calculate the difference between `dirNP`'s facing and the cycle's facing. We store the vector information in `dirVec` using the `set` method, which simply sets the `Vec3` object's three values to the input. Notice that we don't include the Z information. We don't really care about height for this calculation. We're only interested in horizontal facing, not vertical.

```
self.refNP.setPos(self.cycle, 0, 1, 0)
self.cycleVec.set(self.refNP.getX(), self.refNP.getY(), 0)
```

These two lines perform the same function as the last two lines, with one little difference. This time, we're finding the vector that describes what direction the cycle is facing in. We store that information in `cycleVec`.

```
self.refVec.set(0,0,1)
```

This line simply sets `refVec` to point straight up. We need a reference vector for the method we're about to call, and straight up is the direction we need it to point. Now, we have that.

```
vecDiff = self.dirVec.signedAngleDeg(self.cycleVec,
    self.refVec)
```

This is where the real magic happens. We use the method of `Vec3`, `signedAngleDeg()`, to find the angle from `dirVec` to `cycleVec` if we were rotating around `refVec`. That sounds complicated, so let's break it down. Since we call the method on `dirVec`, `dirVec` is our starting point. The first argument we passed was `cycleVec`, so that's the direction we want to reach. Our reference vector is `refVec`, so that is what we rotate around. Basically, what we're asking is: "If `refVec` is up, then how far do I have to turn to go from the direction `dirVec` is facing to the direction `cycleVec` is facing?" `signedAngleDeg()` gives us an answer in a number of degrees. It even tells us if we need to turn left or right, based on if its return is positive or negative.

```
if(vecDiff < .1 and vecDiff > -.1):
    self.dirNP.setH(self.cycle.getH())
else: self.dirNP.setH(self.dirNP, vecDiff * dt * 2.5)
```

Now that we know how far `dirNP` needs to turn to match the facing of the cycle, we check to see if it's a very small amount. If it is, we can just set `dirNP`'s facing to exactly match the cycle model's facing. If not, then things get exciting. We rotate `dirNP` based on how big the difference between the two headings is. This means that the further the cycle turns away from the direction it's moving, the faster the direction of its motion changes. Just like real drift. We also base it on the passage of time by multiplying it by `dt`, and because `dt` is typically a very small decimal, we multiply it all by 2.5 to make `dirNP` catch up to the cycle a little faster. Otherwise, it would turn too slowly, and our drift amount would be enormous.

```
self.dirNP.setP(self.cycle.getP())
self.dirNP.setR(0)
```

These two lines are insurance against the `dirNP` misbehaving as we rotate it around. We always want the pitch of `dirNP` to be the same as the cycle model's, and we never want it to roll at all, so here we enforce those rules.

After we added in `simDrift()`, we made some changes to move to take advantage of our hard work. What we wanted from these changes was to make `root` move in the direction of `dirNP`'s facing. It might be simple to think, "Well, just rotate `root` to match `dirNP`'s heading, and then move it forward and you're good." But, remember that `dirNP` and the cycle model are both children of `root`. If `root` is rotated, they will rotate along with it!

To get around that problem, we once again used `refNP` to get `dirNP`'s facing in vector form and stored it in `dirVec`. That's nothing new, we've done that before. The next step is to move `root` in that direction. Well, remember that `dirVec` now holds a unit vector. That means that it represents one unit of movement in the direction `dirNP` is facing. All we need to do is multiply that by our speed and the passage of time, and `root` will zoom off exactly like it's supposed to. That's what the following lines do:

```
self.root.setPos(self.root,
    self.dirVec.getX() * dt * mps,
    self.dirVec.getY() * dt * mps,
    self.dirVec.getZ() * dt * mps)
```

With one call to `setPos()`, we move `root` along all three axes an amount equal to the direction multiplied by time and speed. There you have it, our rotation problem is solved. `root` doesn't need to rotate at all!

Pop quiz – using custom classes with NodePaths

`NodePath` integration with custom classes is often needed in programming, so we should make sure to go over some of the important points.

1. Why can't we inherit directly from `NodePath`?
2. How do we get around the problem discussed in question 1?

Accessing classes from within another class

We've got one more topic to discuss in this chapter. What do we do if we want classes to talk to each other? There's a fairly simple solution to the problem. We need to give them access to each other.

Time for action – adding an input manager

To illustrate how this works, we're going to take the keyboard controls out of the Cycle class, put them in a new class, and give the `Cycle` class access to those controls.

1. To start with, save `CycleCLass_03.py` as `InputManagerClass_01.py`. Since we're taking pretty much all of the code we need from the `Cycle` class, we might as well use it as a starting point.

2. Delete the line where we import `Vec3`. We don't need `Vec3` for this class, so we don't need to import it.

3. Change the class definition line to reflect our new class name: `InputManager`:

   ```
   class InputManager(DirectObject):
   ```

4. Delete the first two lines in the `__init__` method. We don't need to set up any variables or `NodePaths`, so we don't need to call `setupVarsNPs()`. We also don't need to add a task for this class.

5. Delete everything below the line `setKey()` method. We don't need any of the class methods other than `setKey()`. That's all the work we need to do on the `InputManager` class. Go ahead and save the file.

6. Reopen `CycleClass_03.py`.

7. In `CycleClass_03.py`, delete the following lines we left in the `InputManager`. We don't need them here anymore.

   ```
   self.keyMap = {"w" : False,
           "s" : False,
           "a" : False,
           "d" : False,
           "mouse1" : False,
           "mouse3" : False}
   self.accept("w", self.setKey, ["w", True])
   self.accept("s", self.setKey, ["s", True])
   self.accept("a", self.setKey, ["a", True])
   self.accept("d", self.setKey, ["d", True])
   self.accept("mouse1", self.setKey, ["mouse1", True])
   ```

```
        self.accept("mouse3", self.setKey, ["mouse3", True])
        self.accept("w-up", self.setKey, ["w", False])
        self.accept("s-up", self.setKey, ["s", False])
        self.accept("a-up", self.setKey, ["a", False])
        self.accept("d-up", self.setKey, ["d", False])
        self.accept("mouse1-up", self.setKey, ["mouse1", False])
        self.accept("mouse3-up", self.setKey, ["mouse3", False])
    def setKey(self, key, value):
        self.keyMap[key] = value
```

8. We need to pass another argument to the __init__ method of the Cycle class. Change the __init__ method definition line to:

   ```
   def __init__(self, inputManager):
   ```

9. Right below the line we just modified, add a new line of code that looks like the following line of code:

   ```
   self.inputManager = inputManager
   ```

10. Use *Ctrl+F* to open the **Find and Replace** window. Select the **Replace** tab, and in the **Find What** box, type self.keyMap. In the **Replace With** box, type self. inputManager.keyMap. Click the **Replace All** button. A dialog box will inform you that six occurrences have been replaced.

11. The Cycle class isn't registering any events anymore so we don't need to inherit from DirectObject. Delete the import line that imports DirectObject. Also, change the class declaration to:

    ```
    class Cycle:
    ```

12. That's all the changes we need to make to the Cycle class. Save the file as CycleClass_04.py and move over to the World class file.

13. World class doesn't register any events either. Delete the line that imports DirectObject and change the class declaration to:

    ```
    class World:
    ```

14. Update the Cycle class import to reference the new file, CycleClass_04 instead of CycleClass_03.

15. Add a new import statement to the imports section at the top of the file. It should look like this:

    ```
    from InputManagerClass_01 import InputManager
    ```

16. Right before we instantiate our track, instantiate an `InputManager()` like so:

```
self.inputManager = InputManager()
```

17. Change the line where we instantiate a cycle to pass a reference to the new `InputManager` into the `Cycle` class instance we're creating:

```
self.cycle = Cycle(self.inputManager)
```

18. That's it. Save the file as `WorldClass_05.py` and run it.

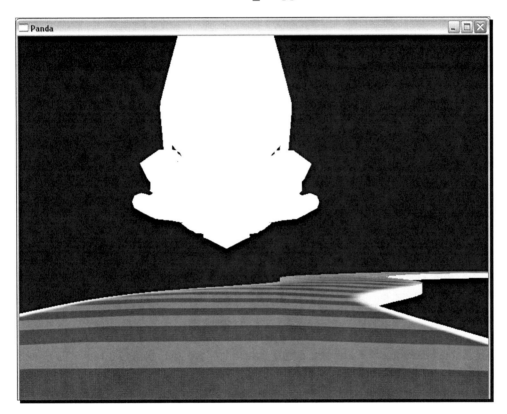

What just happened?

On the surface, nothing has changed. All of our controls still work, even though we moved them over to a new class. That's because we have the `Cycle` class using the `keyMap` in the `InputManager`.

It's important to note that the `self.inputManager` variable in our `Cycle` class is pointing to the same object in memory as the `self.inputManager` variable in our `World` class. There is only one `InputManager` in memory. That's good for the sake of efficiency, but it can also be dangerous. In Python, objects in memory are garbage collected when all of the references to them are removed. It means that if we want to get rid of our `InputManager` now, we need to clear out the references to it in both the `Cycle` class and the `World` class.

 When passing class instance references into other classes like this, keep track of what is referencing what to avoid memory leaks.

Have a go hero – Adding AI to the cycle

Designing an artificial intelligence is a little beyond the scope of this book, but our game obviously needs one so we can have computer-controlled cycles to race against. In the `Chapter05/AdditionalCode` folder there are several files that have been provided to resolve this. Both of these files are needed to create AI-controlled cycles.

One of the files is called `TrackLaneClass`. This file is an add-on to the `Track` class that will add invisible markers to the track that the AI can use to navigate turns. Add this new class to the `Track` class the same way we added the `InputManager` to the `Cycle` class. Store it in a variable called `self.trackLanes` in the `Track` class.

There is also a file called `CycleAIClass`. The class contained in that file will take control of a cycle and drive it along the track. Add it into the `Cycle` class. Make sure to put in an option so that a cycle can be created to use AI or player control. Also, make sure to read the comments in `CycleAIClass` to see what additional information needs to be passed into the AI so it can properly control the cycle.

This is a tall order, but there are examples of this working in the `Chapter05/Examples` folder that we can look at if we need a little assistance. We just need to take a little peek at the files that have the word Hero in their names.

Once you have those add-ons set up, create a second cycle to race against!

Pop quiz – accessing custom classes from other custom classes

Building a game out of custom classes wouldn't be very useful if we couldn't get them to communicate. We need to make sure we know how to set up that communication before we move on.

1. How do we allow one class to access another?
2. What is the danger associated with classes that access each other?

Summary

The lessons in this chapter were focused on custom classes and how to use them.

We covered all of these topics:

- Making custom classes
- Importing custom classes
- When inheritance isn't an option, and how to get around it
- Communication between classes

In the next chapter, we'll finally solve the problem of when our cycle reaches the hill in the track, and passes through it. We're going to introduce collision detection to our game, and learn how to make objects in the game world interact with one another!

6
The World in Action: Handling Collisions

Collision detection is a fundamental part of any game. Without it, objects would just pass through each other, finding the right height to place figures above the ground would be very difficult, and checking if a bullet hits its target would be a trial.

To make sure we get a good understanding of collision detection, we'll talk about:

- Collision basics: Our first collision system
- Creating inter-cycle collisions
- Using BitMasks to organize collisions
- Using PythonTags to get colliding objects
- Setting up ground collision
- Overview of additional collision solids and handlers

Covering these topics will allow us to fully understand how the collision system works, and how we can use it.

Collision basics: Our first collision system

Before we dive into creating collisions in our game, we need to talk a little bit about the collision system in Panda3D or we're going to get in over our heads and get confused. To do that, we'll start with a little example of the collision system.

Time for action – creating a simple collision detection system

For this exercise, we won't be using our game. Instead, we're going to start with a blank document and make a quick little collision system to see things in action before we start on the more complicated collisions in the game.

1. Create a blank document in Notepad++ and save it as chp06_01.py.

2. Add this block of code to the beginning of the file:

```
import direct.directbase.DirectStart
from direct.showbase.DirectObject import DirectObject
from pandac.PandaModules import *

class World(DirectObject):
  def __init__(self):
```

3. Right after that, type in these lines:

```
self.colNode1 = CollisionNode("colNode1")
colSphere1 = CollisionSphere(4.1,30,0,1)
self.colNode1.addSolid(colSphere1)
self.colNP1 = render.attachNewNode(self.colNode1)
self.colNP1.show()
```

4. Now, copy and paste the block of code from step 3, and modify it to look like this:

```
self.colNode2 = CollisionNode("colNode2")
colSphere2 = CollisionSphere(0,30,0,1)
self.colNode2.addSolid(colSphere2)
self.colNP2 = render.attachNewNode(self.colNode2)
self.colNP2.show()
```

5. Next, we have another three lines to add to the __init__ method:

```
self.cTrav = CollisionTraverser()
self.cHan = CollisionHandlerQueue()
self.cTrav.addCollider(self.colNP1, self.cHan)
```

6. And then the last three lines to go in the __init__ method:

```
self.accept("a", self.move, extraArgs = [-.5])
self.accept("d", self.move, extraArgs = [.5])
taskMgr.add(self.checkCollisions, "Check Collisions")
```

7. Next, we need to add two methods to the World class. One to respond to the events that we're accepting and the other will be the task we're adding to the task manager.

```
def move(self, dir):
  self.colNP1.setX(self.colNP1, dir)

def checkCollisions(self, task):
  self.cTrav.traverse(render)
  print(self.cHan.getNumEntries())
  return task.again
```

8. The last thing we need to do is create an instance of the World class and call run. Add these lines to the bottom of the file:

```
W = World()
run()
```

9. Save the file and run it from the command prompt using the command python chp06_01.py.

10. Use the *A* and *D* keys to move collision sphere 1 right and left. Note the output in the command prompt when the spheres are overlapping and when they aren't.

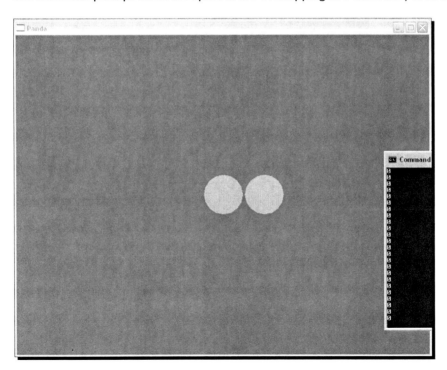

In the previous screenshot we see that the output is **0** when the spheres don't overlap, and in the following screenshot we see that the output is **1** when the spheres do overlap.

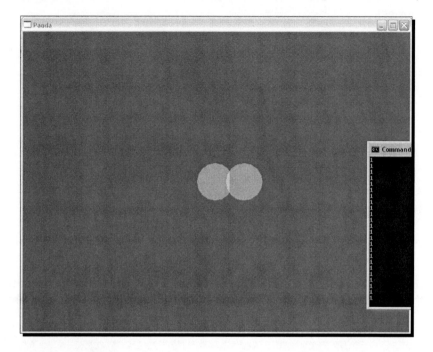

What just happened?

We've got a lot of new things going on here, so let's go through it line-by-line and break it down until we understand it.

As far as the imports go, there's nothing really new here except for the PandaModules import:

```
from pandac.PandaModules import *
```

For this line, we're using the wildcard * to import everything in the PandaModules package for our little program. This can make the program take a bit longer to load, but it save us from having to use a lot of specific imports for different things.

Moving right along, we have our class definition and our __init__ method definition, nothing new there, and then we come to this line:

```
self.colNode1 = CollisionNode("colNode1")
```

Here, we are creating an instance of a new class, the CollisionNode. A CollisionNode is a special type of node in Panda3D that integrates into the collision system. These nodes are designed to contain geometry that is specifically optimized for use in collision detection.

It's also possible to use visual geometry for collision, but this isn't recommended. The reason being that visual geometry tends to be more detailed than collision geometry needs to be, and each polygon used for collision adds to the processing expense. Even when defining an odd shape for collision, it's better to use several collision spheres or a less detailed version of the shape.

`CollisionNodes` are very important to the collision detection process because they contain important variables that help us define how our collisions will operate. We'll be going into more detail about those variables as we further explore collision detection.

Next, we have a call to create an instance of another class we haven't seen before: the `CollisionSphere`.

```
colSphere1 = CollisionSphere(4.1,30,0,1)
```

The `CollisionSphere` is one of many different collision solids available in Panda3D's collision detection system, and it's also the simplest and most efficient. It's great to use for things that collide into other things, and for things that get collided into. It's so efficient, in fact, that we can check collisions with about 3-4 collision spheres in the same time it takes to check one collision polygon. That's a big difference in processing time, and we should bear it in mind going forward.

Basically, the `CollisionSphere` call creates a sphere at the location defined by the first three arguments it's given: x, y, and z, with a radius equal to the last argument. The `CollisionSphere` by itself isn't useful to us at all, though. To use it, we have to put it into a `CollisionNode`. That's what the next line is for:

```
self.colNode1.addSolid(colSphere1)
```

This line puts the `CollisionSphere` into the `CollisionNode`. This is also the reason why we can create the `CollisionSphere` as a temporary variable. Once we put it into the `CollisionNode`, the `CollisionNode` keeps a reference to it and it won't be garbage collected.

Putting collision solids into `CollisionNodes` does two important things: first, it gives the `CollisionNode` a shape to define the space it occupies so we can tell if it's colliding with anything. Secondly, it gives the collision solid a wrapper to integrate into the collision system with. Another way to put it is that the `CollisionNode` is the object that can collide with things, and the collision solid is the shape that defines that object.

We aren't limited to putting a single solid into each `CollisionNode`, either. We can add as many of them as we'd like to by calling `addSolid` for each solid we want to put in. The different solids will still be checked for collision individually, but the collision system will consider them all a part of the greater object, the `CollisionNode`. Our next example will go into more detail about this.

Before we get into our next example, we've got more to talk about regarding the previous one. The next line we run into uses an old friend, `attachNewNode`:

```
self.colNP1 = render.attachNewNode(self.colNode1)
```

This call creates a `NodePath` to point to the `CollisionNode` we've created and populated with a solid, and it also inserts the `NodePath` into the scene graph as a child of `render`.

After that, we call the show method on that new `NodePath` we've just created:

```
self.colNP1.show()
```

This actually doesn't have anything to do with the collision system itself. We do it because by default, collision solids are invisible. By calling `show` on the `NodePath`, we tell it and all of its children, including the collision solid, to be visible to the camera. That way, we can see the collision spheres.

In the next five lines we do it all over again to create the second `CollisionNode` and `CollisionSphere`, and add them to the scene. Once we have that done, we create a new instance of another new class, the `CollisionTraverser`.

```
self.cTrav = CollisionTraverser()
```

The `CollisionTraverser` is the workhorse of the collision system. This is the object that actually performs the calculations that determine if a collision is happening. Internally, they're very complicated, but in practice they are very simple and easy to use.

We then create a collision handler:

```
self.cHan = CollisionHandlerQueue()
```

The collision handler is used to determine what's done with the collisions that are detected. In our case, we're using the `CollisionHandlerQueue`, which just stores a list of the collisions for us to use as we see it.

Once we have a `CollisionNode`, a `CollisionTraverser`, and a collision handler, we need to set up the `CollisionTraverser`. That's what the next line does for us.

```
self.cTrav.addCollider(self.colNP1, self.cHan)
```

This very important call tells the `CollisionTraverser` that when it checks collisions, it needs to check and see if the `CollisionNode` pointed to by `self.colNP1` is colliding with anything, and if it is, `self.chan` should be used to handle those collisions. Just like adding solids, we can add more than one collider to a `CollisionTraverser`, but the performance difference between doing that and using a different traverser for each collider is pretty negligible.

When we start looking at collision data, we're going to run into some nomenclature that we should talk about. In every collision, there is a **From** object and an **Into** object. The **From** object is always the `CollisionNode` that's added to the `CollisionTraverser`. The **Into** object is the `CollisionNode` that it's collided with. **Into** objects don't need to be added to the traverser; they are determined by what we tell the `CollisionTraverser` to check collisions with, which we'll talk about in a moment. This is very important when we start trying to identify what objects are colliding in a more complicated system.

Not too much left to go over. We've only got two new things left to talk about before we can move on. The first is this line, in the `checkCollisions` method:

```
self.cTrav.traverse(render)
```

This is the call that makes it all happen. The `traverse` method of the `CollisionTraverser` is what tells the `CollisionTraverser` to work its magic. It also tells it what to work its magic on. The argument we give it needs to be a `NodePath`, and it's that `NodePath` and all of its children that will be checked for collisions with the collider that was added to the `CollisionTraverser`. Using clever scene graph setups and only traversing the branches you want to is one way to limit the amount of collision detection happening in a game, but it's not the only way. Note that the `NodePath` we give to the traverse method, and all of its children, become the potential **Into** objects. The `CollisionNodes` added to the `CollisionTraverser` are the **From** objects, and the `NodePath` (and its children) that we give to the traverse method are the potential **Into** objects. We say "potential" **Into** objects because the **From** and **Into** designations only matter if a collision is actually detected.

Whew! Finally we come to the last new operation in our example here:

```
print(self.cHan.getNumEntries())
```

Remember how we said the `CollisionHandlerQueue` stores the collisions for later use? Well, `getNumEntries` returns the number of collisions that were detected on the last traversal. We can use this to determine if there were any collisions, and how many, and it helps to keep us from trying to get information on collisions that didn't happen.

Pop Quiz – regarding basic collision detection

Collision detection is one of the most difficult parts of Panda3D to understand. To make sure we've got it down, we're going to have to answer some hard questions about it.

1. What are collision solids?
2. What purpose is served by `CollisionNodes`?
3. What is a `CollisionTraverser`?
4. What is the argument given to the `traverse` method of a `CollisionTraverser`, and why does it matter?

Creating inter-cycle collisions

Now that we have a basic understanding of how collision detection works, we're going to start taking things to the next level by adding collisions to our game. The first thing we'll do is add collisions between cycles to keep them passing through one another.

Time for action – inter-cycle collisions

We're going to use the files from last chapter's *Have a Go hero* section to proceed. If we didn't complete that section, that's fine. Files have been provided that we can use instead.

1. Open the cycle class file we made during the previous chapter's *Have a Go hero* section, or open the file `CycleClassHero.py` in the `Chapter06` folder.

2. Resave the file as `CycleClass_01.py` in the `Chapter06` folder.

3. For this collision system, we're going to have a unique name for each cycle on the track. We also need to be able to put the cycles in different spots on the track so they don't start on top of each other. Change the definition of the `__init__` to look like this:

   ```
   def __init__(self, inputManager, track, startPos, name, ai =
   None):
   ```

4. Change the line where we call `setupVarsNPs` to accept the new `startPos` and `name` information, like so:

   ```
   self.setupVarsNPs(startPos, name)
   ```

5. Naturally, we have to update `setupVarsNPs` to use this data. Replace the definition for that method with these lines of code:

   ```
   def setupVarsNPs(self, startPos, name):
     self.name = name
   ```

6. To make use of `startPos,` add this code right after we create the `root NodePath`:

   ```
   if(startPos == 1):
     self.root.setPos(5,0,0)
   elif(startPos == 2):
     self.root.setPos(-5,-5,0)
   elif(startPos == 3):
     self.root.setPos(5,-10,0)
   elif(startPos == 4):
     self.root.setPos(-5,-15,0)
   ```

7. Also, remove the line where we set `self.root`'s position to (2,15,0).

8. We'll also need access to a few more of Panda3D's modules. Change the line where we import `Vec3` to:

```
from pandac.PandaModules import *
```

9. The next step is to create the shield around the cycle that we will use for collisions. We'll use three spheres to approximate the shape of the cycle. For the sake of tidiness, we'll also make a new method called `setupCollisions` right after `setupVarsNPs`. Add this code between `setupVarsNPs` and `cycleControl`:

```
def setupCollisions(self):
    self.shieldCN = CollisionNode(self.name + "_ShieldCN")
    CS1 = CollisionSphere(0, -.025, .75, .785)
    CS2 = CollisionSphere(0, -1.075, .85, .835)
    CS3 = CollisionSphere(0, 1.125, .6, .61)
    self.shieldCN.addSolid(CS1)
    self.shieldCN.addSolid(CS2)
    self.shieldCN.addSolid(CS3)
    self.shieldCNP = self.cycle.attachNewNode(self.shieldCN)
```

10. Without a `CollisionTraverser` and a collision handler, the shield won't do us any good. Let's put those into the `setupCollisions` method next, immediately below the code we just added.

```
    self.bumpCTrav = CollisionTraverser()
    self.bumpCTrav.showCollisions(render)
    self.bumpHan = CollisionHandlerPusher()
    self.bumpHan.addCollider(self.shieldCNP, self.root)
    self.bumpHan.addAgainPattern("%fn-again")
    self.bumpCTrav.addCollider(self.shieldCNP, self.bumpHan)
```

11. The collision handler we're using this time will trigger events when collisions occur. We want to receive those events, so we'll need to have our `Cycle` class inherit from `DirectObject` again. Add the import to the top of the fall.

```
from direct.showbase.DirectObject import DirectObject
```

12. Also, change the class definition statement to make the inheritance happen.

```
class Cycle(DirectObject):
```

13. Now that we have the ability to register events, we need to do so. We'll add one more line to the `setupCollisions` method, right at the end:

```
self.accept(self.name + "_ShieldCN-again", self.bump)
```

14. Now, we'll add the bump method we're calling when the event occurs right above the `getPos` method at the bottom of the file:

```
def bump(self, entry):
    print(entry)
```

15. Right now, nothing is actually checking for collisions. Nor are we calling `setupCollisions` anywhere. Right after the call to `setupVarsNPs`, add a call to `setupCollisions`:

```
self.setupCollisions()
```

16. Right after the call to `move` in `cycleControl`, add this line:

```
self.bumpCTrav.traverse(render)
```

17. The final modification to the `Cycle` class will be to add an option for neither artificial intelligence nor player control. Near the end of the __init__ method we have an `if` statement that checks what the input for the AI variable is. Change that line to this one:

```
if(ai == True):
```

18. Change the `else` statement that corresponds to that `if` statement into an `elif` that looks like this:

```
elif(ai == None)
```

19. Save the file, and then open the `WorldClassHero.py` in the `Chapter06/Examples` folder. Resave this one as `WorldClass_01.py` in the `Chapter06` folder.

20. Our first order of business here is to make sure we're importing the correct version of the `Cycle` class. Change the import line to read such as the following:

```
from CycleClass_01 import Cycle
```

21. Next, we need the line that creates our cycle to give the cycle a name. Also, since we'll want more than one cycle, we need to change the variable name. Modify the line so it looks like this:

```
self.cycle1 = Cycle(self.inputManager, self.track, 1, "Bert",
ai = False)
```

22. We want a second cycle as well so they can collide. Copy the line that you just modified and paste it right below, then change this new line to look like this:

```
self.cycle2 = Cycle(self.inputManager, self.track, 1, "Ernie")
```

23. Resave `WorldClass_01.py`, and run it from the command prompt and pilot one cycle to run it into the other one.

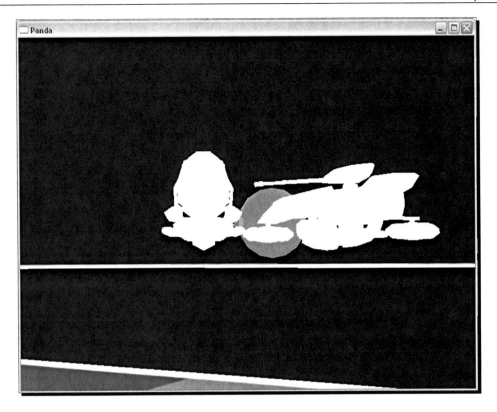

What just happened?

There we have it! One cycle bumps into the other instead of passing through. Let's talk about how this collision system is different from the first one we made.

This system uses `CollisionSpheres`, too, but this time we added three of them to the `CollisionNode`. Because they have all been added to the same `CollisionNode`, Panda3D treats the three `CollisionSpheres` as a single collision object. In our case, we use them as the invisible shields that surround our vehicles.

The bigger change is the collision handler we're using. Instead of a `CollisionHandlerQueue`, we're using the `CollisionHandlerPusher`. This is a specialized handler that automatically prevents the colliding objects from passing through each other. Let's talk about the code we used to set it up.

```
self.bumpHan = CollisionHandlerPusher()
self.bumpHan.addCollider(self.shieldCNP, self.root)
self.bumpHan.addAgainPattern("%fn-again")
```

The first line creates the handler for us. The second line is a call to the handler's `addCollider` method. Don't confuse this with the call to `addCollider` for the `CollisionTraverser`; they do very different things. For the `CollisionHandlerPusher` to do its job, it needs to know what `NodePath` to push back against when a collision occurs. For each **From** object it will handle, we need to tell it what `NodePath` to adjust. In our system, we want to push against the cycle's `self.root` `NodePath` when the collision occurs, so we tell the handler that when `self.shieldCNP` is the **From** object for a collision, it needs to adjust `self.root` to prevent objects from overlapping. That's what this call to `self.bumpHan.addCollider` does for us.

The last line is important for using events tied to the collision system. `CollisionHandlerPusher` uses the same system as `CollisionHandlerEvent` to generate events when collisions occur. For this to work, we have to tell the handler what we want the name of the event to be. The string for the name event is called a **pattern**. When making **patterns**, there are some special sequences we can use to get specific information about the collision. The two most useful sequences are:

- `%fn`—This sequence will be replaced by the name of the **From** `CollisionNode`
- `%in`—This sequence will be replaced by the name of the `Into` `CollisionNode`

Because our **pattern** is `"%fn-again"`, and the only **From** object we add into the `CollisionTraverser` is `self.shieldCNP`, the event the handler generates will always be the name of `self.shieldCN` followed by `"-again"`, or `self.name + "_ShieldCN-again"`, because we named `self.shieldCN` `self.name + "_ShieldCN"`. This is the reason we needed to have unique names for our cycles; so that each cycle's `CollisionHandlerPusher` would create a uniquely named event to register and respond to.

`CollisionHandlerPusher` and `CollisionHandlerEvent` don't automatically generate events. When we add a **pattern** to the handler, we're also telling it to generate events. We have three options for when we want the handler to create an event:

- `addInPattern` – This event is generated when the **From** node collides with a node that it was *not* colliding with in the previous frame
- `addAgainPattern` – This event is generated when the **From** node collides with a node that it *was* colliding with in the previous frame
- `addOutPattern` – This event is generated when the **From** node *doesn't* collide with a node that it *was* colliding with in the previous frame

This gives us great control over our responses to collisions. We could have an event for when an object first collides with anything, using `addInPattern("%fn")`, or we could have an event only for when one object stops colliding with another using `addOutPattern("%fn-%in")`, for example.

In our case, we want to know when our cycle is continuously colliding with something so we can print out the collision entry for the collision. That's why we used `addAgainPattern`. Speaking of the collision entry, we should take a look at it.

```
CollisionEntry:
    from render/Root//c/BGP3D/Chapter06/../Models/Cycle.bam/Ernie_ShieldCN
    into render/Root//c/BGP3D/Chapter06/../Models/Cycle.bam/Bert_ShieldCN []
    at 4.68144 1.63434 0.705784
    normal -0.522231 0.834986 0.173417
    interior 4.68321 1.63152 0.705197 <depth 0.00338486>
    respect_prev_transform = 0
```

A collision entry is an object that contains information about a collision, such as the **From** `NodePath`, the **Into** `NodePath`, what point in space the collision occurred at, and more. Both `CollisionHandlerPusher` and `CollisionHandlerEvent` pass the collision entry into any methods that are used to respond to their events. The collision entry is also what is stored by `CollisionHandlerQueue`. We're going to put these entries to use when we set up ground collision later in this chapter.

There's one more line of code that's worth mentioning in this example:

```
self.bumpCTrav.showCollisions(render)
```

This line tells the `CollisionTraverser` to make the collisions visible. That's why, when the collision occurs, we see the sphere appear and the red box with a line coming out of it. We're seeing the point of contact where the collision occurred.

Pop quiz – understanding handlers that generate events

Using `CollisionHandlerPusher` or `CollisionHandlerEvent` is a powerful technique for responding to collisions, but to use it, we have to fully understand how the events generated by these handlers work.

1. When do `CollisionHandlerPusher` and `CollisionHandlerEvent` generate events? What must we do to control what events they generate and what names those events have?

2. What Python object is passed into methods that respond to events generated by `CollisionHandlerPusher` and `CollisionHandlerEvent`?

3. What special options are there for event name **patterns** used with `CollisionHandlerEvent` and `CollisionHandlerPusher`?

Have a go hero – using collision events

Try modifying our original collision system, the simple one with two spheres, to use a `CollisionHandlerEvent` or `CollisionHandlerPusher`. Set it up to do different things with the events that those handlers can generate.

Using BitMasks to organize collisions

Collision detection can very easily become a severe drain on the computer's resources. The best way to prevent this is by limiting what objects are checked for collision with which other objects. One way to do this is by controlling which segments of the scene graph collision checks are performed on, but this can be impractical because there are so many other things that scene graph organization can be used to accomplish.

Fortunately, we have another solution to this problem. We can use BitMasks to limit which CollisionNodes can interact. A BitMask is a series of 32 bits that can be either 0 or 1. Here is an example of a BitMask:

```
0000 0000 0000 0000 0000 0010 0000 1000
```

The BitMask works by limiting only those CollisionNodes that have one of the same bits set to 1 to interact. That means if you set bit number 4 to 1 on two CollisionNodes, they'll be able to collide. If that bit is set to 1 for one of them and 0 for the other, they won't be checked for collision. To clarify, if the two BitMasks have any bits matching bits set to 1 then the CollisionNodes will be checked for collision. If the BitMasks don't share any bits set to 1 then they won't be checked for collision. Here's an example of two BitMasks that will allow collision:

```
0000 0000 0000 0000 0000 0011 0000 1000
0000 0000 0000 0000 0000 0000 0000 1000
```

The following two BitMasks won't allow collision:

```
0000 0000 0000 0000 0000 0000 0000 0100
0000 0000 0000 0000 0000 0000 0000 1010
```

Although it isn't terribly important for our purposes, we should mention that BitMasks are numbered from right-to-left, and the numbering starts with 0. That means that if you set bit 0 to 1, the right-most bit will be 1.

In Panda3D, we have the option of setting both the **From** and **Into** BitMasks on each collision node. This means we can have CollisionNodes that can cause collisions on one set of bits, and be collided with on a different set of bits. This can be particularly useful with things like explosions. Right now, if our cycle detects a collision with something, it won't be able to move through that object. If we use different BitMasks, we can allow explosions to collide with the cycle without letting the cycle collide with the explosions. That may seem like a small semantic difference, but it means the explosion can detect the cycle without the cycle crashing into the explosion as if it were a brick wall.

Time for action – implementing BitMasks

Using `BitMasks` is actually pretty easy. This example will show us how.

1. In the `setupCollisions` method of our `Cycle` class, add the following code right after the lines where we add our `CollisionSpheres` to the `CollisionNode`:

   ```
   self.shieldCN.setIntoCollideMask(BitMask32.bit(3))
   self.shieldCN.setFromCollideMask(BitMask32.bit(2))
   ```

2. Save the file as `CycleClass_02.py`.

3. Modify `WorldClass_01.py` to import `CycleClass_02.py` instead of `CycleClass_01.py`. Then, save it as `WorldClass_02.py` and run it from the command prompt. Attempt to collide the two cycles together and we'll see them pass through each other, like in the following screenshot:

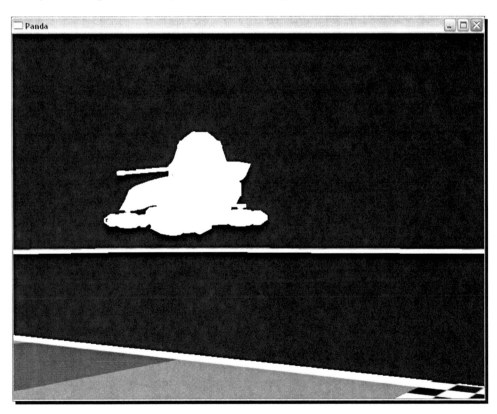

What just happened?

Our cycles don't collide anymore! That's because they are set to have different **From** and **Into** BitMasks. BitMask.bit creates a BitMask that has the indicated bit set to 1, and all other bits set to 0. The calls to setIntoCollideMask and setFromCollideMask apply the masks created by BitMask.bit to the CollisionNode.

In order for our cycles to be able to collide with one another, and for our weapons to detect cycles without being collided into, we'll need to expand the **Into** BitMask on self.shieldCN. We can use BitMask.range for this. It takes two arguments: the first is the lowest bit in the range you want to specify, and the second is the number of bits in the range. For example, BitMask.range(2,3) would set bits 2, 3, and 4 to 1 and all other bits to 0.

Time for action – setting a range of bits with BitMask.range

Let's fix our BitMasks to work better for our purpose.

1. In the setupCollisions method of our Cycle class, change the line where we set the **Into** collide mask for self.shieldCN to this:

   ```
   self.shieldCN.setIntoCollideMask(BitMask32.range(2,3))
   ```

2. Save the file as CycleClass_03.py.

3. Modify WorldClass_02.py to import CycleClass_03.py instead of CycleClass_02.py. Then, save it as WorldClass_03.py and run it from the command prompt. Attempt to collide the cycles together and we'll see that the collision is detected again, like in the following image:

What just happened?

Now our cycles can collide with each other again because they share bits on their BitMasks.

Pop quiz – understanding BitMasks

BitMasks are often misunderstood because they are both an esoteric concept and also largely invisible when being used. We never really see the BitMasks themselves, just the result of their use. For that reason, we should make certain of our understanding before we move on.

1. What is a BitMask?
2. To what purpose do we employ BitMasks?
3. How do we apply BitMasks?
4. What is the difference between a **From** mask and an **Into** mask?
5. Will these two BitMasks allow a collision to occur?

    ```
    0000 0000 0000 0000 0000 0000 0110 0000
    0000 0000 0000 0000 0000 0000 0010 1010
    ```

Using Python tags to get colliding objects

Very commonly, games developers will want to be able to get a reference to the objects that have collided so they can modify some attribute of one or the other, such as a character taking damage when they are hit by an attack. In Panda3D, we can easily get the **From** and **Into** CollisionNodes from the collision entry with getFromNodePath and getIntoNodePath.

```
myCollisionEntry.getFromNodePath()
myCollisionEntry.getIntoNodePath()
```

But, that doesn't give us the class instance that actually owns the CollisionNode. For that, we need to attach a reference to the class instance to the CollisionNode using PythonTags.

A PythonTag is a way to attach a reference of one thing to another. We use setPythonTag to create them.

```
myObject.setPythonTag([tagName], [tagContents])
```

To get the contents of the PythonTag, use getPythonTag.

```
myObject.getPythonTag([tagName])
```

A PythonTag can contain any Python object in it. Strings, numbers, class instances, anything goes.

Note that using PythonTags can cause a circular reference. For example, if we have a class instance that owns a CollisionNode and we attach a reference to that class instance to the CollisionNode, the class instance now has a reference to itself. Python will only garbage collect objects that have no references to them, so as long as the class instance has a reference to itself, it won't be garbage collected. We'll talk about this more when we discuss garbage collection in *Chapter 12, Finishing Touches: Getting the Game Ready for the Customer*.

Time for action – setting and getting PythonTags

Let's add a PythonTag to our CollisionNodes so we can print out the names of the cycles when they collide.

1. In the setupCollisions method of our Cycle class, add the following line of code right after we create self.shieldCN:

```
self.shieldCN.setPythonTag("owner", self)
```

2. In the `bump` method, replace the `print` statement we have with the following:

```
print(entry.getFromNodePath().getPythonTag("owner").name)
print("has bumped into:")
print(entry.getIntoNodePath().getPythonTag("owner").name)
print("")
```

3. Save the file as `CycleClass_04.py`.

4. Modify `WorldClass_03.py` to import `CycleClass_04.py` instead of `CycleClass_03.py`. Then, save it as `WorldClass_04.py` and run it from the command prompt. Make sure to watch the command prompt when the cycles collide and you see something similar to the following screenshot:

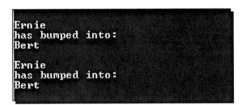

What just happened?

When we bump our cycles together, we see the output in the command prompt that tells us who is bumping into whom. That's because we are getting the `CollisionNodes` from the collision entry, and then getting the class instances from the `PythonTags`, and finally we get the names from the class instance. Easy as pie!

Have a go hero – gaining experience with BitMasks and PythonTags

Hop back over to that simple collision system we made at the beginning of the chapter. Add a couple more collision spheres to it and give them `PythonTags` with strings in them, and different `BitMasks`. Use `CollisionHandlerPushers` or `CollisionHandlerEvents` and play around with `BitMasks` and `PythonTags` until you feel comfortable with how they work. These concepts are important to using collision detection so we have to make sure we understand them.

Pop quiz – using Python Tags

PythonTags are a very useful utility available to us, both for collision detection systems and other applications as well. Let's take a moment to test our understanding of how to use them.

1. How do we create a PythonTag?

2. What can we put in a PythonTag?

3. How do we retrieve things from a PythonTag?

4. What is the inherent danger of using PythonTags that we must be careful of?

Setting up ground collision

Panda3D comes equipped with a special collision handler that is designed to keep characters at a fixed height above the ground, or cause them to slowly fall toward that height if they are too high. Unfortunately, CollisionHandlerFloor doesn't have a component to ensure that our cycle's pitch will match the angle of the track. It's designed for use with a vertical character, such as a person, where that isn't so much of an issue.

To cover this lapse, we're going to construct our own system for ground collision.

Time for action – creating a ground collision system

This is going to be another long example, so let's pay close attention to each step and make sure we get everything right.

1. To begin with, we're going to make some modifications to our Track class to prepare it. Open the TrackClassHero.py file in the Chapter06 folder and resave it as TrackClass_01.py.

2. The first change to make is to remove the line that resets the track's position to 5 units lower.

3. Once that is gone, add in these lines at the end of the class:

```
self.gravity = 1
self.groundCol = loader.loadModel("../Models/Ground.egg")
self.groundCol.reparentTo(render)
mask = BitMask32.range(1,3)
mask.clearRange(2,1)
self.groundCol.setCollideMask(mask)
```

4. We also need an import to use BitMask. Add this line to the very top of the file:

```
from pandac.PandaModules import *
```

5. Resave the file again.

6. The rest of the changes we need to make will be in the `Cycle` class, so open `CycleClass_04.py` up again.

7. Our first addition will be to the end of the `setupCollisions` method. Add all of these lines there, at the bottom:

```
self.gRayCN = CollisionNode(self.name + "_GRayCN")
self.fRay = CollisionRay(0, .5, 10, 0, 0, -1)
self.bRay = CollisionRay(0, -.5, 10, 0, 0, -1)
self.gRayCN.addSolid(self.fRay)
self.gRayCN.addSolid(self.bRay)
self.gRayCN.setFromCollideMask(BitMask32.bit(1))
self.gRayCN.setIntoCollideMask(BitMask32.allOff())
self.gRayCNP = self.cycle.attachNewNode(self.gRayCN)

self.gCTrav = CollisionTraverser()
self.gHan = CollisionHandlerQueue()
self.gCTrav.addCollider(self.gRayCNP, self.gHan)
```

8. The next step is to add two variables and a `NodePath` to our `setupVarsNPs` method. Place these three lines at the bottom of that method:

```
self.freeFall = False
self.fallSpeed = 0
self.trackNP = render.attachNewNode(self.name + "_TrackNode")
```

9. With that, we've got everything we need for checking ground collision, tracking the height of our cycle, and controlling its pitch. Let's go ahead and start working on the method that will do all of that for us. Add in this code right after the `simDrift` method to get us started:

```
def groundCheck(self, dt):
  self.gCTrav.traverse(render)
  points = [None, None]
  if(self.gHan.getNumEntries() > 1):
    self.gHan.sortEntries()
    for E in range(self.gHan.getNumEntries()):
      entry = self.gHan.getEntry(E)
      if(entry.getFrom() == self.fRay and points[0]== None):
        points[0] = entry.getSurfacePoint(render)
      elif(entry.getFrom() == self.bRay and points[1]== None):
        points[1] = entry.getSurfacePoint(render)
```

10. That code will check ground collisions and get us the data we need. Now, we have to put that data to use. The first step of that is to make sure the data is valid. Add this code right after the code we just wrote:

```
if(points[0] == None or points[1] == None):
  self.teleport()
  return
else:
```

11. This gives us an escape in case our data is bad. The first thing we'll do with our data is use it to control the pitch of the cycle. Write this code right after that last `else` statement:

```
if(self.freeFall == False):
  self.refNP.setPos(points[1])
  self.refNP.lookAt(points[0])
  pDiff = self.refNP.getP()- self.cycle.getP()
  if(pDiff < .1 and pDiff > -.1):
    self.cycle.setP(self.refNP.getP())
  else:
    self.cycle.setP(self.cycle, pDiff * dt * 5)
elif((self.cycle.getP() - (dt * 10)) > -15):
  self.cycle.setP(self.cycle, -(dt * 10))
else:
  self.cycle.setP(-15)
```

12. To control the height of the cycle, we're going to put the new `trackNP` we've created at the actual track surface and use it for our height reference. We want to consider the height at the leading end of the cycle; that is, the front when moving forward and the back when moving in reverse, so we'll check the speed of the cycle to determine which to use. This code should immediately follow the previous code again.

```
if(self.speed >= 0):
  self.trackNP.setPos(points[0].getX(),
    points[0].getY(), points[0].getZ())
else:
  self.trackNP.setPos(points[1].getX(),
    points[1].getY(), points[1].getZ())
```

13. With the `trackNP` set, we can get the height of our cycle relative to the `trackNP` to see how far above the track we are. If we're too high, we need to enter a freefall state. This code will do that for us. It belongs right after the code we just wrote.

```
height = self.root.getZ(self.trackNP)
if(height > 2 and self.freeFall == False):
  self.freeFall = True
  self.fallSpeed = 0
```

14. Since we know if we're in a freefall state now, we can calculate a new height for the cycle. Continue adding to `groundCheck` with this code:

```
if(self.freeFall == True):
  self.fallSpeed += (self.track.gravity * 9.8) * dt
  newHeight = height - (self.fallSpeed * dt)
else:
  hDiff = 1 - height
  if(hDiff > .01 or hDiff < -.01):
    newHeight = height + (hDiff * dt * 5)
  else:
    newHeight = 1
```

15. Next, we decide what to do with that new height. Add this to the end of `groundCheck` as well:

```
if(newHeight >= 0):
self.root.setZ(self.trackNP, newHeight)
    else:
      self.root.setZ(self.trackNP, 0)
      self.freeFall = False
```

16. We're almost done with `groundCheck`! We just need one more line at the end to constrain our cycle to a roll of 0:

```
self.cycle.setR(0)
```

17. We need to adjust the `speedCheck` method to degrade the cycle's speed over time. To start with, select all the lines of code within the method, but not the definition itself, and hit *Tab*. That will indent all the lines at once. Another handy feature of NotePad++. After you've done that, put this line at the beginning of the method, just under the definition line:

```
if(self.freeFall == False):
```

18. Then, add this code to the very bottom of the `speedCheck` method:

```
else:
  self.speed -= (self.momentum * .125) * dt
```

19. We also need to call `groundCheck` to actually put in use. Add this line to the `cycleControl` method, right underneath the call to `simDrift` and right above the call to `move`:

```
self.groundCheck(dt)
```

20. In `groundCheck`, we have a call to a method called `teleport`. This method is meant to return the cycle to the track if it goes off of it. Let's add this method in right below the `checkMarkers` method.

```
def teleport(self):
    marker = self.track.trackLanes.getNearestMarker(self)
    markerPos = marker.getPos()
    self.root.setPos(markerPos.getX(),
markerPos.getY(), self.root.getZ())

    self.gCTrav.traverse(render)
    points = [None, None]
    if(self.gHan.getNumEntries() > 1):
      self.gHan.sortEntries()
      for E in range(self.gHan.getNumEntries()):
        entry = self.gHan.getEntry(E)
        if(entry.getFrom() == self.fRay and points[0]== None):
          points[0] = entry.getSurfacePoint(render)
        elif(entry.getFrom() == self.bRay and points[1]== None):
          points[1] = entry.getSurfacePoint(render)

      if(self.speed >= 0):
        self.trackNP.setPos(points[0].getX(),
          points[0].getY(), points[0].getZ())
      else:
        self.trackNP.setPos(points[1].getX(),
          points[1].getY(), points[1].getZ())

      self.root.setZ(self.trackNP, 1)
    self.dirNP.setHpr(marker.getHpr())
    self.cycle.setHpr(marker.getHpr())
    self.speed /= 2
```

21. Resave the file as `CycleClass_05.py`.

22. The last step is to change `WorldClass_04.py` to use our new `TrackClass_01.py` and `CycleClass_05.py` files. Once we've done that, resave it as `WorldClass_05.py` and run it from the command prompt. Take the cycle around the track, and see what happens when we reach the hills. Run the cycle off the track, too, to see the `teleport` method move the cycle back onto the track, as it did in the following screenshot:

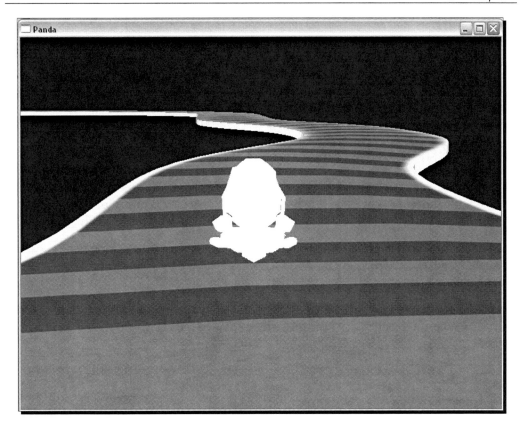

What just happened?

That was a real monster of a *Time for action*. To talk about it, we'll have to break it down piece-by-piece. We'll go over the steps we took to make this happen, and within the steps we'll go over the code line-by-line.

To start with, we added some new code to our `Track` class:

```
self.gravity = 1
self.groundCol = loader.loadModel("../Models/Ground.egg")
self.groundCol.reparentTo(render)
mask = BitMask32.range(1,3)
mask.clearRange(2,1)
self.groundCol.setCollideMask(mask)
```

The first line is a variable that stores the percentage of normal earth gravity this track will have. Since it's at 1, we're using 100 percent Earth gravity.

The next two lines load an egg file and reparent it to render. We've seen this before, but there's something under the hood here. The egg we're loading doesn't contain visual geometry, like the ones we've loaded before. This egg was created using the `EggOctree` script developed by the Panda3D community. It takes an egg and breaks it down into an octree of collision polygons. This minimizes the number of collision checks needed for the object. This script is most appropriate to large objects that will be checked for collision from within, such as our track. The important thing to understand is that we aren't getting visual geometry, we're getting collision geometry.

The next line creates a new `BitMask` with bits 1, 2, and 3 all at 1, and the other bits at 0. The following line, where we call `clearRange` on the `BitMask`, sets a series of bits back to 0. In this case, the range starts at 2 and is only 1 bit long, so only bit 2 is reverted. That's because we don't want the cycles to check collision against the ground with their shields.

The last line is a call that can be made on any `NodePath`. It sets both collision masks on the `NodePath` and its children to the provided `BitMask`. This is only appropriate for `NodePaths` that contain collision geometry, and we won't use it very often.

We finished off the `Track` class with a new import line; we've seen that before. After we did that, we moved on to our `Cycle` class and added some new code to our `setupCollisions` method:

```
self.gRayCN = CollisionNode(self.name + "_GRayCN")
self.fRay = CollisionRay(0, .5, 10, 0, 0, -1)
self.bRay = CollisionRay(0, -.5, 10, 0, 0, -1)
self.gRayCN.addSolid(self.fRay)
self.gRayCN.addSolid(self.bRay)
self.gRayCN.setFromCollideMask(BitMask32.bit(1))
self.gRayCN.setIntoCollideMask(BitMask32.allOff())
self.gRayCNP = self.cycle.attachNewNode(self.gRayCN)

self.gCTrav = CollisionTraverser()
self.gHan = CollisionHandlerQueue()
self.gCTrav.addCollider(self.gRayCNP, self.gHan)
```

The first line creates a new `CollisionNode` to store the collision solids we'll be using to collide with the ground. This isn't new to us either.

The next two lines both create a collision solid we haven't seen before: the `CollisionRay`. This "solid" is actually an infinitely thin line that starts at a specific position and extends out into infinity in a given direction. The first three inputs tell the ray where to start, and the last three are a vector that tells the ray which direction to extend in.

```
myCollisionRay([posX], [posY], [posZ], [vecX], [vecY], [vecZ])
```

The values we put into these rays place them slightly forward and backward of the centre of their parent and tell them to point straight down. We also put them 10 units above their parent.

This time, we used permanent variables instead of temporary variables to store the collision solids. We did this because later on, in groundCheck, we need a reference to them.

The next two lines add the CollisionRays to the CollisionNode. There's nothing new there. After that, we set the **From** and **Into** collision masks on the CollisionNode. We use bit 1 for our **From** mask because that's a bit shared by the ground we added to the track. For the **Into** mask, we called BitMask32.allOff, which sets all the bits to 0. A CollisionRay should never be collided into; it should only be used to collide into other things. We turned off all the bits in the **Into** mask to make sure the ray would never be collided into.

The next line attaches our new CollisionNode to self.cycle. We use self.cycle here instead of self.root because we want our rays to tilt and turn with the cycle as it goes around the track. Because of the values we gave our CollisionRays when we created them, they will be placed appropriately relative to the origin of self.cycle.

The next two lines of this block create a new CollisionTraverser and a CollisionHandlerQueue. Remember that the CollisionHandlerQueue stores all of the collisions detected in a pass for us to use. Since we want information on the collisions for both rays, the queue is ideal for our purpose.

Lastly, we have a line that adds the CollisionNode's NodePath and the collision handler into the CollisionTraverser. Again, that's nothing new to us.

Following that change, we shifted over to the setupVarsNPs method and added some new things there:

```
self.freeFall = False
self.fallSpeed = 0
self.trackNP = render.attachNewNode(self.name + "_TrackNode")
```

The variable self.freeFall is used to tell the cycle if it is in a state of freefall or not. We need this to make the cycle fall gracefully onto the track when it's too high above it. The next variable we create here, self.fallSpeed, will control the rate of descent for the cycle while it is in freefall.

The last thing we added was a new proxy NodePath called self.trackNP. This NodePath is used as a reference for the height of the track beneath the cycle, and also as a reference to place self.root above. This makes the final placement of self.root considerably easier than it would be otherwise.

We started working on the real meat of this system next, by creating the `groundCheck` method:

```
def groundCheck(self, dt):
  self.gCTrav.traverse(render)
  points = [None, None]
  if(self.gHan.getNumEntries() > 1):
    self.gHan.sortEntries()
    for E in range(self.gHan.getNumEntries()):
      entry = self.gHan.getEntry(E)
      if(entry.getFrom() == self.fRay and points[0]== None):
        points[0] = entry.getSurfacePoint(render)
      elif(entry.getFrom() == self.bRay and points[1]== None):
        points[1] = entry.getSurfacePoint(render)
```

The method takes `dt` because we want to use delta time to smoothly adjust our cycle's height based on time instead of frame rate. The first line in the method tells our ground `CollisionTraverser` to check for collisions between our rays and the ground.

Our next step is to create a short, two-item list to hold the collisions for the two rays. We initialize it with `None` so that if we don't get a collision from one of the rays we'll have a `None`-type object left in the list.

After our list is prepped, we check the number of entries in the `CollisionHandlerQueue`. If we don't have more than one collision entry in the queue, it's pointless to evaluate the entries since we can't possibly have one from each ray. Our cycle must have gone off the track, at least partially.

If we have enough entries, we want to evaluate them in order from the nearest to the `CollisionNode` to the farthest. To make sure they're in that order, we call `sortEntries` on the `CollisionHandlerQueue`. Next, we use a `For` loop to iterate through every entry in the queue.

The first line inside the loop stores the entry in a temporary variable called `entry`. Once we have that, we perform two checks on it. For each check, we call `getFrom` on entry, which is not quite the same thing as the `getFromNodePath` method we used before. `getFromNodePath` returns the `CollisionNode`, but `getFrom` returns the actual collision solid involved in the collision. We check the return of `getFrom` against the references we kept of our collision solids to figure out which ray is involved in the collision. This lets us make sure that we put the data from the front ray into `points[0]` and the data from the back ray into `points[1]`. We also make sure that the spot in the list still holds a `None`-type object because we don't want to overwrite any data we've already collected. We want the data from the nearest collisions, so we don't want to overwrite it with any further away collisions that might have been detected.

The two lines that are used when the checks are true do the actual work of collecting and storing the data. To do this, we are calling `entry.getSurfacePoint(render)`. This call returns the x, y, z position where the collision actually occurred on the surface of the **Into** object, which is the ground in our case. Because we passed in `render`, the position we get is in `render`'s coordinate system. That's the same coordinate system `self.root` and `self.trackNP` are using, so that's the one we want.

If the cycle is properly on the track, this will give us two positions in the points list. `points[0]` will be the collision point for the front ray, and `points[1]` will be the collision point for the back ray.

Before proceeding any further, we need to verify that we got collision data for both of the rays. That's what the next block of code we added is for:

```
if(points[0] == None or points[1] == None):
  self.teleport()
  return
else:
```

Remember that we set up our list to contain a `None`-type object in both spots by default? This, as well as the overwriting check we already performed, is the reason. If we still have `None`-type objects in the list now, instead of positions, then one or both of our rays didn't collide with the track. That means the cycle has gone off the track, and we need to put it back. That's why we call the `teleport` method, and abort the `groundCheck` method. The `teleport` method will handle the rest, this frame.

Our next code block handles the pitch of the cycle, and it's made up of two parts. One part is what happens when the cycle is not in freefall, and the other handles the pitch if the cycle is in freefall.

```
if(self.freeFall == False):
  self.refNP.setPos(points[1])
  self.refNP.lookAt(points[0])
  pDiff = self.refNP.getP()- self.cycle.getP()
  if(pDiff < .1 and pDiff > -.1):
    self.cycle.setP(self.refNP.getP())
  else:
    self.cycle.setP(self.cycle, pDiff * dt * 5)
elif((self.cycle.getP() - (dt * 10)) > -15):
  self.cycle.setP(self.cycle, -(dt * 10))
else:
  self.cycle.setP(-15)
```

The first line checks for freefall. If the cycle isn't in freefall, we go to the next two lines. These lines place our cycles reference NodePath, self.refNP, at the point on the track where the back ray collided with it. We then tell self.refNP to lookAt the point on the track where the front ray collided with it. This reorients self.refNP so that the point we gave to the lookAt method is straight down self.refNP's Y-axis. That means that the pitch of self.refNP is set such that it accurately reflects the up or down angle of the track beneath the cycle.

Once we have the pitch of the track, we compare it to the pitch of the cycle and put the difference in a temporary variable called pDiff. If pDiff is really small, we just set the cycle's pitch to the pitch of self.refNP exactly to prevent excessive wobbling in the cycle's pitch as it tries to perfectly match the pitch of the track. If pDiff is significant, we adjust the cycle's pitch according to pDiff and delta time to smoothly adjust it to the pitch of the track.

That takes care of the pitch when we aren't in freefall, but what if we are? Well, in that case, we want the nose of the cycle to slowly drift down, but not too far. We don't want the cycle to turn upside down! The four lines starting with the elif statement take care of that. With the elif statement, we check to see if lowering the nose of the cycle according to dt would make it drop too low. If not, we reduce the cycle's pitch based on time. If that would take it too low, we just set it to our minimum value, -15.

Now that we have the pitch sorted out, we need to deal with the actual height of the cycle. We have two track points to use as a reference, the front and back, but what we really want to use is the leading end of the cycle. This would be the front when moving forward, and the back when going in reverse, so we have some code to get the right one for us based on the cycle's speed.

```
if(self.speed >= 0):
  self.trackNP.setPos(points[0].getX(),
    points[0].getY(), points[0].getZ())
else:
  self.trackNP.setPos(points[1].getX(),
    points[1].getY(), points[1].getZ())
```

This uses the positive or negative nature of self.speed to determine if the cycle is moving forward or backward, and then it puts self.trackNP at the appropriate collision point with a call to setPos. Now, we have our track reference in place, and we're ready to start calculating how the cycle's height should change, or if it should change at all.

```
height = self.root.getZ(self.trackNP)
if(height > 2 and self.freeFall == False):
  self.freeFall = True
  self.fallSpeed = 0
```

The first line of this code block finds the Z position of `self.root` relative to `self.trackNP`. That means we get the difference in height between the two. If `self.root` is higher, we get a positive; if `self.trackNP` is higher, we get a negative. We put this value in a temporary variable called `height`, which we'll be using several times before `groundCheck` is finished.

The first thing we want to do is check to see if we need to enter a new freefall state. To determine that, we need to see if `height` is greater than 2 and we aren't in a freefall already. We want to give the cycle a bit of leeway before going into freefall, so a height of 2 meters is a good number (remember that our game is scaled so one unit is one meter).

If we do need to enter a new freefall state, the last three lines of this code block takes care of it for us by adjusting our three freefall-related variables. `self.freeFall` is set to `True`, so we know we're in a freefall state. Since we're starting a new fall, we want to reset `self.fallSpeed` to 0.

Now we know if we're in a freefall or not, we can calculate what our cycle's new height should be. We do that with this code:

```
if(self.freeFall == True):
  self.fallSpeed += (self.track.gravity * 9.8) * dt
  newHeight = height - (self.fallSpeed * dt)
else:
  hDiff = 1 - height
  if(hDiff > .01 or hDiff < -.01):
    newHeight = height + (hDiff * dt * 5)
  else:
    newHeight = 1
```

Again, this code is divided into two parts: one for when we're in freefall and one for the rest of the time. The first line checks if we're in a freefall. If we are, the second line accelerates `self.fallSpeed` based on the amount of gravity on this track and time. The third line takes the freshly accelerated `self.fallSpeed` and uses it, with time, to figure out how much the cycle would fall within this frame. Note that we don't immediately set the cycle to the new height. That comes later. Instead, we store the new height in a variable called, unsurprisingly, `newHeight`.

If we aren't in freefall, the rest of this code block comes into play. The first thing we do is find the difference between the cycle's height and our target height, which is one meter off the ground. We subtract `height` from one so that we get a value that we can use to directly calculate a new height. If height is too high, we get a negative that will lower the cycle, and vice versa. We store this value in another temporary variable, this one called `hDiff`.

Once we've got `hDiff`, we again check to see if it's actually significant. If so, then we use it and the time to calculate a new height for the cycle. Our goal with this is to smoothly adjust the cycle back to a height of one meter. If `hDiff` isn't significant, we just set the `newHeight` variable directly to one.

Now we have a value in `newHeight` to set the cycle at, but we can't just apply it right away. If we really look at the code we've gone over so far, we might notice something important. We don't have anything in our code so far to stop a freefall once it starts! To keep our cycle from plummeting right through the track and into oblivion, we need to have a trigger to end a freefall. That's what the last big block of code in the `groundCheck` method is for.

```
if(newHeight >= 0):
  self.root.setZ(self.trackNP, newHeight)
else:
  self.root.setZ(self.trackNP, 0)
  self.freeFall = False
```

Our first line here checks if `newHeight` is greater than 0. Remember that `newHeight` is relative to `self.trackNP`, so 0 would be the exact height of `self.trackNP`, which is the height of the track under the cycle. If `newHeight` is greater than or equal to 0, it's safe to set the cycle to that height. We call `self.root.setZ(self.trackNP, newHeight)` to place `self.root newHeight` meters above `self.trackNP`, and consequently, the track.

If `newHeight` isn't greater than or equal to 0, that means our `newHeight` would put the cycle beneath the surface of the track! We can't have that, so instead we set `self.root` to the same height as `self.trackNP` with `self.root.setZ(self.trackNP, 0)`. If we weren't in a freefall, our cycle would be gravitating toward a height of one meter, so if it's gotten this low we're probably in a freefall. Regardless of that, we can't fall any farther, so we'll set `self.freefall` to `False` with the last line. This will take us out of the freefall state if we were in it, and the cycle will start gravitating back to a height of one meter next frame.

The next change we made was to the `speedCheck` method. This change is a fairly simple one. If the cycle is in freefall, it doesn't have any ground to push against to adjust its speed on its own, so we don't want to do the regular part of `speedCheck` during a freefall. Instead, we'll execute this line:

```
self.speed -= (self.speed * .125) * dt
```

This will degrade our speed at a rate of 12.5 percent per second. While not a realistic expression of friction with whatever atmosphere is on our track, it will satisfy for our purposes.

After that, we added a call to `groundCheck` to our `cycleControl` method. We don't need to go over that.

The last chunk of code we added to our `Cycle` class was a new method, `teleport`:

```
def teleport(self):
  marker = self.track.trackLanes.getNearestMarker(self)
  markerPos = marker.getPos()
  self.root.setPos(markerPos.getX(),
    markerPos.getY(), self.root.getZ())

  self.gCTrav.traverse(render)
  points = [None, None]
  if(self.gHan.getNumEntries() > 1):
    self.gHan.sortEntries()
    for E in range(self.gHan.getNumEntries()):
      entry = self.gHan.getEntry(E)
      if(entry.getFrom() == self.fRay and points[0]== None):
        points[0] = entry.getSurfacePoint(render)
      elif(entry.getFrom() == self.bRay and points[1]== None):
        points[1] = entry.getSurfacePoint(render)

    if(self.speed >= 0):
      self.trackNP.setPos(points[0].getX(),
        points[0].getY(), points[0].getZ())
    else:
      self.trackNP.setPos(points[1].getX(),
        points[1].getY(), points[1].getZ())

    self.root.setZ(self.trackNP, 1)
  self.dirNP.setHpr(marker.getHpr())
  self.cycle.setHpr(marker.getHpr())
  self.speed /= 2
```

The first line of this method finds the nearest track marker to our cycle. We want to place the cycle back on the track with this method, so we need to figure out where the track is. Finding the closest marker is how we do that. Once we have the marker we want, we get its position and place `self.root` on top of it.

The next big block of code should look familiar. This is a duplicate of part of `groundCheck`, right down until the line where we call `setZ` on `self.root`. What we're doing with these lines is finding the height of the track, and setting the cycle to be one meter above it.

The last three lines of this method do a little maintenance to prevent the cycle from going right off the track again. The track marker is facing the correct direction down the track, so we copy that direction to `self.dirNP` and `self.cycle` so we'll be facing and moving in the right direction when we come out of the teleport. The last line is the penalty for going off the track: the cycle's speed is halved.

Pop quiz – complex collision detection

Now that we've put together a more complicated collision detection system, let's go over some questions about how we put it together.

1. How do we sort the entries in a `CollisionHandlerQueue` from nearest to farthest?

2. How do we get the **From** and **Into** `CollisionNodes` from a collision entry? How do we get the collision solids?

3. How did we use collision detection to tell if the cycle went off the track?

4. What method of what object did we use to find the point in space where a collision was detected? How did we determine what coordinate system the point was given to us in?

5. How did we use collision detection to figure out what pitch our cycle should be at?

Overview of additional collision solids and handlers

Panda3D offers many more options for collision solids and handlers than we used in this chapter. Most of these have specific uses that won't apply to our game, but we should talk about them briefly so we know when to use them.

Collision solids

The different collision solids in Panda3D are:

◆   `CollisionSphere` – A simple sphere, the most basic collision solid. This solid is excellent as both a **From** object and an **Into** object. A sphere is defined by a position and a radius.

   ❑   mySolid = CollisionSphere([posX], [posY], [posZ], [radius])

◆   `CollisionTube` – A tube is formed by a cylinder with hemispherical end caps. This shape is sometimes referred to as a capsule. The tube is only suitable for use as an **Into** object. Define a tube with its two end points, and a cylinder radius.

   ❑   mySolid = CollisionTube([pos1X], [pos1Y], [pos1Z], [pos2X], [pos2Y], [pos2Z] , [radius])

◆   `CollisionInvSphere` – This is very similar to the regular `CollisionSphere`, but instead of considering anything on its exterior as not colliding, and everything in its interior as colliding, it's reversed. Things inside the sphere are not colliding, and things that protrude out of the sphere are colliding. One way to think of this shape is a solid mass that fills everything, except for one little bubble of space in the middle. The `CollisionInvSphere` is defined exactly like the `CollisionSphere`. This solid is meant to be an **Into** object.

❏ mySolid = CollisionInvSphere([posX], [posY], [posZ], [radius])

◆ CollisionPlane – This shape is a flat plane extending infinitely in all directions. This shape actually divides the universe into two regions: the one behind the plane that is considered solid, and the front of the plane that is not. The CollisionPlane is constructed from the Plane object, which has several constructors of its own. One example uses a point to be the centre of the plane, and a vector to be its facing. This solid is also meant for use as an **Into** object.

❏ mySolid = CollisionPlane(Plane(Vec3([facingX], [facingY], [facingZ]), Point3([posX], [posY], [posZ])))

◆ CollisionPolygon – This is the most general of the collision solids. It is also the most expensive and the least accurate, being the most likely to let collisions slip through. It is not recommended to create CollisionPolygons in code; it's better to use a modeling package. Collision polys may only be used as **Into** objects.

◆ CollisionRay – This solid represents an infinite ray that shoots from a point out in a given direction. This can only be used as a **From** object.

❏ mySolid = CollisionRay([posX], [posY], [posZ], [dirX], [dirY], [dirZ])

◆ CollisionLine – This is the same as a CollisionRay, with the only difference being that the CollisionLine extends in both directions. This is a **From** object only.

❏ mySolid = CollisionLine([posX], [posY], [posZ], [dirX], [dirY], [dirZ])

◆ CollisionSegment – Another variant on the CollisionRay, a CollisionSegment only extends out to a second point and then stops. Another **From** object only.

❏ mySolid = CollisionSegment([pos1X], [pos1Y], [pos1Z], [pos2X], [pos2Y], [pos2Z])

◆ CollisionParabola – A final variant on the CollisionRay, this solid represents a parabolic arc. It isn't used often, and is only suitable for objects that would travel instantly along an arc, or possibly for aiming such objects. It is only valid as a **From** object, and its constructor requires a Panda3D Parabola object.

Collision handlers

- ◆ `CollisionHandlerQueue` – The most basic of the collision handlers, this handler stores all of the detected collisions for a frame as collision entries.

- ◆ `CollisionHandlerEvent` – Another basic collision handler, this triggers an event when a collision is detected. Classes that inherit from `DirectObject` can register that event and react to it.

- ◆ `CollisionHandlerPusher` – This is a more advanced handler that will automatically prevent colliding objects from passing through each other. It can also trigger events, like a `CollisionHandlerEvent`.

- ◆ `PhysicsCollisionHandler` – This handler is designed to integrate with Panda3D's physics system.

- ◆ `CollisionHandlerFloor` – This is a special handler used to keep objects on a defined floor, or falling gracefully toward it.

Summary

This chapter was all about collision detection. It was a big, meaty topic, but we cleaned our plate.

We talked about these major points:

- ◆ `CollisionNodes`
- ◆ Collision solids
- ◆ Collision handlers
- ◆ `CollisionTraversers`
- ◆ `BitMasks`
- ◆ `PythonTags`

Now that our game is starting to act all high and mighty, we need to give it the appearance to match. Next chapter we delve into the world of lighting, textures, and Panda3D's `autoShader`. Get ready for a fun ride!

7
Making it Fancy: Lighting, Textures, Filters, and Shaders

Modern games can't get away with the graphics of the old Atari classics. Players have a certain level of expectation, and it's our duty as developers to live up to that expectation. That's the focus of this chapter: making our game as visually appealing as it will be fun.

There are a few different topics to cover when talking about the game's appearance:

◆ Adding lighting
◆ Applying textures to models
◆ Creating filters
◆ Using a sky sphere

With an understanding of these concepts under our belt, we'll really be able to give our game some visual jazz.

Adding lighting

Panda3D has a very practical approach to lighting. There are two aspects: first, we create the light, and second, we set what things will be illuminated by it. On the surface, that's all there is to it. Of course, that's just the surface.

We have to decide what kinds of light we need, and how many, and set their options to get the effect we want. Also, it's important to keep in mind that we should use as few lights as possible because they can be a serious drain on our system resources.

Time for action – adding lights to the game

To get a feel for lights, let's go ahead and throw some into our game!

1. Open up the `TrackClass_00.py` file in the `Chapter07` folder.

2. We'll start with a new method that will create two lights for us and assign them to illuminate the entire scene. Add this method to the bottom of the `Track` class:

```
def setupLight(self):
    primeL = DirectionalLight("prime")
    primeL.setColor(VBase4(.6,.6,.6,1))
    self.light = render.attachNewNode(primeL)
    self.light.setHpr(45,-60,0)
    render.setLight(self.light)

ambL = AmbientLight("amb")
    ambL.setColor(VBase4(.2,.2,.2,1))
    self.ambLight = render.attachNewNode(ambL)
    render.setLight(self.ambLight)
    return
```

3. Of course, we need to call that new method in order for it to do anything. Add this line of code to the bottom of the `__init__` method:

```
self.setupLight()
```

4. Resave the file as `TrackClass_01.py`.

5. Since our cycles have components that glow on the bottom, it makes more sense for them to cast light instead of shadow. To do that, we'll put a light on our cycle as well. Open the `CycleClass_00.py` file in the `Chapter07` folder, and add this method right beneath the `setupCollisions` method:

```
def setupLight(self):
    self.glow = self.cycle.attachNewNode(
PointLight(self.name + "Glow"))
    self.glow.node().setColor(Vec4(.2,.6,1,1))
    self.glow.node().setAttenuation(Vec3(0,0,.75))
    render.setLight(self.glow)
    return
```

6. Next, we need to call that method as well. Add this line to the end of the `__init__` method:

```
self.setupLight()
```

7. Resave the file as `CycleClass_01.py`.

8. Once that's done, open `WorldClass_00.py` in the `Chapter07` folder and modify it to use the new files we just made for the track and cycle, then resave it as `WorldClass_01.py`. Run it from the command prompt.

9. Things are looking quite a bit different already, but notice that the blue light doesn't seem to be illuminating the track. To fix that, we need to turn on the auto shader. Add this line to the bottom of the __init__ method for the World class:

```
render.setShaderAuto()
```

10. Save the file and run it from the command prompt.

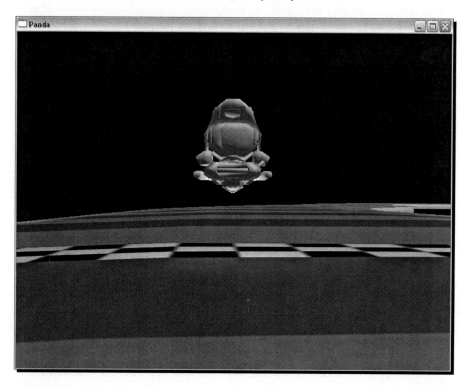

What just happened?

Creating lights really isn't very difficult. We start by calling the constructor and giving it a name for the light. Once we have that, we can use `setColor` to control the nature of the light that it emits.

Once the light was created, we needed to package it up in a `NodePath` to add it to the scene graph. We used `attachNewNode` to do that, as we've done in the past. We can aim and position lights by rotating and repositioning the `NodePath` we place them in.

The values we give to `setColor` control not only the hue of the light, but also its brightness. The closer the color is to a pure white, the brighter the light will be. That means if you want a bright red light, you could use (1, 0, 0), but if you give it a pinkish tinge with (1, .5, .5) it will be even brighter.

We used `setAttenuation` to better control the point light we created on the cycle. Attenuation is defined as the decrease in a property that occurs as the distance from the source increases. With `setAttenuation`, we can control how far the light spreads. The three numbers we supply to `setAttenuation` are, in order, the constant, linear, and quadratic falloff based on the distance from the source. The best way to better understand this would be to adjust the numbers up and down and see how the light changes.

Once the light is set up, we need to use `setLight` to tell Panda3D what needs to be illuminated by it. The `NodePath` we call `setLight` on, and all of its children in the scene graph, will be illuminated. `NodePaths` in other branches of the scene graph will not. The argument is the `NodePath` that contains the light itself, so `setLight` knows what light it's working with.

We made one more addition that bears mentioning. In `World` class, we added this line:

```
render.setShaderAuto()
```

This is a very special call that turns on Panda3D's built-in automatic shader generation. Turning on automatic shader generation makes it possible to use a wide variety of effects to improve the visuals in the game. In our case, we turned it on to allow per-pixel lighting, which made the glow of the cycle's light show up on the track. Per-pixel lighting is also necessary for normal maps and gloss maps, among other things.

Types of lights

We've got a few different options when selecting what lights we'll use in our game.

- `AmbientLight`: This is the only type of light that ignores position and direction. An ambient light strikes all surfaces everywhere exactly the same. This is generally used as a filler light, to give detail to the shadows where other lights don't shine.

- `DirectionalLight`: These lights are meant to represent a very large or very far away source of light, such as the sun. They shine onto everything from a particular direction, which is determined according to where the `NodePath` they are in is facing.

- `PointLight`: This light type shines light out in all directions, like a light bulb. The amount the light spreads is controlled with `setAttenuation`, and the light's position is controlled with the `NodePath` it's in.

- `SpotLight`: The last type of light is kind of like a combination of the `DirectionalLight` and the `PointLight`. It works very much like the way a spotlight in the real world does. You can control the falloff with `setAttenuation`, and the position and direction through the `NodePath`.

Have a go hero – adding more lights to the scene

Try creating more lights in the scene, adjusting their settings, and otherwise manipulating them to create different lighting environments. Keep playing with them until you've got a good feel for how they work, and what can be done with them.

 The automatic shader generation system will impose a limit on the number of lights in the scene. Try to only have five or six in existence at a time.

Pop quiz – using lights

Here are some questions to help us figure out how well we understand lighting.

1. What controls the position and direction of a light, if they are applicable?
2. What kinds of lights are there?
3. What difference does turning on automatic shader generation do for lights?

Applying textures to models

Textures play a very important role in the visual appearance of any game. They are the images that are wrapped around the models to add color and detail to the polygons that form the model. To use textures properly, a model has to be given texture coordinates that tell Panda3D how to apply the texture to the model. It is possible to automatically generate these coordinates, but this is rarely done in practice. The best way to create these coordinates is in a modeling package, such as Blender. For our game, the models we use will already have the texture coordinates created.

We have two options for applying textures to our model. The first method we've already used, and that is to have the texture applied in the modeling package when we export an egg file, so that when the egg is loaded the texture is already there. That's what we've done with our track.

The second method is to apply the texture with code at runtime. This method is best when we want to use some of Panda3D's texturing effects, such as normal, gloss, or glow maps. Applying several textures to use all of these effects every time a model is loaded is not very practical, though. To get around this, we're going to use another feature of Panda3D that we talked about back when we were discussing eggs and bams. Panda3D can save out a bam file that contains a model and all of its texturing that we can load later on, so we don't have to reapply the textures every time we load the model. This will help us keep our `Cycle` class as simple as possible, too, because we won't have to put all of the code for creating and applying the textures into that class.

Time for action – creating a bam writer

Instead of loading and applying textures to our models in the game, we're going to create a new Panda3D application that we'll call a bam writer. This application will load up our models and texture them, then save out a bam file that will retain all the work we've done. Then, we'll just need to load the bams into the game. While we're at it, we'll set up the bam writer to give us a good preview of the models to make sure they look nice.

1. Open a blank document in Notepad++. Save the file as `BamWriter_01.py`.

2. Our first step is to import all the components we'll need for this application. Add this code to the new file:

```
import direct.directbase.DirectStart
from pandac.PandaModules import *

from InputManagerClass_00 import InputManager
```

3. Next, we'll create a new class to perform the work of the bam writer, and put some code in its `__init__` method to get the ball rolling:

```
class BamWriter:
  def __init__(self):
    base.setBackgroundColor(0, 0, 0)
    base.disableMouse()
    base.camera.setPos(0, -7.5, .75)
    self.inputManager = InputManager()
    taskMgr.add(self.inputTask, "Input Task")

    self.setupLight()
    render.setShaderAuto()

    self.modelRoot = render.attachNewNode("Model Root")
    self.setupModels()
```

4. We have a couple of method calls in our `__init__` now that we need to create the methods for. First, we'll tackle the `setupLight` method by copying the `setupLight` method we created for the `Track` class into our `BamWriter` class. This will give us the same lighting environment in the `BamWriter` as we have in our game. Hop over to the `TrackClass_01.py` file, copy the `setupLight` method, and paste it into the bottom of `BamWriter_01.py`.

5. Next, we'll create the `inputTask` we're adding to the task manager. This task will use the `InputManager` we've created to let us spin the model around and see it from various angles. Add this code to the bottom of the `BamWriter` class:

```
def inputTask(self, task):
  if(self.inputManager.keyMap["w"] == True):
```

```
    self.modelRoot.setP(self.modelRoot, .5)
elif(self.inputManager.keyMap["s"] == True):
    self.modelRoot.setP(self.modelRoot, -.5)
if(self.inputManager.keyMap["a"] == True):
    self.modelRoot.setH(self.modelRoot, .5)
elif(self.inputManager.keyMap["d"] == True):
    self.modelRoot.setH(self.modelRoot, -.5)
return task.again
```

6. None of this will work if we don't create an instance of the `BamWriter` class and tell the program to run, so add these two lines to the very bottom of the file:

```
BW = BamWriter()
run()
```

7. The last method we need to fill in is the `setupModels` method, which is where we'll actually load our models, apply textures, and so forth. To really see our `BamWriter` in action, let's load a model with no textures and apply one to it. Add these three lines to the bottom of the `BamWriter` class, just above the two lines we added in the last step:

```
def setupModels(self):
    self.moulding =  loader.loadModel("../Models/Moulding.egg")
    self.moulding.reparentTo(self.modelRoot)
```

8. Save the file and run it from the command prompt.

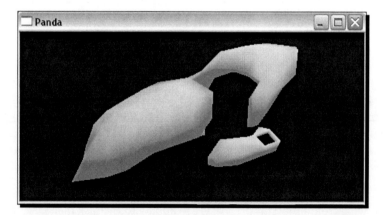

9. Here, we are looking at another untextured flat, grey model. Let's spice it up with some nice red paint, shall we? Add this code to the end of the `setupModels` method:

```
        self.teamTex = loader.loadTexture("../Images/RedTeamTex.png")
    self.moulding.setTexture(self.teamTex)
```

10. The whole purpose of this system is to write out a bam file that contains our texture changes to the model, so let's do that now, too. Add this line to the bottom of the __init__ method, below the call to setupModels:

```
    self.modelRoot.writeBamFile("RedCycle.bam")
```

11. Resave the file, and then run it from the command prompt.

What just happened?

When the application opens, we see the model for the moulding with a new texture added to it. If we look in the Chapter07 folder, we also see a new RedCycle.bam file. It didn't take much work to do this, either.

We loaded and applied the red and striped texture with this code:

```
        self.teamTex = loader.loadTexture("../Images/RedTeamTex.png")
    self.moulding.setTexture(self.teamTex)
```

The first line tells the loader to go find the image file that we want and turn it into a texture object. The second line replaces the current texture of self.moulding (that was empty) with the new texture we just loaded.

The only other new thing we saw in this code was the line to write the bam file:

```
    self.modelRoot.writeBamFile("RedCycle.bam")
```

The call to `writeBamFile` creates a bam file with the name we supply as the argument. It fills that bam file with the `NodePath` it's called on *and all of that* `NodePath's` *children*. This is an important note because it means that we can use `writeBamFile` to save out an entire branch of our scene graph into a single file. We're going to use this to build our cycle out of several pieces that use different textures, and then save it all into a single, easy-to-load file.

Have a go hero – loading the bam file

Don't take my word for it about the contents of the bam file. Try loading it into our game, just like you would with an egg file, and see that we get the textured version of the moulding.

 Make sure to change the game files back to how they were before we move on, though!

Texture stages

A `TextureStage` is a kind of slot for a texture on a model. It's similar to a `NodePath` in that it has settings for a texture, but it's also a bit different because the same `TextureStage` can be added to multiple models and contains a different texture on each model. Basically, the `TextureStage` doesn't contain the texture itself, it just contains the settings.

Every model has a base `TextureStage` by default. When we call `setTexture`, as we did in the last example, we are replacing the texture in that default `TextureStage`. We can also give `setTexture` a `TextureStage`, and if we do, the texture we're applying will be put in that `TextureStage` instead of the default one.

```
myModel.setTexture(myTextureStage, myTexture)
```

The primary reason for this is to apply textures with different settings, or to apply multiple textures to a single model. For our game, we'll be doing both. We create new `TextureStages` by calling their constructor and giving it a name for the `TextureStage`.

```
myTextureStage = TextureStage("My Texture Stage")
```

The main setting that we'll be using for our different `TextureStages` will be the texture mode. The mode controls how the texture is used on the model. We've got several different options we can use.

The first two texture modes represent different ways to mix multiple textures together. Note that if they are used with only a single texture on the model, there won't be anything to mix, so we'll just see the texture applied as it is.

- ◆ `Modulate`: This is the default mode for textures. In this mode, the texture is multiplied with the textures already on the model. This means that the resulting look will be dark, or at least no brighter, than the original textures. In this mode, the alpha channel of the texture will create a cutout of the model through which things behind it can be seen.

- ◆ `Add`: In this mode, the texture is added to the textures already on the model, and clamped to go no higher than 1 (white). This means that the look will be lighter, or at least no darker, than the original textures. In this mode, the alpha channel of the texture produces a cutout just like in modulate mode.

 In order for the alpha channel to create a cutout as mentioned in the above descriptions, transparency needs to be activated on the model's `NodePath`.

The next three modes are used for applying a color texture without altering the colors in the texture being applied:

- ◆ `Replace`: This mode is rarely used. This causes only this texture to show up on the model.

- ◆ `Decal`: This is a handy mode for applying additional textures like stickers onto the model. In this mode, the texture is placed on top of the textures already on the model without any mixing, and any alpha channel in the texture will allow the textures already present to show through. It does not create a cutout in the model, like Modulate and Add do.

- ◆ `Blend`: This mode is meant for use with a grey-scale image. The black parts of the image will be transparent, like in the Decal mode, while the white parts of the image will show up in whatever color is specified by `TextureStage.setColor`. For the grey parts of the image, there will be a smooth blend between the textures already present and the color specified.

There are also three modes that are used to adjust the lighting on the model. None of the three will work if Panda3D's automatic shader generation isn't turned on because they require per-pixel lighting to operate.

- ◆ `Normal`: This mode uses a grey-scale image to create a Normal map for the model. A Normal map is an image that represents height on the model, and can be used to create complex bumps and ridges that would be difficult to create in the modeling process, or would result in too many polygons. The dark parts of the image will be considered lower, and the white parts of the image will be considered higher. Normal maps are sometimes referred to as Bump maps. Currently, Panda3D only supports the use of a single Normal map on each model; further Normal maps will be ignored. Lastly, Normal maps also require that binormals and tangents be calculated on the model. This should be taken care of when the model is exported from the modeling package, or when it's converted into an egg.

- ◆ Gloss: This mode uses a grey-scale image to indicate what parts of the model should be shiny and what parts should be dull. The black parts of the image won't be shiny at all, and the white parts will be very shiny indeed. Like Normal maps, Panda3D only supports one Gloss map per model.

- ◆ Glow: This mode also uses a grey-scale image, this time to indicate which parts of the model should glow. The black parts of the image will result in spots on the model where it responds normally to the lighting in the scene, while the white spots will always be fully illuminated, regardless of the scene's lighting. Like Normal and Gloss maps, only one Glow map can be applied to a model. Additional ones are ignored.

 A Normal map will only affect the way the model reacts to lighting; it does not actually move vertices or polygons to create bumps or crevices. That means that while the Normal map may create the illusion of bumps and crevices by changing the light and shadows on a model, those bumps and crevices aren't really there. They may vanish entirely when looking at the model from a different angle, such as the side.

There are also a couple of combined modes that we can use to do multiple things at once. They are:

- ◆ ModulateGloss: This mode combines the Modulate mode and the Gloss mode. The RGB components of the texture are used for Modulate mode, while the alpha component is used to control the Gloss mode.

- ◆ ModulateGlow: This mode combines the Modulate mode and the Glow mode. The RGB components of the texture are used for Modulate mode, while the alpha component is used to control the Glow mode.

To set the mode of a TextureStage, we use the setMode method and give it the mode object, which we also get from the TextureStage. This may sound a little confusing, so here are a couple of examples:

```
myTextureStage.setMode(TextureStage.MModulate)
myTextureStage.setMode(TextureStage.MNormal)
myTextureStage.setMode(TextureStage.MModulateGloss)
```

Note that we aren't using any specific instance of the TextureStage class to get the modes; we're using the global name TextureStage that we imported from Panda3D's modules. Also note that the mode names are prefaced by an uppercase M.

Time for action – using TextureStages

That's enough talk about TextureStages. It's about time we saw them at work. Let's start putting our cycle together with all the right textures so we can make use of these things.

1. Open the file `BamWriter_01.py`.

2. We'll start by applying a gloss map to `self.moulding`. Add this code to the very beginning of the `setupModels` method:

```
self.glossTS = TextureStage("glossTS")
self.glossTS.setMode(TextureStage.MModulateGloss)
```

3. We have our new `TextureStage` set to use `ModulateGloss` mode, which requires an image with an alpha channel. However, the texture we're using is in the PNG format, which doesn't support alpha channels. We can fix that by changing the line where we load `RedTeamTex.png` to the following:

```
self.teamTex = loader.loadTexture("../Images/RedTeamTex.png",
   "../Images/HighGloss.png")
```

4. By telling the loader to load two images at once, we're actually combining them into a single texture object. The first image becomes the RGB section of the texture, and the second image becomes the alpha channel. Let's apply this new texture to `self.moulding` by adding this line to the end of the `setupModels` method:

```
self.moulding.setTexture(self.glossTS, self.teamTex)
```

5. Save the file as `BamWriter_02.py` and run it from the command prompt.

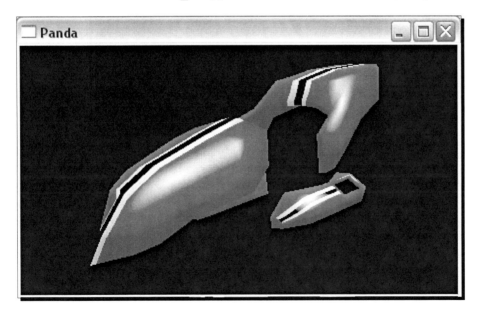

6. Now, we're seeing some shiny highlights on the moulding, but we won't stop there. We can also use a normal map to help make the stripes pop a bit more. Create a new `TextureStage` for normal maps right below where we created the `TextureStage` for the `ModulateGloss` texture, using this code:

```
self.normalTS = TextureStage("normalTS")
self.normalTS.setMode(TextureStage.MNormal)
```

7. Now, we'll load up another texture and apply it to the model with the new `TextureStage`. This code goes at the bottom of the `setupModels` method:

```
self.normalTex = loader.loadTexture("../Images/Normal.png")
self.moulding.setTexture(self.normalTS, self.normalTex)
```

8. Save the file as `BamWriter_03.py` and run it from the command prompt.

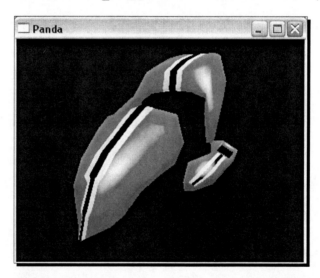

9. Now, our highlights are following the contour of the stripes on the front. It's a subtle change, but effective. Our next step is to try out a Glow map. For this, we'll load two separate models for the cycle's power plant and apply a Glow map to one and a Gloss map to the other. Start by adding this code to where we are creating our `TextureStages`, at the beginning of the `setupModels` method:

```
self.glowTS = TextureStage("glowTS")
self.glowTS.setMode(TextureStage.MModulateGlow)
```

10. Then, add this code to the bottom of the method:

```
self.pp1 = loader.loadModel("../Models/PP1.egg")
self.pp1.reparentTo(self.modelRoot)
self.pp2 = loader.loadModel("../Models/PP2.egg")
```

```
self.pp2.reparentTo(self.modelRoot)
self.metalTex = loader.loadTexture("../Images/Metal.png",
    "../Images/HighGloss.png")
self.pp1.setTexture(self.glossTS, self.metalTex)
self.glowTex = loader.loadTexture("../Images/Blue.png",
    "../Images/HighGlow.png")
self.pp2.setTexture(self.glowTS, self.glowTex)
```

11. Resave the file as `BamWriter_04.py` and then run it from the command prompt.

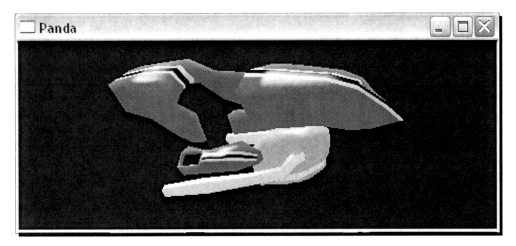

12. Notice how the blue parts of the power plant ignore the lighting in the scene. That's our glow map at work. We've got all the tools we need now, so let's go ahead and add the other cycle pieces we need. Add this code to the bottom of the `setupModels` method:

```
self.coffin = loader.loadModel("../Models/Coffin.egg")
self.coffin.reparentTo(self.modelRoot)

self.coffinTex = loader.loadTexture("../Images/Coffin.png",
    "../Images/HighGloss.png")

self.coffin.setTexture(self.glossTS, self.coffinTex)

self.frame = loader.loadModel("../Models/Frame.egg")
self.frame.reparentTo(self.modelRoot)
self.fuelTank = loader.loadModel("../Models/FuelTank.egg")
self.fuelTank.reparentTo(self.modelRoot)
self.sp1 = loader.loadModel("../Models/SP1.egg")
self.sp1.reparentTo(self.modelRoot)
self.sp2 = loader.loadModel("../Models/SP2.egg")
self.sp2.reparentTo(self.modelRoot)
```

```
self.frame.setTexture(self.glossTS, self.metalTex)
self.fuelTank.setTexture(self.glossTS, self.metalTex)
self.sp1.setTexture(self.glossTS, self.metalTex)
self.sp2.setTexture(self.glowTS, self.glowTex)
```

13. Save the file as `BamWriter_05.py` and run it.

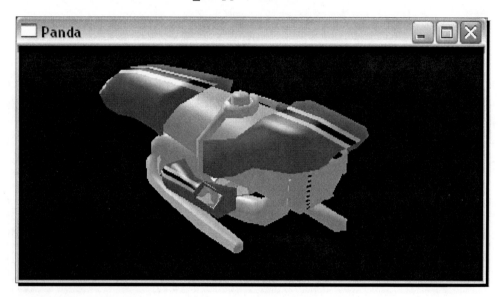

What just happened?

Now, our cycle is really coming together. We haven't added the turret or the discs yet, because those parts are going to be animated. We'll add them in the upcoming animation chapter.

Most of what we did in this example we had covered beforehand, but there is one thing that we should note:

```
self.coffinTex = loader.loadTexture("../Images/Coffin.png",
    "../Images/HighGloss.png")
```

In this call, we are loading two images into a single texture. When we do that, we are taking the first image and using it for the RGB part of the texture, and we are using the second image for the alpha channel of the texture.

When we use the loader to load an image that we've already loaded once before, it doesn't actually go get the file. It returns the same texture that it returned the first time. That means if we have images called A, B, and C, and we make these calls to the loader:

```
loader.loadTexture(A, B)
loader.loadTexture(A, C)
```

We'll get a texture with A in the RGB portion and B in the alpha portion from *both* calls. That's because the second call to load image A will return the texture that was already created, which has B in the alpha channel. This is just one of the quirks of Panda3D that we need to know about and plan for. One way to get around this problem is to unload texture A before loading it the second time. We can do that with `loader.unloadTexture(A)`.

The bam file we've made has relative path names for the texture files it loads, so it needs to be left in the `Chapter07` folder to load correctly. We can correct that by moving `BamWriter_05.py` to the `Models` folder and creating the bam file there.

Have a go hero – apply textures

For an easy little exercise, alter the `BamWriter` to create bam files that use `GreenTeamTex.png`, `BlueTeamTex.png`, and `YellowTeamTex.png` instead of `RedTeamTex.png`. While you're at it, move `BamWriter_05.py` over to the `Models` folder so the bams it writes will have the correct relative paths for the texture files. You'll have to either move `InputManager_00.py` over as well, or comment out some lines so it isn't needed.

Pop quiz – understanding textures and TextureStages

We've covered a lot of material, so let's check ourselves on it before we continue.

1. What is a `TextureStage`?
2. What are `TextureStages` used for?
3. What different modes can be used with textures?
4. What does the `NodePath` method `writeBamFile` do?

Creating filters

Panda3D offers us some handy, built-in postprocessing filters that we can use to get some neat effects in our game. These filters work by editing the rendered frame before displaying it. The best way to think of it is by imagining the filter as an additional step between rendering the scene and actually displaying it because that's exactly what it is.

Time for action – adding a bloom filter

Let's go ahead and add a bloom filter to our game so we can see how to set these guys up. The bloom filter automatically integrates with glow maps, so it's easy to use it to make halos around glowing objects.

1. Open a `WorldClass_01.py`.

2. We need to import the filters before we can use them, so add this code to our import section at the top of the file:

```
from direct.filter.CommonFilters import CommonFilters
```

3. Now that we're importing `CommonFilters`, we need to create an instance of it. Add this code right before the `render.setShaderAuto` call. It doesn't really have to precede that call, but that's as good a place as any.

```
self.filters = CommonFilters(base.win, base.cam)
```

4. Next, we'll turn on the bloom filter and give it some parameters to work with. Add these lines right below the line we added in step 3:

```
filterok = self.filters.setBloom(blend=(0,0,0,1),
    desat=-0.5, intensity=3.0, size=2)
```

5. Okay, now we just need something to bloom. We've got a glow effect in our new cycle bam files, so let's change the `Cycle` class to use those. Open `CycleClass_01.py` and find the line where we load `cycle.bam`, down in the `setupVarsNPs` method. Remove that line. Then, scroll up to where we set the position of `self.root` based on the position the cycle is starting in. Change that section to look like this:

```
if(startPos == 1):
  self.root.setPos(5,0,0)
  self.cycle = loader.loadModel("../Models/RedCycle.bam")
elif(startPos == 2):
  self.root.setPos(-5,-5,0)
  self.cycle = loader.loadModel("../Models/BlueCycle.bam")
elif(startPos == 3):
  self.root.setPos(5,-10,0)
  self.cycle = loader.loadModel("../Models/GreenCycle.bam")
elif(startPos == 4):
  self.root.setPos(-5,-15,0)
  self.cycle = loader.loadModel("../Models/YellowCycle.bam")
```

6. Resave the file as `CycleClass_02.py`, then bounce back over to the `World` class and modify the imports to use `CycleClass_02.py` instead of `CycleClass_01.py`. Then, resave this file as `WorldClass_02.py` and run it from the command prompt.

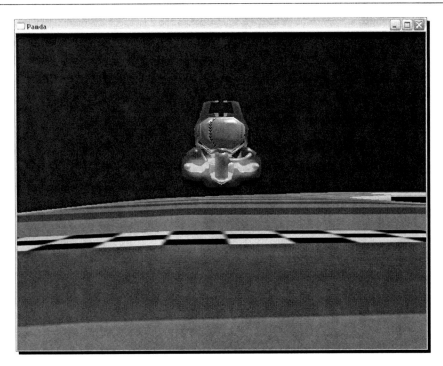

What just happened?

That's all it took! We've got a nice blue halo around our glowing bits. Let's talk about the code we used to set up the filter real quick, and then we can move on.

The first line we added was this one:

```
self.filters = CommonFilters(base.win, base.cam)
```

This line sets up the CommonFilters class and makes it ready to use. It needs to know which window we're outputting to, and which camera we're using to render the scene from, so we passed those into it. The other two lines set up the bloom filter by itself.

```
filterok = self.filters.setBloom(blend=(0,0,0,1),
    desat=-0.5, intensity=3.0, size=2)
```

The properties of the bloom filter aren't very complicated. Blend determines how the bloom filter measures the brightness of pixels. The values we give it are weights that tell it how much emphasis to put on the R, G, B, and A channels respectively. Since we only want our Glow maps to be considered, we put R, G, and B to 0 and put A to 1. The Desat property tells the filter how much it should desaturate the halo it creates. A value of 0 means the halo is the same color as the pixel that created it. A value of 1 makes the halo white. Intensity is a variable that controls how bright the halo is. The last property, size, determines how far the halos spread.

The `filterok` temporary variable will receive the return of the call to `setBloom`, which tells us if the graphics card responded favorably to our attempt to turn on the bloom filter. If we have trouble getting the filter to work, we can print out `filterok` to see if the graphics card is preventing us from using it.

Using a sky sphere

The last thing we'll add to our game in this chapter is a backdrop, to get rid of that ugly black background we've had for so long. We'll do this by loading up an enormous sphere and setting it up to imitate a background. By doing so, we'll create a seamless sky that surrounds our scene.

To learn how to create a bam file like the one we'll be loading for our sky sphere, check out *Appendix A, Creating a Sky Sphere with Spacescape*.

Time for action – adding a sky sphere

We'll be putting the sky sphere in the track class since it's a piece of scenery, technically.

1. Open `TrackClass_01.py`.

2. Resave the file as `TrackClass_02.py`.

3. Let's just dive right in, now. Add these two methods to the very bottom of the `Track` class:

```
def setupSkySphere(self):
    self.skySphere = loader.loadModel(
"../Models/LinearPinkSkySphere.bam")
    self.skySphere.reparentTo(render)
    self.skySphere.setBin('background', 1)
    self.skySphere.setDepthWrite(False)
    self.skySphere.setShaderOff()

    self.skySphere.setAlphaScale(0)
    taskMgr.add(self.skySphereTask, "SkySphere Task")
    return
def skySphereTask(self, task):
    self.skySphere.setPos(base.camera, 0, 0, 0)
    return task.cont
```

4. Right beneath the call to `setupLight` in the `__init__` method, add a call to `setupSkySphere`:

```
self.setupSkySphere()
```

5. Save the file then change `WorldClass_02.py` to use `TrackClass_02.py`. Once you've made the change, resave the `World` class file as `WorldClass_03.py` and run it.

What just happened?

There are a number of new calls in that `setupSkySphere` method we just made, so let's go through them one at a time and talk about them.

To start with, we have the call to `setBin`. This `NodePath` method is used to place geometry in a named rendering bin. We don't generally use this very often, but by moving `self.skySphere` to the `'background'` bin, we ensure that it's rendered before anything else in the scene. The second argument, 1, is a priority. We have to use a number above 0 to override the default settings.

After that, we call `setDepthWrite` with the argument **False**. This is another `NodePath` method that we're using to turn off depth checking with the sky sphere. That means that the renderer won't bother to try and figure out what is in front of or behind of the sky sphere. Since the sky sphere is rendered into the scene first because it's in the `'background'` bin, and we aren't checking it for depth at all, it will always seem to be further away than everything else in the scene. That's exactly what we want from our sky.

Our next call is to `setShaderOff`. This call is the opposite of `setShaderAuto`; it turns off automatic shader generation for the `NodePath` it's called on, and all of that `NodePath`'s children. We have to turn off the automatic shader generation because the sky sphere uses a special kind of texture, a cube map, which the automatic shader can't handle.

After that, we have this line:

```
self.skySphere.setAlphaScale(0)
```

The purpose of this line is to turn off the alpha channel on the `skySphere` by scaling it down to 0. We do this because we don't want the `skySphere` to be affected by the bloom filter, and our bloom filter is working off the alpha channels of our textures. By scaling the alpha down to 0, we prevent the bloom filter from affecting the `skySphere`. To see the difference, comment this line out and re-run `WorldClass_03.py`.

Pretty ugly, huh? So, why does this happen if the `skySphere`'s alpha channel isn't scaled down to 0? It's because we had to turn off automatic shader generation for the `skySphere`. Without the automatic shader to keep the bloom filter in check, it's running wild all over the `skySphere`.

We also added a little task that moves the sky sphere to the position of the camera each frame. This simulates the sensation of far away things standing still while nearby things move. It's just a little camera trick, really.

Pop quiz – setting up a sky sphere

Here are some questions to help us figure out how well we understand lighting.

1. What rendering bin did we put the sky sphere in, and why?
2. What does the call to `setAlphaScale` do, and why did we us it?

Summary

The focus of this chapter was spicing up the visuals. We used a few different tools to meet that goal.

- Lights
- Textures
- Filters

We also set up a sky sphere to act as a backdrop for our level.

Since we're putting textures to use, we should also use them to create a GUI for the game. Thankfully, that's the focus of the next chapter!

8

GUI Goodness: All About the Graphic User Interface

Now is the time to start giving the player more options and more information. We've almost got a playable racing game at this point, though we don't have the weapons yet. If we add in a Graphical User Interface, we'll be that much closer to our goal of a complete game.

The GUI components we'll need to create are:

- Menu system
- Putting menus to use
- In-game HUD

To create these elements, we'll be using Panda3D's `DirectGUI` system. This system includes all the tools we'll need to make our GUI and get it running.

Creating a menu system

Rather than creating menus individually, it would be wiser to create a system that will allow us to make all the menus we need. We can do this if we rely on the handy feature of Python that allows us to pass functions and methods between objects.

We'll create a menu system that takes functions or methods as arguments and executes them when menu options are selected. We'll also need to take in the arguments for those functions and methods.

About DirectGUI

The `DirectGUI` system in Panda3D is a series of tools for constructing a graphical user interface. Among the objects in `DirectGUI` we can find `DirectFrames` to act as the backgrounds of menus, `DirectLabels` that will put text on the menus, `DirectButtons` that will serve for the menu buttons, and more.

All of the `DirectGUI` objects inherit from `DirectGUIBase`, so they share many of their features. The typical method for creating a `DirectGUI` object is to fill the constructor with keyword/value pairs, like the following:

```
myDirectGuiObject = DirectGUIObject(keyword = value, keyword = value,
keyword = value)
```

For that reason, it's a good idea to know what the keywords that are shared by most, if not all, of the `DirectGUI` objects. Here's a list of those keywords for reference. It's taken from the Panda3D manual on the Panda3D website, with a couple of updates.

Keyword	Description	Value
text	Text to be displayed on the object	string
text_bg	Background color of text on the object	(R,G,B,A)
text_fg	Color of the text	(R,G,B,A)
text_pos	Position of the displayed text	(x,y,z)
text_roll	Rotation of the displayed text	number
text_scale	Scale of the displayed text	(sx,sy,sz)
text_*	Parameters to control the appearance of the text	Any keyword parameter appropriate to `OnscreenText`.
frameSize	Size of the object	(left, right, bottom, top)
frameSize	Size of the object	(Left,Right,Bottom,Top)
frameVisibleScale	Relative scale of the visible frame to its clickable bounds. Useful for creating things such as the paging region of a slider, which is visibly smaller than the acceptable click region	(hscale, vscale)
frameColor	Color of the object's frame	(R,G,B,A)
relief	Relief appearance of the frame	SUNKEN, RAISED, GROOVE, RIDGE, FLAT, or None
invertedFrames	If true, switches the meaning of SUNKEN and RAISED	0 or 1
borderWidth	If relief is SUNKEN, RAISED, GROOVE, or RIDGE, changes the size of the bevel	(Width,Height)

Keyword	Description	Value
image	An image to be displayed on the object	image filename or Texture object
image_pos	Position of the displayed image	(x,y,z)
image_hpr	Rotation of the displayed image	(h,p,r)
image_scale	Scale of the displayed image	(sx,sy,sz)
geom	A geom to represent the object's appearance. This is usually a textured polygon created with egg-texture-cards.	NodePath
geom_pos	Position of the displayed geom.	(x,y,z)
geom_hpr	Rotation of the displayed geom.	(h,p,r)
geom_scale	Scale of the displayed geom.	(sx,sy,sz)
pos	Position of the object	(X,Y,Z)
hpr	Orientation of the object	(H,P,R)
scale	Scale of the object	(sx, sy, sz)
pad	When frameSize is omitted, this determines the extra space around the geom or text's bounding box by which to expand the default frame	(Width,Height)
state	The initial state of the object	NORMAL or DISABLED
frameTexture	Texture applied directly to the frame generated when relief is FLAT	image filename or Texture object

Time for action – creating a menu system

Armed with that knowledge of the DirectGUI system, we're ready to start building a Menu class that we can use to create all of our game menus.

1. Open a blank document in NotePad++ and save it as MenuClass_01.py.

2. Our first step is to import some things we'll need to make this menu happen. Type in this code:

```
from direct.gui.DirectGui import *
from pandac.PandaModules import *
```

3. Now, we need to define the class and give it an __init__ method. Add this code in next:

```
class Menu:
    def __init__(self, menuGraphics, fonts, inputManager = None):
        self.menuGraphics = menuGraphics
```

```
        self.fonts = fonts
        self.inputManager = inputManager
        self.self = self
```

4. Now, we're going to create a method that initializes the menu. This may seem silly, when we already have an __init__ method, but it will help keep the arguments we give the menu from getting even more confusing. The system will take a complicated list of arguments, but with two different methods we can separate some of them and make the menu easier to use. Here is the start of the new method. Place this into the class below the __init__ method.

```
    def initMenu(self, args):
        type = args[0]
        if(args[1] != None):
            self.title = args[1]
        else:
            self.title = None
        self.items = args[2]
      self.funcs = args[3]
      self.funcArgs = args[4]
        self.buttons = []
```

5. Now for the most complicated part. This is the code that will actually construct the menu from `DirectGUI` components. It's a big piece of code, so we should go over it carefully as we type it in to minimize mistakes. It goes right beneath the code we just added.

```
        if(type == 0):
            self.frame = DirectFrame(
              geom = self.menuGraphics.find("**/Menu0"),
              relief = None, scale = (1.5,1,1.5),
              frameColor = (1,1,1,.75),
              pos = (.2625,0,.43125), parent = base.a2dBottomLeft)
          framePadding = .1
          height = self.frame.getHeight() - framePadding
          for N in range(len(self.items)):
            xPos = 0
            zPos = height/2 - (height / (len(self.items)-1)) * N
            self.buttons.append(DirectButton(
              command = self.activateItem, extraArgs = [N],
              geom = (self.menuGraphics.find("**/BttnNormal"),
                  self.menuGraphics.find("**/BttnPushed"),
                  self.menuGraphics.find("**/BttnNormal"),
                  self.menuGraphics.find("**/BttnNormal")),
                relief = None, clickSound = None,
```

```
            rolloverSound = None, parent = self.frame,
            pos = (xPos, 0, zPos)))
        self.items[N] = DirectLabel(text = self.items[N],
          text_font = self.fonts["silver"],
          text_fg = (1,1,1,.75), relief = None,
          text_align = TextNode.ACenter,
          text_scale = .035, parent = self.buttons[N])
        self.items[N].setPos(0,0,-self.items[N].getHeight()/2)
```

6. There's just one last thing we need to add to this method, to prepare the menu for keyboard interaction. Add the following code below the big block we just put in:

```
if(self.inputManager != None):
  self.itemHL = 0
  self.keyWait = 0
  self.highlightItem(0)
  taskMgr.add(self.menuControl, "Menu Control")
return
```

7. Our `Menu` class needs four more methods to work how we want it to, but none of them are as big as the `initMenu()` method. Here's the first; add it to the bottom of the class. This method controls the changing of which menu item is highlighted when using keyboard controls.

```
def highlightItem(self, item):
  if(item < 0): item = len(self.items) - 1
  if(item == len(self.items)): item = 0
  self.items[self.itemHL]["text_font"] = self.fonts["silver"]
  self.items[item]["text_font"] = self.fonts["orange"]
  self.itemHL = item
  return
```

8. Now, we need the method that will run the functions and methods that the menu needs to execute when an item is selected. The following one goes right below the `highlightItem()` method:

```
def activateItem(self, item):
  if(type(self.funcs[item]) == list):
    for N in range(len(self.funcs[item])):
      if(self.funcArgs[item][N] != None):
        self.funcs[item][N](self.funcArgs[item][N])
      else:
        self.funcs[item][N]()
  else:
    if(self.funcArgs[item] != None):
      self.funcs[item](self.funcArgs[item])
```

```
            else:
                self.funcs[item]()
        self.destroy()
        return
```

9. Our next method will be a task that monitors the `InputManager` to respond to keyboard keys. Note that the keys that are requested from the `InputManager`'s key map are different than what we made it with. Don't worry about that; the `InputManager` in the `Chapter08` folder has been updated already.

```
    def menuControl(self, task):
        if(self.self == None):
            return task.done
        dt = globalClock.getDt()
        if( dt > .20):
            return task.cont
        self.keyWait += dt
        if(self.keyWait > .25):
            if(self.inputManager.keyMap["up"] == True):
                self.highlightItem(self.itemHL - 1)
                self.keyWait = 0
            elif(self.inputManager.keyMap["down"] == True):
                self.highlightItem(self.itemHL + 1)
                self.keyWait = 0
            elif(self.inputManager.keyMap["fire"] == True):
                self.activateItem(self.itemHL)
                self.keyWait = 0
        return task.cont
```

10. The last method we add will remove the menu and the `DirectGUI` objects it creates. We want the menu to be thoroughly cleaned up, so a method such as this is necessary.

```
    def destroy(self):
        for N in range(len(self.items)):
            self.items[0].destroy()
            self.buttons[0].destroy()
        if(self.title != None):
            self.title.destroy()
        self.frame.destroy()
        self.self = None
        return
```

11. Resave the file, and open the `WorldClass_00.py` file in the `Chapter08` folder. Note that this file is a little different from the `World` class we ended last chapter with. We're making four cycles controlled by AI now.

12. We need to add some code here to make use of our new `Menu` class. To start with, we need to import it. Add the following line of code to our imports:

```
from MenuClass_01 import Menu
```

13. At the bottom of the ___init___ method, add the following code:

```
self.menuGraphics = loader.loadModel(
  "../Models/MenuGraphics.egg")
self.fonts = {
  "silver" : loader.loadFont("../Fonts/LuconSilver.egg"),
  "blue" : loader.loadFont("../Fonts/LuconBlue.egg"),
  "orange" : loader.loadFont("../Fonts/LuconOrange.egg")}
menu = Menu(self.menuGraphics, self.fonts, self.inputManager)
menu.initMenu([0,None,
  ["New Game","Quit Game"],
  [[self.printTest],[self.printTest]],
  [[0],[1]]])
```

14. Resave the file as `WorldClass_01.py` and run it from the command prompt.

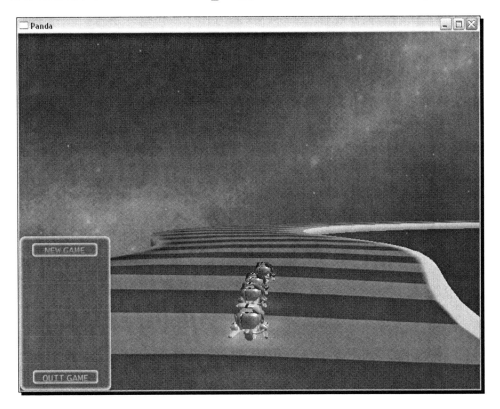

What just happened?

When one of the buttons is clicked, we get a printout on the command prompt. Success! So let's talk about this new `Menu` class and how we made it work.

The first thing to mention is the `DirectGUI` import:

```
from direct.gui.DirectGui import *
```

This gave us access to all the pieces of `DirectGUI`, which we used later on. Note that it isn't in `pandac.PandaModules`.

In the `__init__` method for the class, we pulled an interesting trick that we haven't seen before, and should use sparingly. Since Python will garbage collect objects that don't have any references to them, the best way to remove an object from memory is to remove all the references to it. In order for the menus to clean themselves up, the objects that create them can't have references to them, but if nothing has a reference to it the menu would get garbage collected right away.

To prevent this, we give the menu a reference to itself with the following line:
`self.self = self`

This kind of circular referencing can be dangerous in terms of garbage collection, so it's best to keep it to a minimum. At the very least, we have to make sure we remove that reference when it's time for the object to get cleaned up.

Next, let's talk about the arguments for the `initMenu()` method. This is one of the more potentially confusing parts of how our menus work. The method takes a single argument, which needs to be a list. The first entry in the list is the type of menu to create. Currently, we only have one type of menu, but we'll be able to add more later on. The second entry is a title text for the list. Our first menu type isn't using the title text, but later ones will.

The next three entries in the list are where things get confusing. Each of these three entries is also a list. These three lists need to have their contents in a particular order, because they correspond to the buttons that the menu will create, and the list indexes are used to associate the contents of each list with their respective button.

The first of the three is a list of strings that will be used to put label text on the buttons. This list is also used to determine the number of buttons that will be created. The buttons are given the index of the string when created so they know what button they are.

The next of the three lists, and the fourth entry in the list given to `initMenu()`, contains the functions that each button will execute. Each entry in this list can be a single function or method, or it can be a list of functions and methods. Either way, the functions and/or methods that are put in this list will be performed when the button with the same index is clicked.

The final entry in the list we pass to `initMenu()` is a list as well. It contains the arguments for the functions and methods we assigned to the buttons. If a button was given more than one function or method, the entry in this list must be another list. Every function and method must be associated with either an argument of some kind, or `None`.

The following figure should help explain the structure of the list we give to `initMenu()`:

index: 0	index: 1	index: 2	index: 3	index: 4

List given to initMenu

Menu Type	Menu Title	List of Strings for button Labels	List of Functions	List of Arguments
		0: Bttn0 Label	Bttn0 Func	Bttn0 Arg
		1: Bttn1 Label	List of Funcs	List of Args
			0: Bttn1 Func0	Bttn1 Func0 Arg
			1: Bttn1 Func1	Bttn1 Func1 Arg
		2: Bttn2 Label	List of Funcs	List of Args
			0: Bttn2 Func0	Bttn2 Func0 Arg
			1: Bttn2 Func1	Bttn2 Func1 Arg

Now that we've got all that figured out, let's talk about the next section of code we added:

```
if(type == 0):
  self.frame = DirectFrame(
    geom = self.menuGraphics.find("**/Menu0"),
    relief = None, scale = (1.5,1,1.5),
    frameColor = (1,1,1,.75),
    pos = (.2625,0,.43125), parent = base.a2dBottomLeft)
  framePadding = .1
  height = self.frame.getHeight() - framePadding
  for N in range(len(self.items)):
    xPos = 0
    zPos = height/2 - (height / (len(self.items)-1)) * N
    self.buttons.append(DirectButton(
      command = self.activateItem, extraArgs = [N],
      geom = (self.menuGraphics.find("**/BttnNormal"),
          self.menuGraphics.find("**/BttnPushed"),
          self.menuGraphics.find("**/BttnNormal"),
          self.menuGraphics.find("**/BttnNormal")),
```

```
            relief = None, clickSound = None,
            rolloverSound = None, parent = self.frame,
            pos = (xPos, 0, zPos)))
        self.items[N] = DirectLabel(text = self.items[N],
            text_font = self.fonts["silver"],
            text_fg = (1,1,1,.75), relief = None,
            text_align = TextNode.ACenter,
            text_scale = .035, parent = self.buttons[N])
        self.items[N].setPos(0,0,-self.items[N].getHeight()/2)
```

The if statement at the beginning of this code checks to see what kind of menu we are creating. If it's a menu of type 0, the only type we've created so far, then we proceed to create a DirectFrame.

The best way to think of a DirectFrame is like a bulletin board. The DirectFrame is the rectangle that we post all the components of the menu on. It also forms the backdrop for the menu; in our case, the window that the menu is housed in. We created the DirectFrame with the following long line of code:

```
    self.frame = DirectFrame(
        geom = self.menuGraphics.find("**/Menu0"),
        relief = None, scale = (1.5,1,1.5),
        frameColor = (1,1,1,.75),
        pos = (.2625,0,.43125), parent = base.a2dBottomLeft)
```

When we create a DirectGUI object, we call its constructor and we give it a series of key/ value pairs. That's what's happening here. Our first key is geom. The geom is a piece of visual geometry that will be used to represent the DirectFrame. To get the geometry we need, we turn to the menuGraphics egg. The menuGraphics egg contains several separate polygons, each with its own texture applied, and each within its own group inside the egg. To get the one we want, we use the find to search through the egg for a particular group name. By using the ** wildcard in our search string, "**/Menu0", we are telling the find() method to look as deep in the hierarchy of the egg as it needs to in order to find a group called Menu0. When the find() method finds the group we told it to look for, it returns it, and we get a single rectangular polygon to use as the geom for our DirectFrame. The menuGraphics egg was created with egg-texture-cards so that it could be used for this exact purpose.

The next key/value pair we specified was to set relief equal to None. Most DirectGUI objects will try to create a default visual object for themselves, which is basically a blank rectangle with a bevel of some sort. We have our own object that we are using so we don't want this default behaviour. To turn it off, we set relief to None.

Next, we use the `scale` keyword to increase the size of the `DirectFrame`. After that, we use the `frameColor` keyword with a reduced alpha argument to make the `DirectFrame` slightly transparent. Next is the `pos` keyword, which we use to offset the menu up and right. The amounts we used are based on the actual size of the menu and the rescaling we did. We're moving the menu up an amount equal to half its height, and half its width to the right.

The last keyword we used was parent. This keyword performs the same function as calling the `reparentTo()` method. We don't want to add our `DirectFrame` to the 3D scene graph that `render` serves as the top of. We want it to sit on top of our 3D view, and ignore camera movement and lighting and things like that. We also want it to stay in the same position and maintain the same relative scale, if the window is resized. Fortunately, there's an easy way to make all that happen. We just have to add the `DirectFrame` as a child of `base.aspect2d`.

Very much like render, `base.aspect2d` is the uppermost `NodePath` of a scene graph. The scene graph that extends from `base.aspect2d` is very different from the one that extends from `render`, though. The children of `base.aspect2d` will always be rendered on top of the 3D view, and will ignore changes in lighting, camera, and so on. They will also maintain their scale when the window is resized by clicking and dragging on the border.

Just parenting a `DirectGUI` object directly to `base.aspect2d` will put it right in the center of the screen, but that isn't exactly what we want. We want to put our menu in the bottom-left corner of the screen, so we make our frame a child of one of the many position handles of `base.aspect2d`. By doing this, we ensure that the `DirectFrame` will always be located at that position handle, even if the window is resized. The different position handles available are:

- `a2dBackground`: Special handle appropriate only for full-screen backgrounds.
- `a2dBottom`
- `a2dBottomCenter`
- `a2dBottomLeft`
- `a2dBottomRight`
- `a2dLeft`
- `a2dLeftCenter`
- `a2dRight`
- `a2dRightCenter`
- `a2dTop`
- `a2dTopCenter`
- `a2dTopLeft`
- `a2dTopRight`

So, if we can make our `DirectFrame` a child of `base.a2dBottomLeft` to control its position, why did we need to set the `pos` keyword in the constructor? Good question. The `(0,0,0)` point in our `DirectFrame` is right at its center, so if we just made it a child of `base.a2dBottomLeft` without setting the `pos` keyword, the center of the menu would be glued to the bottom-left corner of the screen, and we'd only see the upper-right corner of the menu. That's why we offset the menu up and right based on its height and width.

 Note that the position handles we just talked about are special cases. They aren't actually `NodePath`, but we can still supply them as parents to our `DirectGUI` objects and to the `reparentTo()` method.

Once our `DirectFrame` is up and running, we created two temporary variables:

```
framePadding = .1
height = self.frame.getHeight() - framePadding
```

These variables will help us dynamically place the buttons on our menu. The first one, `framePadding`, represents the total amount of space that will be left open above and below the buttons. Half of it will be above, half of it will be below. The second, height, is the height of the area we're placing our buttons in; the height of the `DirectFrame` minus the padding. The `getHeight()` method can be called on any `DirectGUI` object to get the height of object, not including any scaling we've done to it. Since any children of the object will inherit that scaling anyway, we don't really want it. Note that we aren't taking the actual height of the buttons themselves into consideration here. The padding we've set will be the amount of space between the top or bottom of the menu and the *center* of the first or last button.

Once we have those two temporary variables, we're ready to start creating the buttons and their labels. A `for` loop is perfect for this purpose; we just need to walk through all the entries in our list of label strings and make a button and label for each one.

The first thing we do in our `for` loop is figure out what position the buttons need to be at. Since we're creating the buttons dynamically, we have two options. We could use a series of `if` statements, or we can use a formula. To keep the code as clean and simple as possible, a formula is the better choice.

```
xPos = 0
zPos = height/2 - (height / (len(self.items)-1)) * N
```

Centering the buttons horizontally is easy; we just leave their X position at 0. To arrange them vertically, we have to get a bit cleverer. We start with `height/2` because that indicates half of the total space we've reserved for buttons up from the center of the `DirectFrame`. That's exactly where we want our first button placed. To find the position of the remaining buttons, we need to determine how far apart we want them to be. To do this, we take the height of our space and divide it by the number of buttons we're creating, minus one. Since the first button will always be at the top, we don't want to take it into consideration. That gives us the amount of space we'll put between buttons, so we just need to multiply that by the index of the button, and that's how far down from the first button we'll place the button we're making. Remember that since list indexes start at 0, this formula will be `height/2 - (height / (len(self.items) -1)) * 0` for the first button. That's the same as `height/2`.

Now that we know where we want to put our button, it's time to actually make it:

```
self.buttons.append(DirectButton(
  command = self.activateItem, extraArgs = [N],
  geom = (self.menuGraphics.find("**/BttnNormal"),
      self.menuGraphics.find("**/BttnPushed"),
      self.menuGraphics.find("**/BttnNormal"),
      self.menuGraphics.find("**/BttnNormal")),
  relief = None, clickSound = None,
  rolloverSound = None, parent = self.frame,
  pos = (xPos, 0, zPos)))
```

We call the `DirectButton` constructor, and the first keyword we set a value for is `command`. This keyword stores the function or method that the button will call when it detects a mouse-click. The next keyword, `extraArgs`, stores the arguments that will be passed to the function or method stored in the `command` keyword. We have to give the `extraArgs` keyword a list, because it passes the contents of the list to the function or method in order. In our case, we want it to pass the index number of the button, because that's what our `activateItem()` method is expecting.

The next keyword we give a value to is `geom`, which we saw previously when we made our `DirectFrame`. This time, however, we're passing in four objects instead of one. That's because a `DirectButton` has four states: `normal`, `pushed`, `rollover`, and `disabled`. These states are used to change the appearance of the button depending on mouse behaviour. Normally, the button will show its `normal` state. When the mouse button is held down over it, the button will show its `pushed` state. When the mouse is just hovering over the button, we'll see its `rollover` state. If we disable the button, we'll see its `disabled` state. We don't really care about the `rollover` or `disabled` state for our menu so we just set them to be the same as `normal`. To get the textured polygons for these four states, we use the `find()` method on our `menuGraphics` egg again.

Again, we don't want a default visual object for our buttons, so we set relief to None. Also, we don't want the default sounds that buttons use, and we don't have our own sounds yet, so we set the `clickSound` and `rolloverSound` keywords to `None`.

We make the button a child of `self.frame` so that it will be attached to, and on top of, our `DirectFrame`. We then set the `pos` keyword according to the position we calculated earlier.

With our button built and in place, it's time to put a text label on it. Buttons can be given text as part of their own constructor, but the bottom of that text would be aligned to the center of the button. Instead of fiddling with the text position to try and get it nicely centered, we can use a `DirectLabel`, which is a `DirectGUI` object that just displays some text. Then, we can use `getHeight` on the `DirectLabel` to easily get the height of the text and figure out how to position it.

```
self.items[N] = DirectLabel(text = self.items[N],
    text_font = self.fonts["silver"],
    text_fg = (1,1,1,.75), relief = None,
    text_align = TextNode.ACenter,
    text_scale = .035, parent = self.buttons[N])
```

Instead of creating a new list to hold the `DirectLabels`, we're going to just replace the contents of `self.items`, which holds the strings for the button labels, with the `DirectLabel` objects. We only needed those strings to create the `DirectLabels` anyway.

In the `DirectLabel` constructor, we use a bunch more keyword/value pairs. The first keyword is `text`, which is the actual string that the `DirectLabel` will display. We fill that with the string from `self.items`. The next keyword is `text_font`. For that, we need a `Font` object. The simplest way to get one of these is to use `loader.loadFont` to load it from a file. To learn how to create font files, have a look at the appropriate Appendix at the end of this book.

`text_fg` is our next keyword. The `fg` in its name stands for foreground, and it sets the color of the text. We want our font colors to show through, so we set it to white, and we use a slightly reduced alpha to make the text partially transparent. To prevent a default visual object from being displayed behind the text, we set `relief` to `None` again.

The `text_align` keyword is mildly annoying, in that it requires a text alignment object as its value. We get the text alignment objects from `TextNode`, which we imported from `pandac.PandaModules`. The options for alignment are `TextNode.ALeft`, `TextNode.ACenter`, and `TextNode.ARight`.

The value we give for the `text_scale` keyword is pretty small. That's because in order to make our font display nicely even when the letters are really big, we had to make the font itself really big. When using custom fonts, this will usually end up being a pretty small value.

The last thing we do in the constructor is assign the `DirectLabel` to be a child of the `DirectButton` with the same index. This will attach the `DirectLabel` to the button, and since we are adding it to the scene graph after the `DirectButton`, the `DirectLabel` is displayed on top.

The last line of code for our `DirectLabel` positions them on the buttons:

```
self.items[N].setPos(0,0,-self.items[N].getHeight()/2)
```

Unlike the other `DirectGUI` objects we've created in the past, the `(0,0,0)` point for a `DirectLabel` is at the bottom of the text, instead of the center. Since we didn't add any padding to the `DirectLabel` with the pad keyword, the bottom of the text is also the bottom of the `DirectLabel` itself. That means we just have to move the `DirectLabel` down half its height to put its center where the bottom used to be. With the `getHeight()` method, that's easily taken care of.

The last bit of code we added to the `initMenu()` method sets up some variables and a task that are all used for keyboard control. We'll talk about them as we go through the rest of the methods in the `Menu` class.

The following code is the next method we added to the `Menu` class:

```
def highlightItem(self, item):
    if(item < 0): item = len(self.items) - 1
    if(item == len(self.items)): item = 0
    self.items[self.itemHL]["text_font"] = self.fonts["silver"]
    self.items[item]["text_font"] = self.fonts["orange"]
    self.itemHL = item
    return
```

The purpose of this method is to highlight one of the menu buttons, so that a player using the keyboard to navigate menus can tell which item they currently have selected. We pass the index of the item we want to highlight into this method, and it first verifies that the index we've passed in is valid. If the index is below zero, we change it to the highest valid index. If the index is too high, we change it to 0. That way, when the player is at the bottom of the menu and presses the down key, the highlight will go to the top of the menu. The reverse is also true.

The actual highlight is a change in font in the `DirectLabel`. The fonts we're using are identical except for their colors, and that difference in color is what we're using to highlight an item. To change the font of a `DirectLabel`, we directly access the `text_font` keyword as if the `DirectLabel` were a dictionary. For example:

```
myDirectLabel["keyword"] = value
```

We can change any keyword's value on any `DirectGUI` object this way.

Once we have a valid index, we remove the highlight from whatever item has it by changing its font to silver with the following line of code:

```
self.items[self.itemHL]["text_font"] = self.fonts["silver"]
```

The `self.itemHL` variable stores the index of the currently highlighted item so we always know which item is highlighted.

Then, we change the font of the item we want to be highlighted now to orange with the following line of code:

```
self.items[item]["text_font"] = self.fonts["orange"]
```

We then update the `self.itemHL` variable to store the index of the newly highlighted item, and we're finished.

The next method we added calls the functions and/or methods when the corresponding button is pressed:

```
def activateItem(self, item):
    if(type(self.funcs[item]) == list):
        for N in range(len(self.funcs[item])):
            if(self.funcArgs[item][N] != None):
                self.funcs[item][N](self.funcArgs[item][N])
            else:
                self.funcs[item][N]()
    else:
        if(self.funcArgs[item] != None):
            self.funcs[item](self.funcArgs[item])
        else:
            self.funcs[item]()
    self.destroy()
    return
```

Just like with `highlightItem()`, we pass the index of the menu item to this method. Before trying to call anything, this method checks to see if the menu item it's been passed is associated with a single function or method, or a list. We use the `type()` function to figure this out:

```
if(type(self.funcs[item]) == list):
```

`type()` is a Python function that tells us what sort of object we've passed to it, and can be very handy in a situation such as this.

If we are dealing with a list, we need to iterate through it. We use a `for` loop for that, but we can't just carelessly call each function or method. First, we need to check if we have arguments to pass to it. To do that, we check if the corresponding index in the list of arguments is a reference to `None`. If not, we call the function or method, passing the argument, with the following line of code:

```
self.funcs[item][N](self.funcArgs[item][N])
```

In those cases where we don't have an argument to pass, we just call the function or method with the following line:

```
self.funcs[item][N]()
```

The rest of this method handles the scenarios where we have a single function or method associated with our menu item, rather than a list. We use the same structure there, but without the `[N]`.

Note that this method always calls `self.destroy` before finishing. This activates the menu's self-cleaning method and ultimately results in the menu going away and getting removed from memory.

The second to last method in our `Menu` class is a task that monitors the `inputManager` for keyboard input. There's nothing really new in this method, except for the use of the `self.keyWait` variable to count the amount of time that has passed since the last key press. We only allow a key press to perform an action if enough time has passed since the last one, because otherwise our menus would respond to a key press every single frame, which could be as often as 60 times per second. That's way too fast to be switching through menu items, and in the event of menus that create submenus, we could accidentally go through several menus with a single stroke of a key.

The last method in our `Menu` class is the first clean-up method we've added to our game. The purpose of the `destroy()` method is to remove all references to all the menu's components so that Python can garbage collect the menu and remove it from memory.

```python
def destroy(self):
    for N in range(len(self.items)):
        self.items[0].destroy()
        self.buttons[0].destroy()
    if(self.title != None):
        self.title.destroy()
    self.frame.destroy()
    self.self = None
    return
```

The first step to destroying an instance of the `Menu` class is removing the `DirectGUI` objects we've created by calling their own `destroy()` methods. This is important because the `DirectGUI` objects may have connections to other parts of Panda3D. For example, a `DirectButton` registers itself to respond to mouse-click events. If we don't remove all of these possible connections, they could result in a lingering reference to our menu that will prevent it from being garbage collected. Whenever we use `DirectGUI` objects in our code, we need to make sure our clean-up method calls `destroy` on them.

Other than calling `destroy()` on the `DirectGUI` objects, the only other thing our clean-up method needs to do is remove the circular self-reference it has by setting the variable to `None`. With that, our keyboard control task will also remove itself from the task manager because of this:

```
if(self.self == None):
    return task.done
```

That will remove the reference the task manager has to the menu, as well.

Now, there are no longer any references to the menu in existence, and it will get garbage collected. Additionally, all of the variables that the menu alone was referencing, such as `self.itemHL` or `self.keyWait`, will no longer have a reference to them when the menu is gone. They'll get garbage collected too.

Before we wrap up, let's talk about the minor changes we made to the `World` class as well. The following lines are used to load up the visual components the menus need to construct themselves:

```
self.menuGraphics = loader.loadModel(
    "../Models/MenuGraphics.egg")
self.fonts = {
    "silver" : loader.loadFont("../Fonts/LuconSilver.egg"),
    "blue" : loader.loadFont("../Fonts/LuconBlue.egg"),
    "orange" : loader.loadFont("../Fonts/LuconOrange.egg")}
```

The only new thing here is the `loader.loadFont()` call, but that's pretty self-explanatory. It loads a font.

Here's the code that actually creates and initializes our menu:

```
menu = Menu(self.menuGraphics, self.fonts, self.inputManager)
menu.initMenu([0,None,
    ["New Game","Quit Game"],
    [[self.printTest],[self.printTest]],
    [[0],[1]]])
```

The first line is nothing special; we just create an instance of the `Menu` class and feed in the basic components it requires, but note that we are storing the instance in a temporary variable. We don't want to use a variable like `self.menu`, or the `World` will retain a reference to the menu and the menu won't be able to destroy itself.

Let's take a closer look at the call to `initMenu()` with some added notes to show which parts of the argument list are which:

```
menu.initMenu([0,None,                        ß Type and
Title
  ["New Game","Quit Game"],                   ß Item Strings
  [[self.printTest],[self.printTest]],    ß Funcs Called
  [[0],[1]]])                               ß Args
for Funcs
```

At this point, the structure of the argument list should be clear enough that we don't need to go over it again. It's a good idea to separate the argument list over several lines like this, to make it easier to understand when reading our code.

Pop quiz – understanding DirectGUI

Ready to test our knowledge?

1. What is `DirectGUI`?
2. Why are `DirectGUI` constructors so long?
3. What is `base.aspect2d`?

Have a go hero – performing additional actions with new menus

The menu system we've created is really robust. Trying using it to perform some different actions, like adding new cycles to the game, or changing the lighting, or something like that. Remember to save any files we change with new names!

Putting menus to use

Okay, now that we have a working menu system and we understand how to use, it's time we did more than just print out a value to the command prompt.

Time for action – using menus

The plan is to set up our game to have a demo race going on the start screen, and create a new race when we click a menu button. That means we'll need to be able to dynamically construct and destroy races, so we should make a `Race` class for that. To further expand our menu use, we'll create a confirmation dialog menu so the player can let the game know when he's ready for the race to start. Roll up those sleeves; it's time to get busy again.

1. Open a blank document in NotePad++ and save it as `RaceClass_01.py`.

2. As always, when creating a new class, we'll start with the imports. Add this code to our blank file:

```
from TrackClass_01 import Track
from CycleClass_01 import Cycle
```

3. To get us rolling, we'll need the class definition and the __init__ method. Here's the code for it:

```
class Race:
  def __init__(self, inputManager):
    self.inputManager = inputManager
    self.cycles = []
    self.track = None
```

4. That's a nice easy start. Next, we'll create a method that will start a demo race for us. Add the following code below the __init__ method we just made:

```
def createDemoRace(self):
  self.destroyRace()
  self.track = Track()
  self.cycles.append(Cycle(self.inputManager,
    self.track, 1, "Bert", ai = True))
  self.cycles.append(Cycle(self.inputManager,
    self.track, 2, "Ernie", ai = True))
  self.cycles.append(Cycle(self.inputManager,
    self.track, 3, "William", ai = True))
  self.cycles.append(Cycle(self.inputManager,
    self.track, 4, "Patrick", ai = True))
  self.setCameraHigh(self.cycles[0])
  self.startRace(1)
  return
```

5. Moving right along, we'll put in a method to create a regular race. The code is pretty similar to what we just added:

```
def createRace(self):
  self.destroyRace()
  self.track = Track()
  self.cycles.append(Cycle(self.inputManager,
    self.track, 1, "Bert"))
  self.cycles.append(Cycle(self.inputManager,
    self.track, 2, "Ernie", ai = True))
  self.cycles.append(Cycle(self.inputManager,
    self.track, 3, "William", ai = True))
  self.cycles.append(Cycle(self.inputManager,
    self.track, 4, "Patrick", ai = True))
 self.setCameraFollow(self.cycles[0])
  return
```

6. Next, we'll put in a couple of methods to set up the camera. They're pretty short and simple.

```
def setCameraFollow(self, cycle):
  base.camera.reparentTo(cycle.dirNP)
  base.camera.setPos(0, -15, 3)
  return

def setCameraHigh(self, cycle):
  base.camera.reparentTo(cycle.dirNP)
  base.camera.setPos(0, 30, 30)
  base.camera.lookAt(cycle.root)
  return
```

7. The next two methods we want to add will give us the ability to delay the start of a race so it isn't in progress the instant it's loaded.

```
def startRace(self, delay):
  taskMgr.doMethodLater(delay, self.startCycles, "Start Cycles")
  return

def startCycles(self, task):
  for C in self.cycles:
    C.active = True
  return task.done
```

8. Our `Race` class only needs one more method, and then it's done. We need a way to remove a race that's already in existence, so we'll make a `destroyRace()` method for that:

```
def destroyRace(self):
  if(self.track != None):
    self.track.destroy()
  for C in self.cycles:
```

```
        C.destroy()
    del self.cycles[0:4]
    return
```

9. We're going to edit some of our other files to make all this work. We'll start with the `Track` class. Save `RaceClass_01.py` and open the `TrackClass_00.py` file in the `Chapter08` folder.

10. The main thing we need to add to our `Track` class is a method that will destroy it. Here's the code for that; put it at the bottom of the file:

```
def destroy(self):
    self.track.removeNode()
    self.planet.removeNode()
    self.groundCol.removeNode()
    self.skySphere.removeNode()
    self.dirLight.removeNode()
    self.ambLight.removeNode()
    self.trackLanes.destroy()
    self.trackLanes = None
    self.skySphere = None
    render.setLightOff()
    return
```

11. You may have noticed that our destroy method calls `removeNode()` on `self.planet`, but our track doesn't have a `self.planet`. Well, we're going to add one now. Put the following two lines of code in our `Track` class's __init__ method, right below the lines where we load up the model for the track:

```
    self.planet = loader.loadModel("../Models/Planet.egg")
    self.planet.reparentTo(render)
```

12. That's it for the `Track`. Save the file as `TrackClass_01.py` and open up the `CycleClass_00.py` file from the `Chapter08` folder. We need to make some changes to this file, too.

13. To start things off, we're going to make a small edit to our __init__ method that will allow a player-controlled cycle to identify the fact that it doesn't have a `CycleAI` object. This is important for the clean-up method we'll be adding. Put the following line of code right above the line where we add the `cycleControl()` method to the task manager:

```
    self.ai = None
```

14. The next thing we need to do is remove the camera control stuff from this class, since we're handing that over to the `Race` class now. Scroll down to the `setupVarsNPs()` method and look for the lines that deal with the camera. Delete them.

15. While we're in the `setupVarsNPs()` method, let's add a new variable that the cycle can use to turn on and off its throttle and turning controls. We'll need that variable to make it impossible for the cycle to move when it isn't supposed to. Add the following line to the bottom of `setupVarsNPs()`:

```
self.active = False
```

16. The next modification is a performance optimization. The planet model we're loading in our `Track` class has a whole bunch of polygons, and we don't want each cycle's glow light to be trying to illuminate that mass of geometry when it isn't necessary. Move down to the `setupLight()` method and look at the end of it for the line where we set render to accept the light. Delete that line, and put in the following two lines instead:

```
self.cycle.setLight(self.glow)
self.track.track.setLight(self.glow)
```

17. The most reliable way to remove a task from the task manager is by having it return `task.done`. We need to set our `cycleControl()` task to do that when the time is right, or our clean-up method won't work. Add these two lines to the very beginning of the `cycleControl()` method, before we even get `dt`:

```
if(self.cycle == None):
    return task.done
```

18. The last change we'll make to our cycle will be the clean-up method. Paste the following code at the very bottom of the file:

```
def destroy(self):
    self.root.removeNode()
    self.cycle.removeNode()
    self.dirNP.removeNode()
    self.refNP.removeNode()
    self.trackNP.removeNode()
    self.shieldCNP.removeNode()
    self.gRayCNP.removeNode()
    self.glow.removeNode()
    self.cycle = None
    if(self.ai != None):
        self.ai = None
    return
```

19. That's it for the `Cycle` class, too. Save the file as `CycleClass_01.py` and let's move on to the `Menu` class. Open `MenuClass_01.py`, the file we made earlier this chapter.

20. The only change we're making to this class is to add a new menu type in
`initMenu()`. We'll number It `3` because it uses the `Menu3` object from the
`menuGraphics` egg. Right below our code for a type `0` menu, in the `initMenu()`
method, add the following block of code. Note that it's very, very similar to the code
we used to create the type `0` menu, but with a few minor differences. The most
major change is the use of the menu title.

```
if(type == 3):
    self.frame = DirectFrame(
        geom = self.menuGraphics.find("**/Menu3"),
        relief = None, scale = (1.5,1,1.5),
        frameColor = (1,1,1,.75), parent = base.aspect2d)
    framePadding = .1
    height = self.frame.getHeight()/2 - framePadding
    self.title = DirectLabel(text = self.title,
        text_font = self.fonts["silver"], text_fg = (1,1,1,.75),
        relief = None, text_align = TextNode.ACenter,
        text_scale = .065, parent = self.frame,
        pos = (0,0,height))
    for N in range(len(self.items)):
        xPos = 0
        zPos = -(height / (len(self.items)-1)) * N
        self.buttons.append(DirectButton(
            command = self.activateItem, extraArgs = [N],
            geom = (self.menuGraphics.find("**/BttnNormal"),
                self.menuGraphics.find("**/BttnPushed"),
                self.menuGraphics.find("**/BttnNormal"),
                self.menuGraphics.find("**/BttnNormal")),
            relief = None, clickSound = None,
            rolloverSound = None, parent = self.frame,
            pos = (xPos, 0, zPos)))
        self.items[N] = DirectLabel(text = self.items[N],
        text_font = self.fonts["silver"],
        text_fg = (1,1,1,.75), relief = None,
        text_align = TextNode.ACenter, text_scale = .035,
        parent = self.buttons[N])
        self.items[N].setPos(0,0,-self.items[N].getHeight()/2)
```

21. Resave this file as `MenuClass_02.py` and open up `WorldClass_01.py` from
the `Chapter08` folder. The `World` class doesn't use the `Cycle` or `Track` classes
anymore, so delete those two imports. Update the import of the `Menu` class to use
the new file. Then, add this new import:

```
from RaceClass_01 import Race
```

22. Scroll down and delete all the lines that create instances of the `Track` or `Cycle` classes.

23. Now, we're going to move the lines that create our menu into their own method. Either cut them, paste them, and edit them, or just delete them and add the following new code to the file, right after the `__init__` method:

```
def createStartMenu(self):
   menu = Menu(self.menuGraphics, self.fonts, self.inputManager)

   menu.initMenu([0,None,
      ["New Game","Quit Game"],
      [[self.race.createRace, self.createReadyDialogue],
        [base.userExit]],
      [[None,None],[None]]])
```

24. We also want a method to create our dialog menu. Add the following code below the method we just created:

```
def createReadyDialogue(self):
   menu = Menu(self.menuGraphics, self.fonts, self.inputManager)

   menu.initMenu([3,"Are you ready?",
      ["Yes","Exit"],
      [[self.race.startRace],[self.race.createDemoRace]],
      [[3],[None]]])
```

25. At the end of the `__init__` method, add a call to the `createStartMenu()` method. We also need to create an instance of the `Race` class and start the demo race. Here's the code:

```
self.race = Race(self.inputManager)
self.race.createDemoRace()
self.createStartMenu()
```

26. We don't need the `printTest()` method any more. So just delete it.

27. Resave the file as `WorldClass_02.py`. We don't need to worry about clean up for any of the other classes; their clean-up methods have been added for this chapter and are all ready to go. If you're curious about them, just open the files and take a look. Run our new `World` class file from the command prompt. Be aware that it's going to take a while to load; Panda3D has to process `Planet.egg`, which is a pretty big file. Since Panda3D caches eggs, the game will load faster in the future.

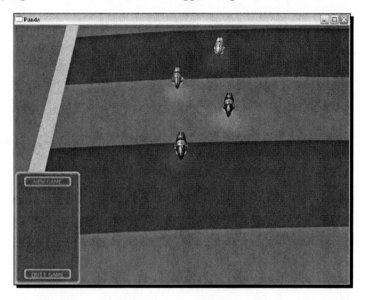

After the program loads and you see the preceding screen, click on the **New Game** button on the menu to proceed to the screen as shown in the following screenshot:

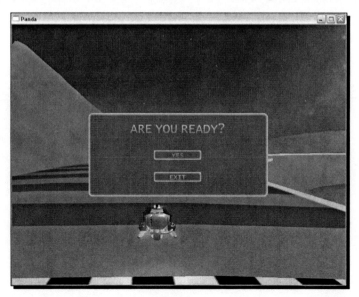

What just happened?

Now, when we load our game we see an overhead view of a demo race in progress. When we click on the **New Game** button, a new race is loaded and a dialog box comes up. Menu's in action!

That was a lot of work, but really there wasn't much new stuff. We only saw two pieces of Panda3D that we hadn't seen before. The first was the call to `removeNode()` that we used in the clean-up methods we created. This is another method of `NodePath` that removes the `NodePath` from the scene graph, so the scene graph doesn't retain a reference to it, and also erases the `NodePath` from the variable it's stored in. If we call `removeNode()` on `self.cycle`, for example, the `NodePath` that `self.cycle` points to will be taken out of the scene graph, along with all its children, and `self.cycle` will be set to **removed** so the `NodePath` it used to contain can be garbage collected. Feel free to print out a `NodePath` that had `removeNode()` called on it to see that for yourself.

If we wanted to remove the `NodePath` from the scene graph while still retaining the reference to it, we would use `detachNode` instead. That only removes the `NodePath` from the scene graph.

The other new call we saw was `base.userExit.` This method causes the game to close itself.

In-game HUD

While playing a game, players expect to have certain pieces of information on their screen, such as their health, or score, or how many lives they have left. These displays can collectively be called the **Heads Up Display**, or **HUD**. Our game is no different, and since we're working on GUI elements, we should start building a HUD to report some information to the player.

Creating our HUD is going to require some `DirectGUI` objects, and also some simple flat polygons with textures on them, just like the ones we gave to our `DirectFrames` and `DirectButtons` when we created the menus.

For things such as the shield and speed bars, our best option for controlling the up and down action is texture manipulation. If we used scaling on curved bars, it would distort the shape of the bar, and it would also compress the nice color gradients when the bars get low. Instead, we'll take advantage of something we learned in the last chapter about textures.

When we were talking about texture modes, we mentioned that putting a texture in the `Modulate` or `Add` modes, when the texture had an alpha channel would create a cutout in the object. We can use those cutouts to chop off parts of the bars, thus creating the illusion of them rising and falling.

Unfortunately, `DirectGUI` objects don't allow that kind of texture manipulation to their `geoms`, so we won't be able to use `DirectGUI` for the bars. We'll just use ordinary textured polygons instead.

Time for action – creating a basic HUD

That's enough talk, let's get to work. To begin with, we're only going to create the bottom-left corner of the HUD, because the items that are tracked by the rest of the HUD haven't been implemented yet. We'll build up the HUD more as we add to the game.

1. Open another blank document in NotePad++ and save it as `HUDClass_01.py`.

2. Once again, our imports come first. Add the following code to our blank file:

```
from direct.gui.DirectGui import *
from pandac.PandaModules import *
```

3. After that, we need the class definition and the `__init__` method. Here's the code for it:

```
class HUD:
    def __init__(self, fonts):
        self.modTS = TextureStage("Modulate")
        self.modTS.setMode(TextureStage.MModulate)
        self.createLLHUD(fonts)
        self.visible = False
        taskMgr.add(self.updateHUD, "Update HUD")
```

4. Notice that the HUD class doesn't take a cycle as an argument. We are going to want to have access to the cycle we're reporting on, though. The plan is to be able to set the cycle at runtime, so let's make a new method for that. Add the following code:

```
def setCycle(self, cycle):
    self.cycle = cycle
    return
```

5. Building all the elements of the HUD in a single method would get messy, fast. Instead, we'll create a couple of methods that will build the different parts for us. To start with, we'll make a method for the lower-left corner and create an invisible `DirectFrame` there to act as a parent for the different pieces. Put the following code at the bottom of the file:

```
def createLLHUD(self, fonts):
    self.llFrame = DirectFrame(frameSize = (0,.60,0,.45),
        frameColor = (1, 1, 1, 0),
        parent = base.a2dBottomLeft)
```

6. Next, we'll load up the textured polygons for our two bars and put them into place. Add the following code to the bottom of the method we just made:

```
shieldEgg = loader.loadModel("../Models/ShieldBar.egg")
self.shieldBG = shieldEgg.find("**/BackgroundBar")
self.shieldBar = shieldEgg.find("**/ShieldBar")
self.shieldFrame = shieldEgg.find("**/BarFrame")
self.shieldBG.reparentTo(self.llFrame)
self.shieldBar.reparentTo(self.shieldBG)
self.shieldFrame.reparentTo(self.shieldBG)
self.shieldBG.setPos(.1,0, .225)
speedEgg = loader.loadModel("../Models/SpeedBar.egg")
self.speedBG = speedEgg.find("**/BackgroundBar")
self.speedBar = speedEgg.find("**/SpeedBar")
self.speedFrame = speedEgg.find("**/BarFrame")
self.speedBG.reparentTo(self.llFrame)
self.speedBar.reparentTo(self.speedBG)
self.speedFrame.reparentTo(self.speedBG)
self.speedBG.setPos(.175,0, .225)
```

7. That will create the bar graphics, but we don't have the alpha cutout texture we were talking about earlier. For our next step, we'll load that image and apply it to the bars. This is code for that; put it right below the code from the last step:

```
alpha = loader.loadTexture("../Images/BarAlpha.png")
alpha.setFormat(Texture.FAlpha)
alpha.setWrapV(Texture.WMClamp)
self.speedBar.setTexture(self.modTS, alpha)
self.shieldBar.setTexture(self.modTS, alpha)
```

8. To indicate the throttle setting for the cycle, we'll add a little bar that will move up and down the speed bar. To make sure it always lines up with the curve of the bar, we'll use another alpha cutout. The following code should be typed in right below the code from the last step:

```
self.throttleBar = speedEgg.find("**/ThrottleBar")
self.throttleBar.reparentTo(self.speedBG)
throtAlpha = loader.loadTexture("../Images/ThrottleAlpha.png")
throtAlpha.setFormat(Texture.FAlpha)
self.throttleBar.setTexture(self.modTS, throtAlpha)
```

9. A couple of text displays will finish off the lower-left section of the HUD. For them, we'll use the method `DirectLabel()`. Here's the code to finish off the method:

```
self.shieldText = DirectLabel(text = "500 R",
  text_font = fonts["blue"], text_scale = .075,
  pos = (.5, 0, .25), text_fg = (1,1,1,1),
```

```
        relief = None, text_align = TextNode.ARight,
        parent = self.llFrame)
    self.speedText = DirectLabel(text = "180 KPH",
        text_font = fonts["orange"], text_scale = .075,
        pos = (.5, 0, .15), text_fg = (1,1,1,1),
        relief = None, text_align = TextNode.ARight,
        parent = self.llFrame)
    return
```

10. The next method we throw in the HUD class will update the lower-left section with cycle information. We'll adjust the throttle bar first. Here's the code to start the method off; put it right below the method we just finished:

```
def updateLLHUD(self):
  if(self.cycle.throttle >= 0):
    self.throttleBar.setColor(0, 1, 0)
    throtRatio = 1 - self.cycle.throttle
  else:
    self.throttleBar.setColor(1, 1, 1)
    throtRatio = 1 + self.cycle.throttle
  self.throttleBar.setTexOffset(TextureStage.getDefault(),
      0, .925 * throtRatio)
```

11. We also need to update the shield bar and the speed bar, so let's put in the code for that:

```
  if(self.cycle.speed >= 0):
    speedRatio = (self.cycle.maxSpeed -
      self.cycle.speed) / self.cycle.maxSpeed
  else:
    speedRatio = (self.cycle.maxSpeed +
      self.cycle.speed) / self.cycle.maxSpeed
  self.speedBar.setTexOffset(self.modTS, 0, .95 * speedRatio)
  shieldRatio = (self.cycle.maxShield -
    self.cycle.shield) / self.cycle.maxShield
  self.shieldBar.setTexOffset(self.modTS,    0, .95 *
shieldRatio)
```

12. Now, we just need to update the text to finish off this method. Here's the end code:

```
  self.speedText["text"] = str(int(self.cycle.speed)) + " KPH"
  self.shieldText["text"] = str(int(self.cycle.shield)) + " R"
  return
```

13. To call this update method every frame, along with the others we'll add later on, we need a `task()` method. Paste the following code right after the method from the last few steps:

```
def updateHUD(self, task):
    dt = globalClock.getDt()
    if (dt > .20):
        return task.cont
    if(self.visible == True):
        self.updateLLHUD()
    return task.cont
```

14. To give us the option of turning the HUD on and off, we want methods to show or hide all the frames. We'll add them next, at the bottom of the file.

```
def hide(self):
    self.llFrame.hide()
    self.visible = False
    return

def show(self):
    self.llFrame.show()
    self.visible = True
    return
```

15. That's it for the `HUD` class for now. Save the file, and let's move on. We need to make a tiny edit to the `Cycle` class, so we'll do that next. Our `HUD` class wants to report on the status of the cycle's shield, but we don't have any variables in the `Cycle` class for that. Open `CycleClass_01.py` and add two more variables into the `setupVarsNPs()` method, right below where the speed variables are created:

```
self.maxShield = 500
self.shield = self.maxShield
```

16. We're done with the `Cycle` class now. Resave the file as `CycleClass_02.py` and we'll move on to the `Race` class. Open `RaceClass_01.py` and change the `Cycle` class import line to use the new file. Then, modify the definition for the `__init__` method to accept a new argument:

```
def __init__(self, inputManager, hud):
```

17. We have to put our new argument into a new variable, so add the following line to the bottom of the `__init__` method:

```
self.hud = hud
```

18. Since we don't want the HUD to be visible during a demo race, we need to add a line at the beginning of the `createDemoRace()` method that will tell the HUD to hide itself. Make this the very first line of the `createDemoRace()` method:

```
self.hud.hide()
```

19. To make sure the HUD class is never trying to update when it doesn't have a cycle to report on, we need to add the same line to the very beginning of the `createRace()` method as well. This way, the HUD will stop updating itself, and we can safely destroy the cycles to create new ones.

20. Once we have our normal race all set up, we want to give the HUD class a cycle to report on and make the HUD visible. Add the following lines to the `createRace()` method, right below the lines that create our cycles:

```
self.hud.setCycle(self.cycles[0])
self.hud.show()
```

21. That's all the changes we need to make here. Resave the file as `RaceClass_02.py` and open `WorldClass_02.py`. We need to make a couple of changes here. First, we need to import the HUD class:

```
from HUDClass_01 import HUD
```

22. Update the import for the `Race` class so it uses the new file.

23. We also need to create an instance of the HUD class and give it the fonts it needs to create `DirectLabels`. Add this code to the `__init__` method, right below the lines that load our fonts:

```
hud = HUD(self.fonts)
```

24. Finally, change the line where we create an instance of our `Race` class to pass in the instance of the HUD class.

```
self.race = Race(self.inputManager, hud)
```

25. Alright, we're done. Resave the file as `WorldClass_03.py` and run it from the command prompt:

What just happened?

The first elements of our HUD are up and running, pretty as posies. We can call that a job well done, but first we need to talk about what we did to make sure we've got a good handle on how it works.

The main topic for this discussion will be the bars, and how they function. To start with, let's have a look at all the images we used to create them.

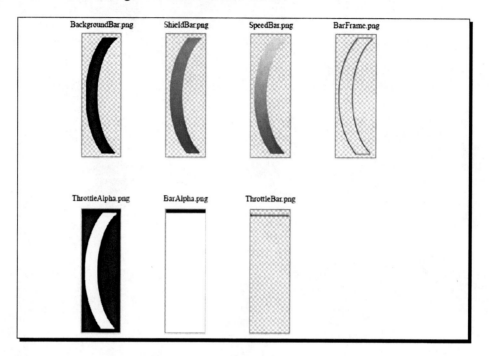

We created the bars by layering either the shield bar or the speed bar on top of the background bar, and then putting the bar frame on top of both of them. We controlled which item was on top by the order in which we inserted them into the scene graph of `base.aspect2d`.

Once we had the bars made, we loaded the bar alpha and changed it to an alpha channel texture using the `setFormat()` method. This little trick will only work if the image has only one channel. If it has an R, G, and B channel, the format change won't take. Then, we changed another texture setting with the `setWrapV()` method. This method is used to change the way a texture that doesn't completely cover the object is treated. We set it to `WMClamp`, which means that the pixels on the edge of the texture are duplicated into infinity; meaning, if the texture is black on the top, and you move the texture down, the area above it will be black too. This produces a very different result than, for example, `WMRepeat`, which tiles the texture across objects that are too large for it.

After we set up bar alpha, we applied it to the bars in `Modulate` mode. Because it's an alpha texture, the little black section at the top of the image creates a cutout from the bar, allowing the background bar to show through. Since we set the vertical wrap to `WMClamp` with `setWrapV(Texture.WMClamp)`, the black at the top gets stretched out infinitely above the image, as does the white on the bottom.

All we needed to do then was use `setTexOffset()` on bar alpha to move it up and down, and move the cutout up and down as well. That gave us the illusion of bars moving up and down. The method `setTexOffset()` requires us to tell it which `TextureStage` we want to offset, so we kept a handle to `self.modTS` and used that.

We used a similar trick for the throttle bar, but instead of moving the alpha, which is in the shape of the bar and used to trim the edges of the over-wide throttle bar image, we moved the default texture up and down by giving `setTexOffset()` the argument `TextureStage.getDefault()` instead of `self.modTS`.

Pop quiz – creating a Heads Up Display

Time for a few more questions about what we've learned so far.

1. Why are we using `setTexOffset` in our HUD?
2. How do we tell `setTexOffset` which texture we want it to affect?

Have-a-go hero – proper order of images

Here's a quick little challenge. With the way our HUD is set up right now, the throttle bar is actually on top of the speed bar's frame. Change the code for the `createLLHUD()` method so that the throttle bar will be sandwiched between the speed bar and its frame.

Summary

In this chapter, we learned how to give menu choices to the player, and we also learned how to display information related to the game with text and graphics.

We created the following new elements for our game:

- A menu system
- The start menu and a confirmation dialogue
- The first section of the HUD

In the next chapter, we'll start talking about using animation in our game. We'll introduce Actors, and talk about both procedural and premade animations.

9
Animating in Panda3D

Animation is a crucial component of most 3D applications. Our game is a bit of a special case because our characters are vehicles rather than people, and they don't need walking or running animations. For many video games, that won't be the case. In order to be better prepared for those situations, we're going to use a simple proxy program to discuss some of the aspects of animation and how it's used in Panda3D. Once we've covered that material, we'll employ some aspects of the animation system in our game as well. Our hover cycles may not need a walking animation, but there are pieces of the animation system we can make use of. The topics we're going to cover will be:

- Loading Actors and Animations
- Controlling Animation
- Blending Animations
- Creating and using Actor subparts
- Exposing joints

Actors and Animations

An `Actor` is a kind of object in Panda3D that adds more functionality to a static model. `Actors` can include joints within them. These joints have parts of the model tied to them and are rotated and repositioned by animations to make the model move and change. `Actors` are stored in `.egg` and `.bam` files, just like models.

`Animation` files include information on the position and rotation of joints at specific frames in the animation. They tell the `Actor` how to posture itself over the course of the animation. These files are also stored in `.egg` and `.bam` files.

Time for action – loading Actors and Animations

Let's load up an `Actor` with an animation and start it playing to get a feel for how this works:

1. Open a blank document in NotePad++ and save it as `Anim_01.py` in the `Chapter09` folder.

2. We need a few imports to start with. Put these lines at the top of the file:

```
import direct.directbase.DirectStart
from pandac.PandaModules import *
from direct.actor.Actor import Actor
```

3. We won't need a lot of code for our class' `__init__` method so let's just plow through it here :

```
class World:
  def __init__(self):
    base.disableMouse()
    base.camera.setPos(0, -5, 1)
    self.setupLight()
    self.kid = Actor("../Models/Kid.egg",
      {"Walk" : "../Animations/Walk.egg"})
    self.kid.reparentTo(render)
    self.kid.loop("Walk")
    self.kid.setH(180)
```

4. The next thing we want to do is steal our `setupLight()` method from the `Track` class and paste it into this class:

```
def setupLight(self):
  primeL = DirectionalLight("prime")
  primeL.setColor(VBase4(.6,.6,.6,1))
  self.dirLight = render.attachNewNode(primeL)
  self.dirLight.setHpr(45,-60,0)
  render.setLight(self.dirLight)
  ambL = AmbientLight("amb")
  ambL.setColor(VBase4(.2,.2,.2,1))
  self.ambLight = render.attachNewNode(ambL)
  render.setLight(self.ambLight)
  return
```

5. Lastly, we need to instantiate the `World` class and call the `run()` method.

```
w = World()
run()
```

6. Save the file and run it from the command prompt to see our loaded model with an animation playing on it, as depicted in the following screenshot:

What just happened?

Now, we have an animated `Actor` in our scene, slowly looping through a walk animation. We made that happen with only three lines of code:

```
self.kid = Actor("../Models/Kid.egg",
    {"Walk" : "../Animations/Walk.egg"})
  self.kid.reparentTo(render)
  self.kid.loop("Walk")
```

The first line creates an instance of the `Actor` class. Unlike with models, we don't need to use a method of `loader`. The `Actor` class constructor takes two arguments: the first is the filename for the model that will be loaded. This file may or may not contain animations in it. The second argument is for loading additional animations from separate files. It's a dictionary of animation names and the files that they are contained in. The names in the dictionary don't need to correspond to anything; they can be any string.

```
myActor = Actor( modelPath,
{NameForAnim1 : Anim1Path, NameForAnim2 : Anim2Path, etc})
```

The names we give animations when the `Actor` is created are important because we use those names to control the animations. For instance, the last line calls the method `loop()` with the name of the walking animation as its argument.

 If the reference to the `Actor` is removed, the animations will be lost. Make sure not to remove the reference to the `Actor` until both the `Actor` and its animations are no longer needed.

Pop quiz – animation basics

Let's take a moment to quiz ourselves on the material we just covered, shall we?

1. What is the difference between an `Actor` and a regular model? What is the difference in how they are brought into a Panda3D application?
2. How are animations loaded?
3. What kind of files can animations be stored in?

Controlling animations

Since we're talking about the `loop()` method, let's start discussing some of the different controls for playing and stopping animations. There are four basic methods we can use:

- `play("AnimName")`: This method plays the animation once from beginning to end.
- `loop("AnimName")`: This method is similar to play, but the animation doesn't stop when it's over; it replays again from the beginning.
- `stop()` or `stop("AnimName")`: This method, if called without an argument, stops all the animations currently playing on the `Actor`. If called with an argument, it only stops the named animation.

 Note that the `Actor` will remain in whatever posture they are in when this method is called.

- `pose("AnimName", FrameNumber)`: Places the `Actor` in the pose dictated by the supplied frame without playing the animation.

We have some more advanced options as well. Firstly, we can provide option `fromFrame` and `toFrame` arguments to play or loop to restrict the animation to specific frames.

```
myActor.play("AnimName", fromFrame = FromFrame, toFrame = toFrame)
```

We can provide both the arguments, or just one of them. For the `loop()` method, there is also the optional argument `restart`, which can be set to `0` or `1`. It defaults to `1`, which means to restart the animation from the beginning. If given a `0`, it will start looping from the current frame.

We can also use the `getNumFrames("AnimName")` and `getCurrentFrame("AnimName")` methods to get more information about a given animation. The `getCurrentAnim()` method will return a string that tells us which animation is currently playing on the `Actor`.

The final method we have in our list of basic animation controls sets the speed of the animation.

```
myActor.setPlayRate(1.5, "AnimName")
```

The `setPlayRate()` method takes two arguments. The first is the new play rate, and it should be expressed as a multiplier of the original frame rate. If we feed in `.5`, the animation will play half as fast. If we feed in `2`, the animation will play twice as fast. If we feed in `-1`, the animation will play at its normal speed, but it will play in reverse.

Have a go hero – basic animation controls

Experiment with the various animation control methods we've discussed to get a feel for how they work. Load the `Stand` and `Thoughtful` animations from the animations folder as well, and use player input or delayed tasks to switch between animations and change frame rates. Once we're comfortable with what we've gone over so far, we'll move on.

Animation blending

`Actors` aren't limited to playing a single animation at a time. Panda3D is advanced enough to offer us a very handy functionality, called **blending**. To explain blending, it's important to understand that an animation is really a series of offsets to the basic pose of the model. They aren't absolutes; they are changes from the original. With blending turned on, Panda3D can combine these offsets.

Time for action – blending two animations

We'll blend two animations together to see how this works.

1. Open `Anim_01.py` in the `Chapter09` folder.

2. We need to load a second animation to be able to blend. Change the line where we create our `Actor` to look like the following code:

```
self.kid = Actor("../Models/Kid.egg",
    {"Walk" : "../Animations/Walk.egg",
    "Thoughtful" : "../Animations/Thoughtful.egg"})
```

3. Now, we just need to add this code above the line where we start looping the `Walk` animation:

```
self.kid.enableBlend()
self.kid.setControlEffect("Walk", 1)
self.kid.setControlEffect("Thoughtful", 1)
```

4. Resave the file as `Anim_02.py` and run it from the command prompt.

What just happened?

Our `Actor` is now performing both animations to their full extent at the same time. This is possible because we made the call to the `self.kid.enableBlend()` method and then set the amount of effect each animation would have on the model with the `self.kid.setControlEffect()` method. We can turn off blending later on by using the `self.kid.disableBlend()` method, which will return the `Actor` to the state where playing or looping a new animation will stop any previous animations. Using the `setControlEffect` method, we can alter how much each animation controls the model. The numeric argument we pass to `setControlEffect()` represents a percentage of the animation's offset that will be applied, with 1 being 100%, 0.5 being 50%, and so on. When blending animations together, the look of the final result depends a great deal on the model and animations being used. Much of the work needed to achieve a good result depends on the artist.

Blending works well for transitioning between animations. In this case, it can be handy to use Tasks to dynamically alter the effect animations have on the model over time.

Honestly, though, the result we got with blending is pretty unpleasant. Our model is hardly walking at all, and he looks like he has a nervous twitch or something. This is because both animations are affecting the entire model at full strength, so the `Walk` and `Thoughtful` animations are fighting for control over the arms, legs, and everything else, and what we end up with is a combination of both animation's offsets.

> Furthermore, it's important to understand that when blending is enabled, every animation with a control effect higher than 0 will always be affecting the model, even if the animation isn't currently playing. The only way to remove an animation's influence is to set the control effect to 0.

This obviously can cause problems when we want to play an animation that moves the character's legs and another animation that moves his arms at the same time, without having them screw with each other. For that, we have to use subparts.

Creating and using Actor subparts

A subpart is a subsection of the joints in an `Actor`. Think of it like a grouping of some of the joints of the `Actor` that excludes the rest of the joints. Creating subparts doesn't actually change the `Actor` at all; it just creates a grouping that we can use when we want an animation to only affect a specific subset of joints. To create a subpart, we just need to call the `makeSubpart()` method of the `Actor`:

```
myActor.makeSubpart("SubpartName", [Included], [Excluded])
```

We pass three arguments into the `makeSubpart()` method:

- The first is a name for the subpart that we can use to identify it later
- The second is a list of joint names for the joints we want to include in the subpart
- The third is a list of joint names for the joints we want to exclude from the model

We can find these joint names if we open `Kid.egg` and scroll down to the bottom. Here's a joint entry for a joint called `Chest`, for reference:

```
<Joint> Chest {
    <Transform> {
      <Matrix4> {
        0.993033 0 0.117839 0
        0.117839 0 -0.993033 0
        0 1 0 0
        0.212127 0 0 1
      }
    }
}
```

The `makeSubpart()` method automatically includes or excludes the children of any joint it is supplied.

 When making `Actor` subparts, exclusion always overrides inclusion.

Let's take a look at some of the joints in our `Actor` and their hierarchy.

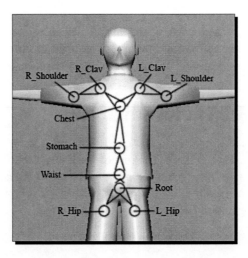

This diagram shows some of our joints, the circles, and their names. It also shows the hierarchy through the connecting arrows. Parents point to their children.

Looking at this, we can tell that the joint named Root is at the top of our joint hierarchy. If we pass Root as an included joint, that will include every joint in the model. If we also pass in Waist as an excluded joint, we'll override part of that inclusion and exclude the Waist joint and its children. Therefore, our subpart will only include Root, R_Hip and its children, and L_Hip and its children, which means only the pelvis and legs.

Time for action – playing animations on subparts

To better understand subparts, we should put them into action.

1. Open Anim_02.py in the Chapter09 folder.

2. Remove the code that enables blending, sets control effects, and loops the two animations.

3. Add this code in place of the code we just removed:

    ```
    self.kid.makeSubpart("Bottom", ["Root"], ["Waist"])
    self.kid.makeSubpart("Top", ["Waist"])
    self.kid.loop("Thoughtful", partName = "Top")
    self.kid.loop("Walk", partName = "Bottom")
    ```

4. Resave the file as Anim_03.py and run it from the command prompt.

What just happened?

We've got a much nicer combination of the two animations now because on the legs of the Actor we're only playing the Walk animation, and on the torso of the Actor we're only playing the Thoughtful animation.

 Note that if we want to play an animation only on a subpart of the Actor, we need to use the partName optional argument for play or loop.

Pop quiz – advanced animation

We've just been exposed to a pretty hefty quantity of information, so let's revisit it in our memories to make sure we don't lose it.

1. What optional arguments can we pass to play, loop, and stop?

2. What do we use if we want to mix animations on an Actor?

3. How do we control the amount of effect an animation has on a model when mixing animations?

4. What do we do if we want to play animations on different parts of a model without letting the animations affect one another?

Exposing joints

We can do more with Actors than just play animations on them. We can also attach other NodePaths to specific joints in an Actor so that they will follow that joint wherever it moves. This technique is often used to put objects in a character's hands. For our game, we'll be using it to attach the discs and turret to our cycle.

This technique works well for us because we want to change the rotation of the discs and turret. For that to work correctly, the models need to have the points they will rotate around at (0, 0, 0) in their own coordinate system. That means we can't reposition them in the modeling software, as we did with the static parts of the cycle such as the power plant.

Instead, we'll load an Actor that only contains three joints. The joints are located at the positions where we want to place our discs and turret. If we attach the Actor to the cycle's model, we can use the joints as mounting points for the discs and turret.

Without the exposeJoint() method of Actor, this technique wouldn't be possible. This method creates a NodePath and attaches it to a joint in the Actor, such that wherever that joint moves, or however it rotates, the NodePath will mimic it exactly. The method exposeJoint() takes three arguments:

- The first is an optional `Node` that is usually set to `None`
- The second is the name of the subpart the joint is a part of, or `modelRoot` if no subparts contain the joint
- The last argument is the name of the joint to expose:

```
jointNP = myActor.exposeJoint(None,
subpartName or "modelRoot", JointName)
```

Once we've used `exposeJoint()` to create `NodePaths`, we can use `reparentTo` to attach things to them, just like any other `NodePath`.

Time for action – animating our cycles

We're going to add two kinds of animation to our cycle. We'll make the discs at the front and rear of the cycle rotate in accordance with the throttle setting, and we'll make the cycle lean left and right when it turns. Because we don't want the `CollisionRays` attached to the cycle to lean as well, we'll have to make accommodations for that.

1. Open `CycleClass_00.py` in the `Chapter09` folder.

2. Add this line to our `import` statements to give us access to `Actors`:

```
from direct.actor.Actor import Actor
```

3. Scroll down to the `setupVarsNPs()` method and look for the section where we use `if` statements to position `self.root` and load the correct model. That section looks like the following code:

```
if(startPos == 1):
  self.root.setPos(5,0,0)
  self.cycle = loader.loadModel("../Models/RedCycle.bam")
elif(startPos == 2):
  self.root.setPos(-5,-5,0)
  self.cycle = loader.loadModel("../Models/BlueCycle.bam")
elif(startPos == 3):
  self.root.setPos(5,-10,0)
  self.cycle = loader.loadModel("../Models/GreenCycle.bam")
elif(startPos == 4):
  self.root.setPos(-5,-15,0)
  self.cycle = loader.loadModel("../Models/YellowCycle.bam")
```

4. Delete that section and replace it with the following code:

```
self.cycle = self.root.attachNewNode("Cycle")

if(startPos == 1):
  self.root.setPos(5,0,0)
```

```
        self.model = loader.loadModel("../Models/RedCycle.bam")
        self.turret = loader.loadModel("../Models/RedTurr.bam")
    elif(startPos == 2):
        self.root.setPos(-5,-5,0)
        self.model = loader.loadModel("../Models/BlueCycle.bam")
        self.turret = loader.loadModel("../Models/BlueTurr.bam")
    elif(startPos == 3):
        self.root.setPos(5,-10,0)
        self.model = loader.loadModel("../Models/GreenCycle.bam")
        self.turret = loader.loadModel("../Models/GreenTurr.bam")
    elif(startPos == 4):
        self.root.setPos(-5,-15,0)
        self.model = loader.loadModel("../Models/YellowCycle.bam")
        self.turret = loader.loadModel("../Models/YellowTurr.bam")
    self.mounts = Actor("../Models/Mounts.egg")

    self.model.reparentTo(self.cycle)
    self.mounts.reparentTo(self.model)

    turretMount = self.mounts.exposeJoint(None,
        "modelRoot", "Turret")
    fdMount = self.mounts.exposeJoint(None,
        "modelRoot", "FrontDisc")
    rdMount = self.mounts.exposeJoint(None,
        "modelRoot", "RearDisc")

    self.fd = loader.loadModel("../Models/Disc.bam")
    self.rd = loader.loadModel("../Models/Disc.bam")

    self.turret.reparentTo(turretMount)
    self.fd.reparentTo(fdMount)
    self.rd.reparentTo(rdMount)
```

5. Scroll down a little to where we set the cycle's speed, shield, and other variables. Right beneath that there is a line that attaches self.cycle to self.root. Delete that line and put the following two lines in its place:

```
self.turning = None
self.lean = 0
```

6. Keep moving down until we're in setupCollisions. Look for the following line:

```
self.shieldCNP = self.cycle.attachNewNode(self.shieldCN)
```

7. Change that line from self.cycle to self.model so it looks like this:

```
self.shieldCNP = self.model.attachNewNode(self.shieldCN)
```

8. Head down to the `cycleControl()` method and find the short block of code that turns the cycle according to user input. It looks like the following code:

```
if(self.inputManager.keyMap["right"] == True):
    self.turn("r", dt)
elif(self.inputManager.keyMap["left"] == True):
    self.turn("l", dt)
```

9. Edit that code so it looks like the following code:

```
if(self.inputManager.keyMap["right"] == True):
    self.turn("r", dt)
    self.turning = "r"
elif(self.inputManager.keyMap["left"] == True):
    self.turn("l", dt)
    self.turning = "l"
else:
    self.turning = None
```

10. Now, skip down to the `move()` method. Add the following code to the bottom of the method, right above the `return` statement:

```
currentLean = self.model.getR()

if(self.turning == "r"):
    self.lean += 2.5
    if(self.lean > 25): self.lean = 25
    self.model.setR(self.model,
        (self.lean - currentLean) * dt * 5)
elif(self.turning == "l"):
    self.lean -= 2.5
    if(self.lean < -25): self.lean = -25
    self.model.setR(self.model,
        (self.lean - currentLean) * dt * 5)
else:
    self.lean = 0
    self.model.setR(self.model,
        (self.lean - currentLean) * dt * 5)

self.fd.setH(self.fd, 5  + (20 * self.throttle))
self.rd.setH(self.rd, -5 + (-20 * self.throttle))
```

11. We've got one more change to make to this file. Go all the way down to the bottom of the file to the `destroy()` method and add these five lines right underneath the call to `self.cycle.removeNode()`:

```
self.mounts.delete()
```

```
        self.model.removeNode()
        self.turret.removeNode()
        self.fd.removeNode()
        self.rd.removeNode()
```

12. Resave the file as `CycleClass_01.py` and run `WorldClass_00.py` from the command prompt. The other files for this chapter have already been updated to look for `CycleClass_01.py` so we don't need to edit any of them.

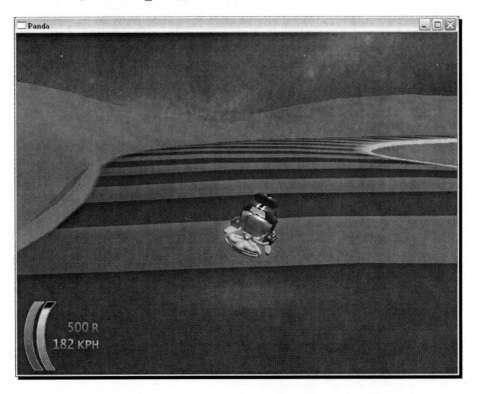

What just happened?

That brings some new life to our cycle! There's one thing we should talk about in this example that we haven't really discussed yet: the reason why we made `self.cycle` an empty `NodePath` and changed the model to be `self.model`. Remember the `CollisionRays` we made back in *Chapter 6*, *The World in Action: Handling Collisions* and how they are children `self.cycle`? Well, when we lean the cycle during a turn, we don't want those `CollisionRays` to lean with it, but the `CollisionRays` still have to turn with the cycle so that the front ray stays in front and the back ray stays at the back. For all that to work out, we need to separate the turning from the leaning, and that's why we are using two `NodePaths` now. Since we want the `CollisionSpheres` for the shield to lean with the cycle, we made them children of `self.model` instead of `self.cycle`.

Summary

We didn't do much work on our game in this chapter, but we learned all kinds of things about animation in Panda3D.

In this chapter, we talked about loading `Actor` and animations and how to control an `Actor`'s animations. We also discussed how we can use blending and subparts to further refine our animation control, and we touched on how to include other objects into our `Actor`'s animations by binding them to joints.

In our next chapter, we'll be adding some shiny new features to our game using intervals. When we're done, our cycles will be armed to the teeth with cannons and machine guns. Look forward to it!

10
Creating Weaponry: Using Mouse Picking and Intervals

The time has come at last to put armaments on our cycles. We'll be using a system very similar to mouse picking for our aiming, and we'll use intervals to control the fire rate of the weapons. For our big cannons, we'll use a special interval to make the projectiles fly correctly.

The topics we're going to cover are:

- Using mouse picking
- Understanding Intervals, Sequences, and Parallels
- Creating machine guns
- Implementing the main cannon
- Adding weapon information to the HUD
- Handling damage response

Using mouse picking

Mouse picking is a term used when the mouse is used to point at something in the game and select or otherwise interact with it. Many types of games use mouse picking for interaction, for example strategy and puzzle games.

For our game, we will use mouse picking to aim our weapons. The general idea is to aim the guns wherever the mouse is pointing to on the screen. We'll set that up first.

Time for action – setting up mouse aim

Mouse picking requires the collision system, so we'll be using collision solids and all that again. Take a look back to *Chapter 6, The World in Action: Handling Collisions* as we go, if it's needed.

1. Have a look in the `Chapter10` folder and open up the `InputMangaer_00.py` file there.

2. A new import comes first. Add this line to our imports section:

```
from pandac.PandaModules import *
```

3. Next, we'll add a call to a new method to the bottom of `__init__` method:

```
self.setupMouseAim()
```

4. Now, let's go ahead and add that new method to the bottom of the class:

```
def setupMouseAim(self):
    self.CN = CollisionNode("RayCN")
    self.cRay = CollisionRay()
    self.CN.addSolid(self.cRay)
    self.CN.setFromCollideMask(BitMask32.bit(8))
    self.CN.setIntoCollideMask(BitMask32.allOff())
    self.CN = base.camera.attachNewNode(self.CN)

    self.aimPlaneCN = CollisionNode("aimPlaneCN")
    self.aimPlane = CollisionPlane(Plane(Vec3(0,-1,0),
        Point3(0,30,0)))
    self.aimPlaneCN.addSolid(self.aimPlane)
    self.aimPlaneCN.setFromCollideMask(BitMask32.allOff())
    self.aimPlaneCN.setIntoCollideMask(BitMask32.bit(8))
    self.aimPlaneCNP = base.camera.attachNewNode(self.aimPlaneCN)

    self.cTrav = CollisionTraverser()
    self.cHanQ = CollisionHandlerQueue()
    self.cTrav.addCollider(self.CN, self.cHanQ)
```

5. Now that we have a method creating the collision components, we need a method that uses them. Add this new method to the `InputManager` class as well:

```
def getMouseAim(self):
    if base.mouseWatcherNode.hasMouse():
        mpos = base.mouseWatcherNode.getMouse()
        self.cRay.setFromLens(
            base.camNode, mpos.getX(), mpos.getY())
        self.cTrav.traverse(self.aimPlaneCNP)
```

```
self.cHanQ.sortEntries()
if(self.cHanQ.getNumEntries() > 0):
  entry = self.cHanQ.getEntry(0)
  colPoint = entry.getSurfacePoint(render)
  return(colPoint)
```

6. Save the file as `InputManager_01.py`.

7. Next, open up `CycleClass_00.py` from the `Chapter10` folder. We have a couple of modifications to make here, too. First, we're going to load an `Actor` with some joints in it for the turret, just like we did for the cycle. The joints will be the mounting points for the guns and for the targeting ray. Scroll down to `setupVarsNPs` and find the line where we reparent `self.turret` to `turretMount`. Replace that line with the following code block:

```
self.turretActor = Actor("../Models/TurretActor.egg")
self.turretActor.reparentTo(turretMount)
self.turret.reparentTo(self.turretActor)
self.trgtrMount = self.turretActor.exposeJoint(None,
   "modelRoot", "TargeterMount")
```

8. Next, scroll down to the `CycleControl()` method and find the block of code that uses the mouse to control the camera. Make sure you find both parts: the stuff that rotates the camera and the code that zooms in and out. Delete all of it. In its place, put the following code:

```
aimPoint = self.inputManager.getMouseAim()
if(aimPoint != None):
  self.turretActor.lookAt(render, aimPoint)
```

9. The last change in the `Cycle` class will happen in the `destroy()` method. We need to call the `delete()` method on our new actor as well. Add this line right after the call to `self.mounts.delete`:

```
self.turretActor.delete()
```

10. Save the file as `CycleClass_00.py`. Finally, open `HUDClass_00.py`. Here, we are going to add a new piece of the HUD: a targeting reticule. Add the following lines of code into the `setCycle()` method:

```
self.targetCone = loader.loadModel("../Models/TargetCone.bam")
self.targetCone.setRenderModeThickness(1)
self.targetCone.reparentTo(self.cycle.trgtrMount)
self.targetCone.setColor(1,.25,.25)
```

11. Save the file as `HUDClass_00.py`. Our other files have already been modified to use the correct names for the files we edited, so we don't need to update any of that. Head to the command prompt and run `WorldClass_00.py`.

What just happened?

Notice how the turret tilts and rotates so that the red cross hairs extending from it always point toward where the mouse is located on the screen. The basic concept behind this is pretty simple. We have a `CollisionPlane` set in front of the camera that moves with the camera so it is always right where it needs to be. Then, we shoot a `CollisionRay` out of the camera, straight through the mouse cursor, and we get the point in space where the ray collides with the plane. From our point of view, the location of that collision will be directly beneath the mouse cursor.

We needed to use the `setFromLens()` method of the `CollisionRay` to make this happen. This method is used to direct a `CollisionRay` from the viewpoint of the camera out into space, through a particular 2D point. Virtually every time this method is used, that 2D point is the position of the mouse cursor.

Also, we needed the `getSurfacePoint()` method of the collision event object to find the point in space we needed. This method returns the point on the surface of the **Into** object where the collision occurred, relative to the `NodePath` that's passed in as an argument.

The only difference between this system and a mouse picking system, where the cursor is used to select objects, is the `CollisionPlane`. Instead of using the plane, we would have the `CollisionRay` collide with objects in the scene to see what's being selected.

Pop quiz – mouse picking

Let's go back over some of the main points we covered to make sure our understanding is absolute.

1. What method of the `CollisionRay` collision solid did we use for mouse picking? How does that method work?

2. What method of the collision event object did we use, and what for?

Understanding Intervals, Sequences, and Parallels

Intervals are very similar to tasks in that they are used to perform an action over time.

 They are also similar to animations because they can be controlled with simple start, loop, and stop methods just like animations.

Unlike tasks, Intervals automatically take into account the passage of time instead of executing on each frame, or waiting an amount of time to then execute in a single frame. They also use a finite duration of time, and stop automatically when that amount of time has passed.

To use Intervals, we need to import them with this import line:

```
from direct.interval.IntervalGlobal import *
```

Then, we can create Intervals by calling the constructor and giving it the necessary arguments:

```
myInterval = Constructor(arguments)
```

The actual constructor varies from `Interval` type to `Interval` type.

Exactly what an `Interval` does depend on the type of `Interval` in question. Here's a list of types of Intervals:

♦ Lerp: A large variety of `Lerp` Intervals are available for use. Lerp stands for linear interpolation, and as the name suggests `Lerp` Intervals are used to smoothly adjust a value over a period of time. Example uses of `Lerp` Intervals include changing position, rotation, or scale of a `NodePath` over time. Here's a list of all the `Lerp` Intervals, taken from the Panda3D manual:

```
LerpPosInterval(NodePath, duration, pos, startPos)
LerpHprInterval(NodePath, duration, hpr, startHpr)
LerpQuatInterval(NodePath, duration, quat, startHpr, startQuat)
LerpScaleInterval(NodePath, duration, scale, startScale)
LerpShearInterval(NodePath, duration, shear, startShear)
LerpColorInterval(NodePath, duration, color, startColor)
LerpColorScaleInterval(NodePath, duration, colorScale,
startColorScale)
LerpPosHprInterval(NodePath, duration, pos, hpr, startPos,
startHpr)
LerpPosQuatInterval(NodePath, duration, pos, quat, startPos,
        startQuat)
LerpHprScaleInterval(NodePath, duration, hpr, scale, startHpr,
 startScale)
LerpQuatScaleInterval(NodePath, duration, quat, scale, startQuat,
startScale)
LerpPosHprScaleInterval(NodePath, duration, pos, hpr, scale,
startPos, startHpr, startScale)
LerpPosQuatScaleInterval(NodePath, duration, pos, quat, scale,
startPos, startQuat, startScale)
LerpPosHprScaleShearInterval(NodePath, duration, pos, hpr, scale,
shear, startPos, startHpr, startScale, startShear)
LerpPosQuatScaleShearInterval(NodePath, duration, pos, quat,
scale,
shear, startPos, startQuat, startScale, startShear)
```

♦ LerpFunc: This is a special Lerp `Interval` that calls a custom function and passes in a data value that is smoothly adjusted over time. Here's an example of the constructor, taken from the Panda3D manual:

```
LerpFunc(myFunction,
        fromData=0,
        toData=1,
        duration=0.0,
        blendType='noBlend',
        extraArgs=[])
```

- ◆ actorInterval: This Interval is used to play an animation on an actor. We won't be using this type of Interval for our game. Here's an example of the constructor, taken from the Panda3D manual:

```
myactor.actorInterval(
    "Animation Name",
    loop=<0 or 1>,
    contrainedLoop=<0 or 1>,
    duration=D,
    startTime=T1,
    endTime=T2,
    startFrame=N1,
    endFrame=N2,
    playRate=R,
    partName=PN,
    lodName=LN)
```

- ◆ SoundInterval: This Interval plays sound files. Here's an example of the constructor, taken from the Panda3D manual:

```
SoundInterval(
    mySound,
    loop = 0 or 1,
    duration = myDuration,
    volume = myVolume,
    startTime = myStartTime)
```

- ◆ MotionPath and particle Intervals: The last two types of Intervals are used with MotionPath and particle systems. Since we aren't covering either of those topics in this book, we won't be discussing these Intervals.

- ◆ ProjectileInterval: This special Interval is used to simulate a projectile that flies under the influence of gravity. Although this Interval has several optional arguments, there are three primary ways to use it. Here's the constructor and the primary usages, taken from the Panda3D manual. The primary usages describe what values should be set for the Interval, and what behavior to expect.

```
ProjectileInterval(<Node Path>,
    startPos = Point3(X,Y,Z), endPos = Point3(X,Y,Z),
    duration = <Time in seconds>, startVel = Point3(X,Y,Z),
    endZ = Point3(X,Y,Z), gravityMult = <multiplier>, name = <Name>)
```

  - ❏ startPos, endPos, duration—go from startPos to endPos in duration seconds

  - ❏ startPos, startVel, duration—given a starting velocity, go for a specific time period

  - ❏ startPos, startVel, endZ—given a starting velocity, go until you hit a given Z plane

Once we have an `Interval`, we have all sorts of methods that we can use to interact with it. The most basic are:

```
myInterval.start()
myInterval.loop()
```

These are the methods that make the `Interval` do its thing. The `start()` method will have `Interval` play through once, while the `loop()` method makes the `Interval` repeat itself each time it finishes. Both of these methods can be given some optional arguments:

```
myInterval.start(startTime, endTime, playRate)
myInterval.loop(startTime, endTime, playRate)
```

Normally, an `Interval` that is started with the `start()` method will finish when its duration has passed. To stop an `Interval` early, you can use the `finish()` method:

```
myInterval.finish()
```

 The `finish()` method will stop the `Interval` and move it to its final state as if it had played through completely.

We can also pause and resume an `Interval` with the `pause()` and `resume()` methods:

```
myInterval.pause()
myInterval.resume()
```

We can also get some useful information from the `Interval` with these methods:

```
myInterval.getDuration()
myInterval.getT()
myInterval.isPlaying()
myInterval.isStopped()
```

The `getDuration()` method returns the duration of the `Interval`, in seconds. The `getT()` method will return the amount of time, in seconds, that has passed since the `Interval` started. The `isPlaying()` method will return `True` if the `Interval` is currently playing, and will return `False` if the `Interval` hasn't been started yet, has already finished, or is paused. By contrast, the `isStopped()` method only returns `True` if the `Interval` hasn't been started or has finished. It won't return `True` if the `Interval` is only paused.

Sequences and Parallels

All of these simple controls for interacting with Intervals are great, but the real benefit of Intervals over tasks lies with Sequences and Parallels. We can use Sequences and Parallels to create groups of Intervals that allow us to perform many different things at once, or one in particular, or both!

Both of these handy utilities are essentially lists of Intervals. They can be started, finished, and so on just like a regular `Interval` can. When started, a `Sequence` will execute the first `Interval` to completion, then execute the second, and so on. A `Parallel` will execute all of the `Interval` it's been given at the same time, but the `Parallel` itself won't be finished until all of the `Interval` in it are finished.

We can even include an already created `Sequence` or `Parallel` in a new `Sequence` or `Parallel`, which allows us to easily make complicated scripts of actions and then run them very easily.

As if that wasn't powerful enough, we also have two very special types of `Intervals` that are just for `Sequences` and `Parallels`:

- `Wait()`: This `Interval` does nothing. The important bit is that it does nothing for a specific period of time. It's very useful for creating delays in a `Sequence`, or extending the overall duration of a `Parallel`.

  `Wait(seconds)`

- `Func()`: This `Interval` is the only `Interval` that doesn't have a duration. Sequences and Parallels only take Intervals as arguments, but sometimes we just want to perform a simple function call during the `Sequence` or `Parallel`. That's what this `Interval` is for. When it comes up in a `Sequence` or `Parallel`, Panda3D executes the function given to `Func()`. We can pass in extra arguments for the function, too.

  `Func(myFunction, arg1, arg2, ..., argN)`

Creating machine guns

The best way to understand the value of Intervals is to see them in action, so we'll put them to use in our cycle's weapons. To start with, we'll make the two machine gun-type lasers that will be mounted on the turret.

Time for action – using Intervals in Sequences and Parallels

We'll be using a `LerpScaleInterval`, a `Parallel`, and a `Sequence` to create a script for when our machine gun lasers fire. Before we start making the `MachineGun` class, though, our `Cycle` class will need some small modifications.

1. Open `CycleClass_01.py` and add this line to our imports section:

   `from GunClasses_01 import *`

2. Scroll down to the `setupVarsNPs()` method and look for the lines where we call `self.fd.reparentTo(fdMount)` and `self.rd.reparentTo(rdMount)`. **Right under those lines, add the following code:**

```
self.LMGMount = self.turretActor.exposeJoint(None,
    "modelRoot", "LMGMount")
self.RMGMount = self.turretActor.exposeJoint(None,
    "modelRoot", "RMGMount")
self.LMG = MachineGun(self, self.LMGMount)
self.RMG = MachineGun(self, self.RMGMount)
```

3. We'll add a little bit of code to the `CycleControl()` method as well so we can actually shoot our `MachineGuns` to test them. Put the following code right below the section where we control turning. Make sure to use the correct indentation level, so this code will only be considered if `self.active == True`.

```
if(self.inputManager.keyMap["mouse1"] == True):
    self.LMG.fire()
    self.RMG.fire()
```

4. Now, scroll down to the `destroy()` method and add the following code right above the line where we set `self.cycle = None`:

```
self.LMG.destroy()
self.LMG = None
self.RMG.destroy()
self.RMG = None
```

5. Go ahead and resave the file as `CycleClass_02.py`. Then, open a new file and save the new file as `GunClasses_01.py`.

6. Start the new file off with the following imports:

```
from direct.interval.IntervalGlobal import *
from direct.actor.Actor import Actor
from pandac.PandaModules import *
from UtilityFunctions import *
```

7. Next, we'll start our `MachineGun` class and its `__init__` method. We'll want to get a reference to the `Cycle` class and load up our `Actor` and models first.

```
class MachineGun:
  def __init__(self, cycle, mount):
    self.cycle = cycle
    self.actor = Actor("../Models/MGActor.egg")
    self.model = loader.loadModel("../Models/MachineGun.bam")
    self.actor.reparentTo(mount)
    self.model.reparentTo(self.actor)
```

```
self.flashModel = loader.loadModel("../Models/LaserFlash.bam")
self.projModel = loader.loadModel("../Models/LaserProj.bam")
self.projModel.setScale(.25, 1, .25)
```

8. We also need a couple of `NodePath` and a temporary variable. Here's the code for them:

```
self.refNP = self.cycle.trgtrMount.attachNewNode("MGRefNP")
self.muzzle = self.actor.exposeJoint(None,
   "modelRoot", "Muzzle")
reloadTime = .25
```

9. The last code we'll put in the `__init__` method will set up our `Interval` script. Here's the code for it:

```
self.flashLerp = LerpScaleInterval(self.flashModel,
   reloadTime * .75, Point3(1,1,1), Point3(.1,.1,.1))

self.firePar = Parallel(
   Func(self.setEffects),
   self.flashLerp)

self.fireSeq = Sequence(self.firePar,
   Func(self.clearEffects),
   Wait(reloadTime * .25))
```

10. Four more methods are needed to complete the `MachineGun` class. Here's the first; add it at the bottom of the file:

```
def fire(self):
  if(self.fireSeq.isPlaying() == False):
     self.refNP.setPos(0,15,0)
    self.fireSeq.start()
  return
```

11. Here are the next two methods, which place and remove the visual effects for the `MachineGun`. Add them beneath the `fire()` method.

```
def setEffects(self):
  self.flashModel.reparentTo(self.muzzle)
  self.projModel.reparentTo(self.muzzle)
  self.projModel.lookAt(self.refNP.getPos(self.muzzle))
  self.projModel.setSy(trueDist(Point3(0,0,0),
    self.refNP.getPos(self.muzzle)) * 2)
  return
def clearEffects(self):
  self.flashModel.detachNode()
  self.projModel.detachNode()
  return
```

12. Lastly, we need to add the cleanup method `destroy()` to our `MachineGun`. Here's the code for it:

```
def destroy(self):
    self.actor.delete()
    self.model.removeNode()
    self.flashModel.removeNode()
    self.projModel.removeNode()
    self.refNP.removeNode()
    self.cycle = None
    self.flashLerp = None
    self.firePar = None
    self.fireSeq = None
    return
```

13. Resave this file. Update `RaceClass_00.py` to use `CycleClass_02.py`, and then resave it as `RaceClass_01.py`.

14. Update `WorldClass_00.py` to use `RaceClass_01.py`, and then resave it as `WorldClass_01.py`.

15. Run `WorldClass_01.py` from the command prompt. Once the race has started, hold down the left mouse button to fire the lasers.

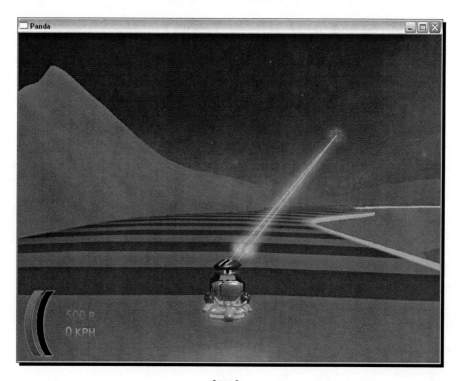

What just happened?

We've got some nice-looking machine gun laser fire going on now! Let's talk about the `Interval` script we used to make it happen.

```
reloadTime = .25
self.flashLerp = LerpScaleInterval(self.flashModel,
   reloadTime * .75, Point3(1,1,1), Point3(.1,.1,.1))
self.firePar = Parallel(
   Func(self.setEffects),
   self.flashLerp)
self.fireSeq = Sequence(self.firePar,
   Func(self.clearEffects),
   Wait(reloadTime * .25))
```

We started off by creating a temporary variable for the machine gun's reload time. Since we're using `reloadTime` in two different places, the variable makes it easier to adjust. We don't need a permanent variable because the value will get stored in the Intervals that use it. We could use a permanent variable if we wanted to change the reload time over the course of the race. If we put in a power up that made weapons shoot faster, for example, then we could change the value and the script would reflect that change.

Next, we created a `LerpScaleInterval()` and called it `self.flashLerp`. This `Interval` adjusts the scale of a `NodePath` over time. In our case, we told it to change the scale of `self.flashModel` from `(.1, .1, .1)` to `(1,1,1)` over `(reloadTime *.75)` number of seconds. When our machine gun lasers are firing, we have a little burst of light right at the muzzle of the gun that grows larger, right? This is the `Interval` that animates the growth of those flashes.

After making `self.flashLerp`, we created `self.firePar`. `self.firePar` is a `Parallel`, so it executes all the Intervals in it at the same time. We gave it two Intervals: `Func(self.setEffects)` and `self.flashLerp`. The `Func(self.setEffects)` Interval simply calls the `setEffects()` method as soon as it's activated, and then it's done. The `setEffects()` method is responsible for placing `self.flashModel`, which is the model for the burst of light at the muzzle of the gun. It also places `self.projModel`, which is the long cylinder that represents the laser itself, at the muzzle as well. It then points `self.projModel` at the impact point of the shot and stretches it so that it will reach all the way from the muzzle to the impact point. We aren't doing any collision testing yet, so we're using a fake impact point. `self.firePar` also starts the `self.flashLerp` Interval that makes the muzzle flash grow. We're using a `Parallel` here because we want both of these actions to occur at the same time.

The last part of the script is `self.fireSeq`. This is a `Sequence` with three pieces in it: `self.firePar`, `Func(self.clearEffects)`, and `Wait(reloadTime * .25)`. Since it's a `Sequence`, it executes the Intervals it's been given one at a time, from first to last. This means that once `self.firePar` and `self.flashLerp` are finished, `Func(self.clearEffects)` will execute. The `clearEffects()` method uses the `detachNode()` method of `NodePath` to remove `self.flashModel` and `self.projModel` from the scene graph without removing the reference to them. That happens virtually instantly, and then `Wait(reloadTime *.25)` starts, forcing the sequence to wait the remainder of the `reloadTime` before finishing. Here's a timeline of what really happens when `self.fireSeq` is started:

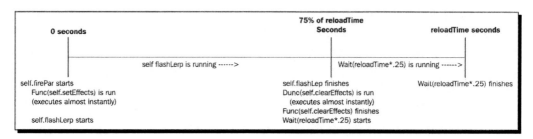

Let's take a look at how we're using this `Sequence` in the `fire()` method.

```
def fire(self):
  if(self.fireSeq.isPlaying() == False):
    self.refNP.setPos(0,15,0)
    self.fireSeq.start()
  return
```

Note that the first thing we do is to see if `self.fireSeq` is already playing. If it is, we don't perform any actions. This simple check, combined with the fact that `self.fireSeq` takes exactly `reloadTime` seconds to complete, limits our machine gun lasers to only fire at their specified fire rate. When `self.fireSeq` isn't playing, we know it's safe for the machine gun lasers to fire again, and we can just call `self.fireSeq.start()` method to make it happen. The only other action we need to perform is to set `self.refNP` to a dummy position so that the `setEffects()` method will have something to aim `self.projModel` at.

The last thing we should talk about is the `destroy()` method. In order for our `MachineGun` class to clean itself up properly, we had to set all of our Intervals equal to `None` type objects. Keep that in mind when using Intervals going forward.

This is an example of the true power of Panda3D's `Interval` system, combining several actions that need to occur over a period of time into a single script that keeps the code clean and easy to use.

Time for action – adding collision detection to the MachineGun

A weapon that can't hit anything isn't much good to us. In order to hit things, we need to use collision detection. Let's go ahead and add collision detection to our MachineGun class so we can shoot some things in the scene.

1. Before we start going hog wild with this, let's create a small explosion effect to use when the laser strikes something. Open a new file and save it as ExplosionClasses_01.py.

2. Place these imports at the top of the file:

```
from direct.interval.IntervalGlobal import *
import random
```

3. Add the class definition and the __init__ method as follows:

```
class Pop:
  def __init__(self, pos):
    rand = random.randint(1,3)
    self.pop = loader.loadModel(
      "../Models/Explosions/Laserburst" + str(rand) + ".bam")
    self.pop.reparentTo(render)
    self.pop.setPos(pos)
    self.pop.find('**/+SequenceNode').node().play(0, 15)

    self.self = self

    self.seq = Sequence(
      Wait(.5),
      Func(self.destroy))
```

4. Now, we just need a destroy() method to clean up after the explosion is finished:

```
  def destroy(self):
    self.pop.removeNode()
    self.self = None
    return
```

5. Resave the file; we're done there. Next, open GunClasses_01.py.

6. Add this line to our section of imports:

```
from ExplosionClasses_01 import *
```

7. Add this new variable to the __init__ method, right underneath our declaration of reloadTime:

```
        self.damage = 10
```

8. Next, change the declaration of `self.firePar` so that it looks like the following code:

```
self.firePar = Parallel(
  Func(self.checkForHit),
  Func(self.setEffects),
  self.flashLerp)
```

9. Scroll down to the `fire()` method. Remove the line that repositions `self.refNP`; we won't need it anymore.

10. Add this new method below the `clearEffects()` method. It will employ a `CollisionRay` we're going to add to the `Cycle` class to check if the laser hit anything.

```
def checkForHit(self):
  self.cycle.trgtrCTrav.traverse(render)
  if(self.cycle.trgtrCHan.getNumEntries() > 0):
    self.cycle.trgtrCHan.sortEntries()
    entry = self.cycle.trgtrCHan.getEntry(0)

    colPoint = entry.getSurfacePoint(render)
    self.refNP.setPos(render, colPoint)

    pop = Pop(colPoint)

    thingHit = entry.getIntoNodePath()
    if(thingHit.hasPythonTag("owner")):
      thingHit.getPythonTag("owner").hit(self.damage)
  else:
    self.refNP.setPos(self.cycle.trgtrCNP, 0, 300, 0)
    pop = Pop(self.cycle.refNP.getPos(render))
```

11. That's it for this file. Resave it as `GunClasses_02.py`.

12. Open `CycleClass_02.py` and update the imports to use the new file for our gun class.

13. Add the following code to the bottom of the `setupCollisions()` method:

```
self.trgtrCN = CollisionNode(self.name + "_TargeterCN")
self.trgtrRay = CollisionRay(0,0,0,0,1,0)
self.trgtrCN.addSolid(self.trgtrRay)
self.trgtrCN.setFromCollideMask(BitMask32.bit(3))
self.trgtrCN.setIntoCollideMask(BitMask32.allOff())
self.trgtrCNP = self.trgtrMount.attachNewNode(self.trgtrCN)

self.trgtrCTrav = CollisionTraverser()
self.trgtrCHan = CollisionHandlerQueue()
self.trgtrCTrav.addCollider(self.trgtrCNP, self.trgtrCHan)
```

14. We'll also add a method that the cycle will perform when it gets hit by something that deals damage. Add this method right below the `bump()` method since it's a similar sort of method to bump:

```
def hit(self, damage):
    print(self.name + " has taken " + str(damage) + " damage!")
    return
```

15. Lastly, scroll down to the `destroy()` method and add the following line right under the line that removes `gRayCNP` to clean up the new `CollisionRay` we've created:

```
self.trgtrCNP.removeNode()
```

16. That's everything in this file. Resave it as `CycleClass_03.py`.

17. Update `RaceClass_01.py` to use `CycleClass_03.py`, and then resave it as `RaceClass_02.py`.

18. Update `WorldClass_01.py` to use `RaceClass_02.py`, and then resave it as `WorldClass_02.py`.

19. Run `WorldClass_02.py` from the command prompt. Try and shoot the AI cycles as they drive past, and try shooting the ground as well.

What just happened?

When we point our lasers at a cycle or the ground and fire them, we see a little explosion at the point of impact. If we hit a cycle, we also get a printout to the command prompt telling us the name of the cycle that got hit, and how much damage it was dealt.

We didn't really have to do anything new to make this work, except for one line in the `Pop` class we made:

```
self.pop.find('**/+SequenceNode').node().play(0, 15)
```

The model that we're loading and referencing with `self.pop` is a flipbook-style animation created with the Panda3D utility **egg-texture-cards**. This line of code is used to tell the animation to play from frame `0` to frame `15`, which is the last frame in the animation. We need this line because without it, the animation may not play as intended. It might be at frame `8` when the explosion appears, and loop around to frame `7` by the time it finishes.

Implementing the main cannon

Next, we'll add the big dog onto our cycles: the main cannon that fires an area of effect blast.

Time for action – creating the main cannon

Fortunately, we'll be able to do a good bit of copying and pasting code we've already written to make the main cannon. Let's get started.

1. Open `ExplosionClasses_01.py`. The first thing we'll do is to make a new kind of explosion for the main cannon.

2. Add a new import to the top of the file:

    ```
    from pandac.PandaModules import *
    ```

3. Copy the entire `Pop` class and paste it into the bottom of the file. Change the class name to `Boom`, and use the find and replace feature of Notepad++ to change `self.pop` into `self.boom` everywhere it appears in the `Boom` class.

4. Change the definition of the `__init__` method for the `Boom` class to look like this:

    ```
    def __init__(self, pos, scale, damage):
    ```

5. Add the following line to the `__init__` method of the `Boom` class, immediately after `self.boom.setPos(pos)`:

    ```
    self.boom.setScale(scale)
    ```

6. At the bottom of the `Boom` class's `__init__` method, add the following block of code:

```
self.boomCN = CollisionNode("BoomCN")
self.boomCS = CollisionSphere(0,0,0,scale)
self.boomCN.addSolid(self.boomCS)
self.boomCN.setIntoCollideMask(BitMask32.allOff())
self.boomCN.setFromCollideMask(BitMask32.bit(4))
self.boomCNP = render.attachNewNode(self.boomCN)
self.boomCNP.setPos(pos)

self.boomCTrav = CollisionTraverser()
self.boomCHan = CollisionHandlerQueue()
self.boomCTrav.addCollider(self.boomCNP, self.boomCHan)

self.checkCollision(damage)
```

7. Now, we need to add the `checkCollision()` method we just put in a call to. Put this method right above the `destroy()` method in the `Boom` class:

```
def checkCollision(self, damage):
  cyclesDamaged = []
  self.boomCTrav.traverse(render)
  if(self.boomCHan.getNumEntries() > 0):
    for E in range(self.boomCHan.getNumEntries()):
      entry = self.boomCHan.getEntry(E)
      cycleHit = entry.getIntoNodePath().getPythonTag("owner")
      if(cycleHit not in cyclesDamaged):
        cycleHit.hit(damage)
        cyclesDamaged.append(cycleHit)
```

8. Finally, we'll edit the `destroy()` method to clean up the collision sphere we made. Add this line, right after `self.boom.removeNode()`:

```
self.boomCNP.removeNode()
```

9. Resave the file as `ExplosionClasses_02.py` and we're done with it. Next, open `GunClasses_02.py`.

10. Update the import to use the new file for explosions.

11. Copy the entire `MachineGun` class and paste it into the bottom of the file. Change the name of this new class to `Cannon`.

12. Change the lines in the __init__ method where we load the `Actor` and model for the gun to look similar to the following code:

```
self.actor = Actor("../Models/CannonActor.egg")
self.model = loader.loadModel("../Models/Cannon.bam")
```

13. Remove this line from the `Cannon` class' __init__ method:

```
self.projModel.setScale(.25, 1, .25)
```

14. Change `reloadTime` to equal `1.5`, and change `self.damage` to equal `75`.

15. Add this new variable to the __init__ method, right underneath our declaration of `self.damage`:

```
self.blastR = 10
```

16. Modify the declaration of `self.flashLerp` to make the flash bigger:

```
self.flashLerp = LerpScaleInterval(self.flashModel,
    reloadTime * .1, Point3(2,2,2), Point3(.2,.2,.2))
```

17. Alter the declaration of `self.fireSeq` to add a longer wait, like this:

```
self.fireSeq = Sequence(self.firePar,
    Func(self.clearEffects),
    Wait(reloadTime * .9))
```

18. Next, change the declaration of `self.firePar` so that it looks like the following code:

```
self.firePar = Parallel(
    Func(self.checkForHit),
    Func(self.setEffects),
    self.flashLerp)
```

19. In the `checkForHit()` method, delete all the lines that contain the `thingHit` variable anywhere in them. Then, edit the method to use `Boom` instead of `Pop`. The method should look similar to the following code when we're finished:

```
def checkForHit(self):
    self.cycle.trgtrCTrav.traverse(render)
    if(self.cycle.trgtrCHan.getNumEntries() > 0):
        self.cycle.trgtrCHan.sortEntries()
        entry = self.cycle.trgtrCHan.getEntry(0)

        colPoint = entry.getSurfacePoint(render)
        self.refNP.setPos(render, colPoint)

        boom = Boom(colPoint, self.blastR, self.damage)
```

```
    else:
      self.refNP.setPos(self.cycle.trgtrCNP, 0, 300, 0)
      boom = Boom(self.refNP.getPos(render),
      self.blastR, self.damage)
```

20. Resave the file as `GunClasses_03.py` and open `CycleClass_03.py`. We need to add the cannons to the cycle, and tie the cannon's fire control to the right mouse button.

21. To start with, update the import of the gun classes to use the new file.

22. Scroll down to the `setupVarsNPs()` method and add the following two lines to it, right underneath where we create our machine guns:

```
    self.CannonMount = self.turretActor.exposeJoint(None,
      "modelRoot", "CannonMount")
    self.cannon = Cannon(self, self.CannonMount)
```

23. Now, scroll down to the `CycleControl()` method and add these lines right above the line where we declare `aimPoint`.

```
      if(self.inputManager.keyMap["mouse3"] == True):
        self.cannon.fire()
```

24. The last edit here is to add these lines to the `destroy()` method, right beneath the lines that remove the machine guns:

```
    self.cannon.destroy()
    self.cannon = None
```

25. Resave the file as `CycleClass_04.py`.

26. Update `RaceClass_02.py` to use `CycleClass_04.py`, and then resave it as `RaceClass_03.py`.

27. Update `WorldClass_02.py` to use `RaceClass_03.py`, and then resave it as `WorldClass_03.py`.

28. Run `WorldClass_03.py` from the command prompt and try out the cannon!

What just happened?

This time we really didn't do anything new at all. By now, we should have noticed that the game tends to skip a little when the guns are first fired. That's because when we use a new explosion, Panda3D needs to load the 16 image files that make up the explosion. Once we've used the explosion already, the images are loaded and the skipping stops. We'll be taking care of this problem in *Chapter 12, Finishing Touches: Getting the Game Ready for the Customer* when we create a pre-loader.

Adding weapon information to the HUD

To make things easier for our player, we're going to add some weapon information to the HUD. We'll also add an energy stat to our cycles that will be used as ammo for the guns, so there's a reason not to just fire everything all the time.

Time for action – adding a new HUD section

For this example we'll mainly be editing the files for our HUD, Cycle, MachineGun, and Cannon classes.

1. Open GunClasses_03.py. First, we have a few small edits to make here.

2. We need labels for the guns to show which HUD elements relate to which gun. Add this line to the __init__ method of the MachineGun class, right under the line that says self.cycle = cycle:

   ```
   self.name = "JR Martin J59 Jabber"
   ```

3. Add this line to the same place in the Cannon class:

   ```
   self.name = "Virtue X-A9 Equalizer"
   ```

4. Each gun needs to have an energy cost associated with it, so add the following line to the MachineGun class, right beneath the line that says self.damage = 10:

   ```
   self.energyCost = 1.25
   ```

5. Add the following line in the same place in the Cannon class:

   ```
   self.energyCost = 5
   ```

6. To actually deduct the energy costs from the cycle's total when the gun is fired, we need to add this line to the fire() method in both the classes, right beneath the line that starts fireSeq:

   ```
   self.cycle.energy -= self.energyCost
   ```

7. Resave the file as GunClasses_04.py and open CycleClass_04.py. Update the gun classes import line to use the new file.

8. Add these two lines to the setupVarsNPs() method, right under the line that says self.handling = 25:

   ```
   self.maxEnergy = 100
   self.energy = self.maxEnergy
   ```

9. Resave the file as CycleClass_05.py and open HUDClass_01.py. It's time to do the real work.

10. Add this line to the __init__ method of the HUD class, right after the line that calls the createLLHUD() method:

    ```
    self.createURHUD(fonts)
    ```

11. Scroll down to `setupCycle` and add the following lines to the bottom of that method:

```
self.guns = [self.cycle.LMG, self.cycle.RMG,
    self.cycle.cannon]
self.gunNames[0]["text"] = self.guns[0].name
self.gunNames[1]["text"] = self.guns[1].name
self.gunNames[2]["text"] = self.guns[2].name
```

12. We need a method to create the new section of the HUD, so add the following method right beneath the `createLLHUD()` method. It's a lot of code, but there's nothing in it that we haven't done before.

```
def createURHUD(self, fonts):
    self.urFrame = DirectFrame(frameSize = (-.6, 0, -.4, 0),
        frameColor = (1,1,1,0),
        parent = base.a2dTopRight)

    energyEgg = loader.loadModel("../Models/EnergyBar.egg")
    self.energyBG = energyEgg.find("**/EnergyBG")
    self.energyBar = energyEgg.find("**/EnergyBar")
    self.energyFrame = energyEgg.find("**/EnergyFrame")
    self.energyBG.reparentTo(self.urFrame)
    self.energyBar.reparentTo(self.energyBG)
    self.energyFrame.reparentTo(self.energyBG)
    self.energyBG.setPos(-.35, 0, -.0375)

    alpha = loader.loadTexture("../Images/ReloadAlpha.png")
    alpha.setFormat(Texture.FAlpha)
    alpha.setWrapU(Texture.WMClamp)

    self.energyBar.setTexture(self.modTS, alpha)

    self.energyText = DirectLabel(text = "100",
        text_font = fonts["orange"], text_scale = .05,
        pos = (-.65, 0, -.0525), text_fg = (1,1,1,1),
        relief = None, text_align = TextNode.ARight,

    self.reloadGreen = loader.loadTexture(
        "../Images/ReloadGreen.png")
    self.reloadRed = loader.loadTexture(
        "../Images/ReloadRed.png").

    self.reloadBars = []
    self.gunNames = []
    for N in range(3):
        self.reloadBars.append(loader.loadModel(
            "../Models/ReloadBar.egg"))
        self.reloadBars[N].reparentTo(self.urFrame)
```

```
    self.reloadBars[N].setPos(-.6, 0, -.1125 + (N * -.05))
    self.reloadBars[N].setScale(.1, 0, .1)
    self.reloadBars[N].setTexture(self.modTS, alpha)
    self.reloadBars[N].setTexOffset(self.modTS, .015, 0)

    self.gunNames.append(DirectLabel(text = "Gun Name",
      text_font = fonts["orange"], text_scale = .035,
      pos = (-.55, 0, -.125 + (N * -.05)),
      text_fg = (1,1,1,1), relief = None,
      text_align = TextNode.ALeft,
      parent = self.urFrame))

return
```

13. Just like with the lower-left corner of the HUD, we need an update method for the upper-right corner. Here's that code; place it in right below the `updateLLHUD()` method:

```
def updateURHUD(self):
  energyRatio = self.cycle.energy / self.cycle.maxEnergy

  self.energyBar.setTexOffset(self.modTS,
    -(1 - energyRatio) + .015, 0)

  self.energyText["text"] = str(int(self.cycle.energy))
  for N in range(3):
    if(self.guns[N].fireSeq.isPlaying() == True):
      if(self.reloadBars[N].getTexture != self.reloadRed):
        self.reloadBars[N].setTexture(self.reloadRed, 1)

      reloadRatio = (self.guns[N].fireSeq.getT()
        / self.guns[N].fireSeq.getDuration())

      self.reloadBars[N].setTexOffset(self.modTS,
        -(1 - reloadRatio) + .015, 0)

    elif(self.reloadBars[N].getTexture() != self.reloadGreen):
      self.reloadBars[N].setTexture(self.reloadGreen, 1)
      self.reloadBars[N].setTexOffset(self.modTS,
        .015, 0)

return
```

14. Scroll down to the `updateHUD()` method and add this line in, right after the call to `updateLLHUD()`:

```
    self.updateURHUD()
```

15. In the `hide()` method, add the following line right beneath the one that hides the lower left `DirectFrame`:

```
    self.urFrame.hide()
```

16. Add this line to the `show()` method as well. It belongs right after the line that shows the lower-left `DirectFrame`:

```
self.urFrame.show()
```

17. Resave the file as `HUDClass_02.py`.

18. Update `RaceClass_03.py` to use `CycleClass_05.py,` and then resave it as `RaceClass_04.py`.

19. Update `WorldClass_03.py` to use `RaceClass_04.py` and `HUDClass_02.py` then resave it as `WorldClass_04.py`.

20. Run `WorldClass_04.py` from the command prompt and fire some of the guns to see the new HUD pieces in action.

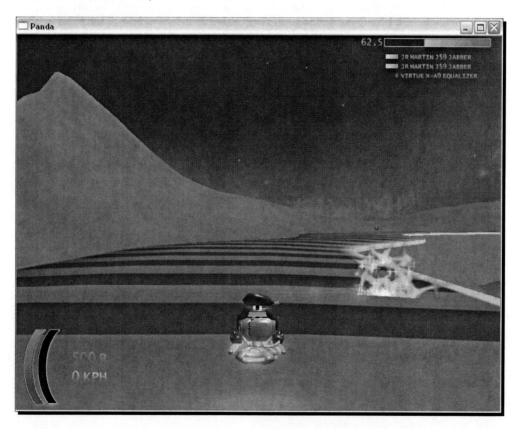

What just happened?

This time we used the `getDuration()` and `getT()` methods of Intervals to take a look at the reload progress on our guns. That allowed us to adjust our reload bars in the HUD according to the status of the guns. These two methods can be very handy for keeping track of our Intervals.

Handling damage response

Before we finish up this chapter, we need to add the elements that will handle damage response to our game. Otherwise, all the guns are meaningless. Here's a list of the things we'll add before we wrap up:

- ◆ Damage impacting shield strength: This is one of the core things we need, to reduce shield strength when the cycle takes damage.
- ◆ Shield and energy recharge: A cycle's shield and energy levels need to be recharged over time, so we'll add in a method to handle that for us.
- ◆ Stability: To keep races tighter and more interesting, we'll add in a system that causes cycles to slow down when they get damaged. That way cycles at the back have a means to slow the cycles up front and catch up to them.
- ◆ Emergency shut down: Because we only have four cycles on the track, it wouldn't be super wise to have a cycle explode or something when its shield drops to zero. We want to keep all the four cycles on the track for the entire race to make it more interesting. Instead, we'll create an emergency shut down mode that a cycle enters when its shield drops to zero.
- ◆ Emergency shut down warning: To notify the player of what's going on when their cycle enters emergency shut down, we'll add a warning message to the HUD.

Time for action – finalizing weapons with damage response

We're almost done with this chapter, but that doesn't mean we still don't have a lot to do. Let's stay focused and finish our cycle combat system so we can move on.

1. Open `CycleClass_05.py`. Most of the changes we need to make will happen here.

2. Our first order of business is with `setupVarsNPs`. We need to add four more variables to our list of cycle attributes. Place the following lines right after the line that says `self.energy = self.maxEnergy`:

```
self.stability = 25
self.shieldRchrg = 10
self.energyRchrg = 5
self.shutDown = False
```

3. Scroll down to `cycleControl` next. The player shouldn't be able to control the cycle during emergency shut down, so change the `if(self.active == True):` line to look like this:

```
if(self.active == True and self.shutDown == False):
```

4. We also need to add a new method call to `cycleControl`. Place this line right after the call to the `checkMarkers()` method:

```
self.recharge(dt)
```

5. Let's go ahead and add the new `recharge()` method we just made a call to. Place this code just below the `checkMarkers()` method:

```
def recharge(self, dt):
  if(self.energy < self.maxEnergy and self.shutDown == False):
    newEnergy = self.energy + (self.energyRchrg * dt)
    if(newEnergy > self.maxEnergy):
      self.energy = self.maxEnergy
    else:
      self.energy = newEnergy
  if(self.shield <= 0 and self.shutDown == False):
    self.shutDown = True
    self.throttle = 0
    self.shield = 0
  if(self.shutDown == True):
    newShield = self.shield + (self.shieldRchrg * dt) * 10
    if(newShield >= self.maxShield):
      self.shutDown = False
  elif(self.shield < self.maxShield):
    newShield = self.shield + (self.shieldRchrg * dt)
  else:
    return
  if(newShield <= self.maxShield):
    self.shield = newShield
  else:
    self.shield = self.maxShield
  return
```

6. The last change we make to the cycle will be an update to the `hit()` method. A rewrite of it, actually. Change the `hit()` method to look like the following code:

```
def hit(self, damage):
  self.shield -= damage
  instability = (damage / 2) - self.stability
  if(instability > 0):
    self.speed -= instability
  return
```

7. Resave the file as `CycleClass_06.py` and open `HudClass_02.py`. To start with, add the following line of code to our imports:

```
from direct.interval.IntervalGlobal import *.
```

8. Next, put the following line in the `__init__` method right after the call to `createURHUD()`:

```
self.createWarning(fonts)
```

9. We'll make the new `createWarning()` method next. Place the following block of code right after the `createURHUD()` method:

```
def createWarning(self, fonts):
  self.warning = DirectLabel(
    text = "*** Emergency Shut Down Active ***",
    text_font = fonts["orange"], text_scale = .1,
    text_fg = (1,1,1,0), relief = None,
    text_align = TextNode.ACenter,
    parent = base.aspect2d)
  self.warningLerp = LerpFunc(self.fadeWarning,
    fromData = 1,
    toData = 0,
    duration = .5)
  self.warningSeq = Sequence(
    Func(self.showWarning),
    Wait(1),
    self.warningLerp,
    Wait(.5))
  return
```

10. Scroll down to `updateHUD()` and add the following code right after the call to `updateURHUD()`. Make sure it's indented far enough to fall under the domain of the `if` statement.

```
if(self.cycle.shutDown == True and
  self.warningSeq.isPlaying() == False):
  self.warningSeq.loop()
if(self.cycle.shutDown == False and
  self.warningSeq.isPlaying() == True):
  self.warningSeq.finish()
```

11. We'll finish up with two little baby methods that go at the end of the class:

```
def showWarning(self):
  self.warning["text_fg"] = (1,1,1,1)
```

```
                    return
                def fadeWarning(self, T):
                    self.warning["text_fg"] = (1,1,1,T)
                    return
```

12. Resave the file as `HUDClass_03.py`.

13. Update `RaceClass_04.py` to use `CycleClass_06.py`, and then resave it as `RaceClass_05.py`.

14. Update `WorldClass_04.py` to use `RaceClass_05.py` and `HUDClass_03.py` then resave it as `WorldClass_05.py`.

15. Run `WorldClass_05.py` from the command prompt. The easiest way to test what we've added is to shoot the cannon at the ground right next to the cycle so the cycle gets hit by the explosion.

What just happened?

We used a new type of Interval in our HUD class this time around. The LerpFunc Interval calls a function or method and passes in a piece of data, which is smoothly adjusted over the duration of the Interval. We took advantage of that to make our warning message slowly fade out after it appears.

Pop quiz – Intervals

Intervals are both simple and complicated, so we should clear up the following points to cement our understanding:

1. What are the differences between an Interval and a task?
2. What is a Sequence? What is a Parallel? What can we put into them?
3. What do we use Func() and Wait() for? What do they do?
4. Which are the two methods that can tell us if an Interval is playing? What is the difference between them?
5. How do we find out how long an Interval is?
6. How do we find out how long an Interval has been playing for?

Summary

We spent a good part of this chapter working on the game to make up for the time we lost in the last chapter. Even so, we talked about some very important things we can do with Panda3D.

We talked about how to implement mouse picking and what we might use it for. We also discussed the different types of Intervals, their strengths, and how to employ them to best effect.

So far, our game has been under a vow of silence. In the next chapter, that vow comes to an end with the introduction of sound effects. Get ready to really hear those engines roaring!

11
What's that Noise? Using Sound

The time has come to add the last piece of our environment: the sound. Using sound in Panda3D is a simple matter, so we'll take care of it quickly.

The topics we cover in this chapter will be:

- ◆ Editing `Config.prc`
- ◆ Adding music
- ◆ Adding sound effects
- ◆ About sound intervals

Editing Config.prc

Before we start using sound in our game, there is something we have to do. By default, Panda3D is set up to use an audio software package called FMOD. This package is very effective, and works marvellously, and is absolutely free for non-commercial use. However, in order to sell a product that uses it, a license fee of several thousand U.S. dollars must be paid.

The purpose of this book is to enable us to create commercial games using free components. For that reason, we can't take advantage of FMOD, and we'll be using the open source audio library called OpenAL. Panda3D comes with OpenAL integration, but it must be selected by editing the `Config.prc` file.

Panda3D's `Config.prc` file is where many default options for Panda3D are set. It decides which rendering system will be used, OpenGL or DirectX; the size of the default Panda window; which audio library will be used, and more. We'll talk about more of these variables in the next chapter when we start packing up our game.

Time for action – selecting an audio library

`Config.prc` is just a text file, so we don't need anything more than Notepad++ to change our audio library.

1. Open a Windows Explorer window and navigate to our Panda3D installation folder. In that folder, there will be a folder called `etc`. The default path is `C:\Panda3D-1.6.2\etc`. Open the `etc` folder.

2. Open the `Config.prc` file in the `etc` folder in Notepad++.

3. Scroll down to the following line:

    ```
    audio-library-name p3fmod_audio
    ```

4. Edit this line so that it looks similar to the following line of code:

    ```
    audio-library-name p3openal_audio
    ```

5. That's it. Resave the file and close it.

What just happened?

Since we aren't using any audio in the game yet, there won't be any sort of difference in the game as a result of this change. All we've done is alter the audio library, which we're making use of, to play sounds.

Adding music

The first thing we'll do is add some background music to our game. Before we do, though, let's talk a little about audio in Panda3D.

The audio system in Panda3D is not the strongest feature of the engine. There are numerous ways to load audio files, and several of the commands can be quite confusing. Even so, it's pretty easy to get the hang of using it. To start with, we'll talk about the two pieces of the audio system:

*   `AudioSound` Objects: Objects that contain individual sounds
*   `AudioManager` Objects: Objects that group multiple sounds together

AudioSound objects

`AudioSound` is the class that contains a specific sound file. An instance of this class is returned when a sound file is loaded. That's really all there is to it. Here are the methods that can be used to control an `AudioSound`:

- `mySound.play()`: Plays the sound.

- `mySound.stop()`: Stops the sound.

- `mySound.status()`: Returns one of three constants that indicate the status of the sound. The constants are `AudioSound.BAD`, which indicates there is a problem with the sound; `AudioSound.READY`, which indicates that the sound is working and is not currently playing; and `AudioSound.PLAYING`, which means the sound is currently playing. The following line of code is an example for how to use status:

  `if(mySound.status() == mySound.PLAYING):`

- `mySound.setVolume([n])`: Sets the volume for the sound. The input should be a float between 0 and 1.

- `mySound.setBalance([n])`: Sets the balance for the sound to determine which speaker the sound is primarily heard from. A value of -1 is all the way to the left speaker, and 1 is all the way to the right speaker.

- `mySound.setLoop([True] or [False])`: Sets the sound either to loop when played, or not. This is the most reliable method for making a sound loop, and should be used instead of looping sound Intervals.

- `mySound.setLoopCount([n])`: This method will tell the sound to loop a given number of times and then stop looping. Passing in a 0 will cause the sound to loop continuously forever, a 1 will play the sound only once, and any higher integer will cause the sound to loop that number of times.

- `mySound.length()`: Returns the length of the sound file in seconds.

- `mySound.getTime()`: Returns the position of the "playback head" in the sound, in seconds. This will tell us how far into the sound the playback currently is.

- `mySound.setTime([n])`: Tells the sound to start playing from the given position, in seconds, into the sound. The sound will play immediately; calling the `play()` method after calling the `setTime()` method will cause the sound to start over at the beginning.

- `mySound.setPlayRate([n])`: Sets the play rate for the sound. Providing a 2 as the argument will make the sound play at double speed, a 0.5 will make it play at half speed, and a -1 will make it play backwards at normal rate. This method can be given any positive or negative number, but numbers close to 1 are the most common.

- `mySound.getPlayRate`: Returns the play rate of the sound.

AudioManager objects

AudioManager objects serve as grouping objects for sounds and allow multiple sounds to be controlled at once. The main reason to use AudioManager objects is to enable, disable, or set the volume on groups of sounds with a single call.

- ◆ myAudioManager.setActive([True] or [False]): Sets whether the AudioManager is currently active or not. An inactive AudioManager won't allow any of its sounds to be played.

- ◆ myAudioManager.setVolume([n]): Sets a master volume control for all sounds in the AudioManager.

- ◆ mySound = myAudioManager.getSound([FilePath]): Loads a sound into the AudioManager.

Panda3D automatically creates an AudioManager object for music during startup. It also creates a list to store AudioManager objects for sound effects, and puts one AudioManager in the list to start with. We can access these AudioManager objects with the following code:

```
sfxMgr = base.sfxManagerList[0]musicMgr = base.musicManager
```

In base, we can find a couple of methods that interact with these two AudioManagers specifically. These methods are used for turning sound on and off. They will affect base.musicManager and/or every AudioManager in base.sfxManagerList.

- ◆ base.disableAllAudio(): Sets base.musicManager and every entry of base.sfxManagerList to inactive

- ◆ base.enableAllAudio(): Sets base.musicManager and every entry of base.sfxManagerList to active

- ◆ base.enableMusic([True] or [False]): Sets base.musicManager to active or inactive depending on input

- ◆ base.enableSoundEffects([True] or [False]): Sets every entry in base.sfxManagerList to active or inactive depending on input

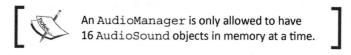

An AudioManager is only allowed to have 16 AudioSound objects in memory at a time.

For music, 16 sounds are generally more than enough, but it is possible for a game to need to play more than 16 sound effects at one time. To handle this, we can create additional AudioManager objects and add them to the list of sound effect managers with this code:

```
from pandac.PandaModules import AudioManager
myMgr = AudioManager.createAudioManager() base.addSfxManager(myMgr)
```

Time for action – creating background music

Enough talk, action speaks louder than words. Let's add some background music to our game.

1. Open `WorldClass_00.py` from the `Chapter11` folder.

2. Scroll down to the bottom of the `__init__` method and add the following four lines of code there:

```
musicMgr = base.musicManager
self.music = musicMgr.getSound(
"../Sound/Loveshadow-Takin_Yo_Time_(The_Wingman_Mix).wav")
    self.music.setLoop(True)
    self.music.play()
```

3. Resave the file as `WorldClass_01.py` and run it from the command prompt.

What just happened?

Now we've got music! That's all there was to it. We just loaded the sound file into the `AudioManager` with `getSound`, set it to loop with `setLoop(True)`, and told it to play with the `play` method.

The song we loaded is called `Takin Yo Time (The Wingman Mix)` and is by an artist named `Loveshadow`. The song was released under a Creative Commons license that allows it to be used in commercial works as long as the artist receives credit for it. There are several websites where music released under this kind of license can be found, but this particular song was taken from `http://dig.ccmixter.org/`.

 Note that we didn't use an MP3 file for the song, but a wav file instead. This is because using MP3 requires a license that costs several thousand dollars, such as FMOD. There is also the alternative format, Ogg Vorbis, but unfortunately OpenAL doesn't play Ogg Vorbis files very well.

Pop quiz – making music

Before we move on to adding sound effects, answer the following questions about the Panda3D sound system to cement our understanding:

1. What is an `AudioManager`?

2. What `AudioManager` objects are created by default, and what can we do with them?

3. What method do we use to load a sound into an `AudioManager`?

4. How do we make a sound loop?

Adding sound effects

Our next step is to add some sound effects for the cycles' engines and weapons. Because these are sounds that are being produced by actual objects in our world, we want their volume to be dependent on how far those objects are from the camera. That will give our sound environment a more realistic feel.

Panda3D comes with a utility called `Audio3DManager` that makes it easy to set this up. Don't let the name confuse you, though; this isn't a new kind of `AudioManager`. It's actually a wrapper that modifies an existing `AudioManager`. Using this wrapper, we can tie a sound to an object, define an object that is the "listener", and the volume of the sound will drop as the object it's attached to gets further from the "listener".

We're going to make four new `AudioManager` objects that we will use for cycles. They'll be owned by the `Race` class because we don't really want to be creating and destroying them each time we make new cycles. Instead, we'll just pass them along from `Race` class into the `Cycle` class, and let the cycles borrow them for a while.

These four `AudioManagers` will have `Audio3DManager` wrappers applied to them. In actuality, it's the wrappers we'll be passing around and making use of instead of the `AudioManagers` themselves.

Time for action – generating 3D audio with Audio3DManager

Are we ready to see how this works? Let's go, then!

1. Open `RaceClass_00.py` from the `Chapter11` folder.

2. We'll start with two new imports. `AudioManager` object is in the `pandac.PandaModules` package, but `Audio3DManager` object is in the `direct.showbase` package.

   ```
   from pandac.PandaModules import *
   from direct.showbase import Audio3DManager
   ```

3. Next, we're going to add a nice block of code to the __init__ method to set up our `AudioManager` objects and their wrappers:

   ```
   self.amList = []
   self.a3DList = []
   for N in range(4):
     self.amList.append(AudioManager.createAudioManager())
     base.addSfxManager(self.amList[N])
     self.audio3D.append(Audio3DManager.Audio3DManager(
       base.sfxManagerList[N + 1], camera))
     self.a3DList[N].setDropOffFactor(.1)
   ```

4. Next, scroll down to the `createDemoRace()` method and change the lines that create our cycles to look like the following code:

```
self.cycles.append(Cycle(self.inputManager,
    self.track, self.a3DList[0], 1, "Bert", ai = True))
self.cycles.append(Cycle(self.inputManager,
    self.track, self.a3DList[1], 2, "Ernie", ai = True))
self.cycles.append(Cycle(self.inputManager,
    self.track, self.a3DList[2], 3, "William", ai = True))
self.cycles.append(Cycle(self.inputManager,
    self.track, self.a3DList[3], 4, "Patrick", ai = True))
```

5. Next, scroll down to the `createRace()` method and change the cycle lines there to look like the following code:

```
self.cycles.append(Cycle(self.inputManager,
    self.track, self.a3DList[0], 1, "Bert"))
self.cycles.append(Cycle(self.inputManager,
    self.track, self.a3DList[1], 2, "Ernie", ai = True))
self.cycles.append(Cycle(self.inputManager,
    self.track, self.a3DList[2], 3, "William", ai = True))
self.cycles.append(Cycle(self.inputManager,
    self.track, self.a3DList[3], 4, "Patrick", ai = True))
```

6. Lastly, change the import line for the `Cycle` class file to load `CycleClass_01`. With that, we're done here. Resave the file as `RaceClass_01.py`. Then, open the `CycleClass_00.py` file.

7. First, update the import of the `GunClasses_00` file to `GunClasses_01`. Then, move down to the `__init__` method and update the definition line to accept a new argument:

```
def __init__(self, inputManager, track, audio3D, startPos,
    name, ai = None):
```

8. Once that is done, update the call to the `setupVarsNPs()` method to pass that new argument along:

```
self.setupVarsNPs(audio3D, startPos, name)
```

9. Now, scroll down to the `setupVarsNPs()` definition and change it to accept that new argument:

```
def setupVarsNPs(self, audio3D, startPos, name):
```

10. Move down right below the line where we store the cycle's name and add a line to store a reference to the `Audio3DManager`:

```
self.audio3D = audio3D
```

11. We'll need to pass the `Audio3DManager` along to the weapons as well. Scroll down to the lines where we create the weapons and change that block of code to look like the following code:

```
self.LMGMount = self.turretActor.exposeJoint(None,
    "modelRoot", "LMGMount")
self.RMGMount = self.turretActor.exposeJoint(None,
    "modelRoot", "RMGMount")
self.LMG = MachineGun(self, self.LMGMount, self.audio3D)
self.RMG = MachineGun(self, self.RMGMount, self.audio3D)
self.CannonMount = self.turretActor.exposeJoint(None,
    "modelRoot", "CannonMount")
self.cannon = Cannon(self, self.CannonMount, self.audio3D)
```

12. Once that's done, add the following block of code right after the lines we just updated. This will give us our engine noise:

```
self.engineSfx = self.audio3D.loadSfx("../Sound/Engine.wav")
self.audio3D.attachSoundToObject(self.engineSfx, self.root)
self.engineSfx.setPlayRate(.5)
self.engineSfx.setLoop(True)
self.engineSfx.setVolume(2)
self.engineSfx.play()
```

13. We want the engine sound to change based on the speed of the cycle, so move down to the `SpeedCheck()` method and add the following two lines of code to the bottom of it:

```
speedRatio = self.speed / self.maxSpeed
self.engineSfx.setPlayRate(.5 + speedRatio)
```

14. Our last change will be in the `destroy()` method. If we destroy `self.root` when the sound is trying to use it as a location reference, we'll create an error, so we need to remove the sound from `self.root`. Add the following line to the `destroy()` method, right before `self.cycle = None`:

```
self.audio3D.detachSound(self.engineSfx)
```

15. Save the file as `CycleClass_01.py` and open `GunClass_00.py`. Update the import in this file to use `ExplosionClasses_01` instead of `ExplosionClasses_00` since we'll be updating the `Boom` class with a noise, too.

16. Next, change the definition for the `MachineGun` class' `__init__` method to accept the `Audio3DManager` we're passing to it:

```
def __init__(self, cycle, mount, audio3D)
```

17. Do the same for the `Cannon` class' `__init__` method definition as well.

18. In the `__init__` method of both the classes, add the following three lines right below the line that exposes the muzzle joint and creates `self.muzzle`:

```
self.audio3D = audio3D
self.fireSfx = self.audio3D.loadSfx("../Sound/LaserShot.wav")
self.audio3D.attachSoundToObject(self.fireSfx, self.muzzle)
```

19. Lastly, we need to add a line that will play the sound effect we've made when the gun is fired. Add the following line into the `fire()` methods of both classes, right after the line that starts `self.fireSeq`:

```
self.fireSfx.play()
```

20. There's only one change that we need to make to the `Cannon` class. Scroll down to the `checkForHit()` method of the `Cannon` class and find the two different spots where we are creating an instance of the `Boom` class. Update both of those lines so that they pass `self.audio3D` as the last argument. That will make them look like this:

```
boom = Boom(colPoint, self.blastR, self.damage,
    self.audio3D)
else:
    self.refNP.setPos(self.cycle.trgtrCNP, 0, 300, 0)
    boom = Boom(self.refNP.getPos(render),
        self.blastR, self.damage, self.audio3D)
```

21. Finally, add this line to the bottom of the `destroy()` method of both the classes:

```
self.audio3D.detachSound(self.fireSfx)
```

22. Save the file as `GunClasses_01.py` and open `ExplosionClasses_00.py`. We need to add a sound to our `Boom` class as well.

23. Scroll down to the definition for the `__init__` method of the `Boom` class. Update it to accept the new argument:

```
def __init__(self, pos, scale, damage, audio3D):
```

24. Add the following four lines to the bottom of the __init__ method:

```
self.audio3D = audio3D
self.boomSfx = self.audio3D.loadSfx("../Sound/LaserBoom.wav")
self.audio3D.attachSoundToObject(self.boomSfx, self.boom)
self.boomSfx.play()
```

25. Still in the Boom class, add this line to the destroy() method right above the line that says self.self = None:

```
self.audio3D.detachSound(self.boomSfx)
```

26. Save the file as ExplosionClasses_01.py and open WorldClass_01.py. Update the imports to use RaceClass_01.py.

27. At the bottom of the __init__ method, add this line just above self.music. play() in order to curb the volume on the background music and make the sounds easier to hear:

```
self.music.setVolume(.5)
```

28. Resave the file as WorldClass_02.py and run it from the command prompt. Listen to the change in the engine noise as the cycle speed increases, and fire the guns to hear the sound effects of them. Shoot the track with the cannon at various distances to hear the difference in volume for the explosion.

What just happened?

This may have seemed like an arduous example, but that's just because we were adding so much. We've got all the sounds we need for our game in place and working exactly how we want, so let's talk a bit about what we used to do it.

Audio3DManager was the shining star this time around. Since it automatically performs the 3D positioning of sounds, we didn't really have to do much with it, but let's talk about the methods and calls we did use.

```
Audio3DManager.Audio3DManager([AudioManager], [Listener NodePath])
```

This is the call that adds an Audio3DManager wrapper to an existing AudioManager. It returns the Audio3DManager wrapper when called, and it takes two arguments. The first is the AudioManager the wrapper will apply to, and the second is the NodePath that will be the listener. If you are using multiple Audio3DManager wrappers, like we are, make sure that they all use the same listener object.

To take advantage of the Audio3DManager wrapper, we had to do two things. The first was to load our sounds through the wrapper, instead of directly from the AudioManager:

```
self.engineSfx = self.audio3D.loadSfx("../Sound/Engine.wav")
```

When we do this, we have to use a method called `loadSfx()` instead of `getSound()`. This can be a source of confusion because it's inconsistent, so be careful about it.

We also had to tie the sounds to an object in the scene graph so that the `Audio3DManager` would know what their position in the world is. For that, we used the `attachSoundToObject()` method of the `Audio3DManager`:

```
self.audio3D.attachSoundToObject(self.engineSfx, self.root)
```

The arguments for this method are simple. The first is the sound object, and the second is the `NodePath` to tie it to.

We also used a method of the Audio3DManager called `setDropOffFactor`. This method controls how quickly a volume's sound fades over distance. It can be given values from `0` to `10`, with values below `1` causing the sound to travel farther, and values above `1` causing the sound to fade over a shorter distance.

About sound intervals

Sound intervals are much like the `Func Interval`, which lets a function or method be called as part of a `Sequence` or `Parallel`. They allow a sound to be played as part of an `Interval`. Unfortunately, they don't provide much functionality beyond that, and trying to loop a sound by putting it in a `SoundInterval` and looping the `Interval` doesn't work very well. Really, the only reason to use a sound interval is when we're using `Sequence` and `Parallel` to create long scripts that need sounds to play at certain parts in them, for example a cinematic sequence in a role-playing game. That's why we didn't use any in this chapter; we don't have any really complicated scripting going on. We already went over the sound interval constructor, but for the sake of completeness we'll repeat it here. This is taken from the Panda3D manual:

```
SoundInterval(
    mySound,
    loop = 0 or 1,
    duration = myDuration,
    volume = myVolume,
    startTime = myStartTime)
```

Pop quiz – sounding off

This was another long chapter, so let's go back to some of the topics we covered to make sure our understanding is absolute.

1. What is an `Audio3DManager`?
2. What method do we use to load a sound into an `Audio3DManager`?

Summary

We're almost done with our game! We spent this chapter putting together the sound environment by adding a background music file and sound effects for our weapons and engines.

Now, we just need to apply a little polish and get the game ready to ship to customers!

12

Finishing Touches: Getting the Game Ready for the Customer

We've had a long, fun trip together through Panda3D and it's both sad and exciting to have it finally coming to an end. That is the fate of all things, and our time together is no exception. Before we go our separate ways, however, we need to put some finishing touches on our game and talk about a few more topics.

Those topics are:

◆ Garbage collection

◆ Creating a Preloader

◆ File handling

◆ Replacing the mouse cursor

◆ Creating an installer

Collecting garbage

Python will automatically garbage collect a custom class instance when all the references to that instance are removed. In theory, this makes garbage collection as simple as cleaning up those references, but because there are so many different places and reasons for these references, garbage collection can quickly grow complicated. Following these steps will help to ensure that a custom class instance is properly garbage collected.

◆ Call `removeNode` on all `NodePaths` in the scene graph—the first step is to clear out the `NodePaths` that the custom class has added to the scene graph. If this step isn't accomplished, it won't necessarily prevent the custom class instance from being garbage collected, but it could. Even if the custom class instance is still garbage collected, the scene graph itself will retain references to the `NodePaths` that haven't been cleared out and they will remain in the scene graph. There is one exception to this rule: when a parent `NodePath` has `removeNode` called on it that ultimately results in the removal of its child `NodePaths`, so long as nothing else retains a reference to them. However, relying on this behavior is an easy way to make mistakes so it's better to manually remove all of the `NodePaths` a custom class adds to the scene graph.

◆ Clean out collision systems—when cleaning up collision systems there are some methods that need to be called to ensure that the collision system doesn't retain references to `NodePaths`. The references we're worried about are created when we call `addCollider` on a traverser or handler. We need to call `removeCollider` on the traversers or handlers to undo that reference.

Note that if the traverse and handler are being garbage collected themselves then we don't need to use `removeCollider`. When the traverser and handler are cleaned up, the references to the colliders will be lost anyway.

◆ Call `delete` on all `Actors`—just calling `removeNode` on an actor isn't enough. Calling `delete` will remove ties to animations, exposed joints, and so on to ensure that all the extra components of the `Actor` are removed from memory as well.

◆ Call `destroy` on all `DirectGui` objects—some `DirectGui` objects, `DirectButtons` in particular, integrate with other Panda3D systems and can result in references that will keep the custom class instance alive. Either way, it's best to remove these objects from the 2D scene graph manually anyway, just like with `NodePaths` and the regular scene graph. The one exception to this is `DirectDialog`. For that `DirectGui` object, we need to use a method called `cleanup` instead of `destroy`.

◆ Set all `Intervals`, `Sequences`, and `Parallels` equal to `None`—it's very common for `Intervals`, `Sequences`, and `Parallels` to retain references to something in the class and prevent the class instance from being cleaned up. To be safe, it's best to remove the references to these `Intervals` so that they get cleaned up themselves and any references they have to the class are removed.

◆ Detach all 3D sounds connected to class `NodePaths`—3D sounds won't actually retain references to the custom class, but if the `NodePaths` they are attached to are removed with `removeNode` and the sounds aren't detached, they'll generate an error and crash the program when they try to access the removed `NodePaths`. Play it safe and detach the sounds.

- End all tasks running in the class—the task manager will retain a reference to the class instance so long as the class instance has a task running, so set up all of the tasks in the custom class to end themselves with `return task.done`. This is the most reliable way to stop them and clear the reference to the custom class in the task manager.

- If the custom class inherits from `DirectObject`, call `self.ignoreAll()`—Panda3D's message system will also retain a reference to the custom class if it is set up to receive messages. To be on the safe side, every class that inherits from `DirectObject` and will be deleted during runtime should call `self.ignoreAll()` to tell the message system that the class is no longer listening to messages. That will remove the reference.

- Remove all direct references to the custom class instance—naturally, the custom class instance won't get cleaned up if something is referencing it directly, either through a self reference like in our Explosion classes, or because it was created as a "child" of another class the way our guns are "children" of our cycles. All of these references need to be removed. This also includes references to the custom class instance placed in `PythonTags`.

We've already done a good bit of garbage collection work with the destroy methods we've added to many of our classes, but now is the time when we put it to the test. We're going to use the `__del__` method to ensure that the classes we create and remove instances of are being properly removed from memory.

The `__del__` method is similar to the `__init__` method in that we don't call it ourselves; it gets called when something happens. `__init__` is called when a new instance of the class is created; `__del__` is called when an instance of the class is garbage collected. It's a pretty common thought to want to put some important clean up steps in the `__del__` method itself, but this isn't wise. In fact, it's best not to have a `__del__` method in any of our classes in the final product because the `__del__` method can actually hinder proper garbage collection. We're just going to create `__del__` methods that print to our command prompt to notify us that our class instances are being identified as ready for removal by Python's garbage collection system. Once we know that they are, we'll get rid of these methods.

Testing one class at a time will make our lives easier, so that's what we'll do. Also, we only need to check for proper clean up on classes that we create and destroy during runtime. We'll start with the Explosion classes, then we'll do the gun classes, and finally we'll do the `Cycle` and `Track` classes.

Time for action – collecting garbage from the Explosion classes

We're starting with the `Explosion` classes because they don't create instances of any other classes. A depth-up kind of strategy is as good as any for this kind of testing.

1. Open the `ExplosionClasses_00.py` file from the `Chapter12` folder.

2. Add the following method to the bottom of the `Pop` class:

```
def __del__(self):
    print("Pop Removed")
```

3. Add this method to the bottom of the `Boom` class:

```
def __del__(self):
    print("Boom Removed")
```

4. Resave the file with the same name and run the game. Watch the command prompt for our prints when `Pops` and `Booms` vanish.

5. We don't see the prints! That's because we have two errors in our classes that need to be fixed. Firstly, we're using a `Sequence` to call our `destroy` method after a set amount of time, but we aren't starting that `Sequence` so our `destroy` method is never called! Add this line of code to the bottom of the `__init__` method for both classes:

```
self.seq.start()
```

6. The second error is a little more subtle. Our `Sequence` is constructed with a `Func Interval`, and we give one of our class methods to that `Func Interval`. That means the `Sequence` is storing a reference to the method in the `Func Interval`, and that reference is enough to keep the class instance alive. Add this line to both `destroy` methods, right above the line that says `self.self = None`:

```
self.seq = None
```

7. Resave the file as `ExplosionClasses_01.py`. Open `GunClasses_00.py` and update its import to use `ExplosionClasses_01.py`, and then resave it with the same name.

8. Run the game again and watch the command prompt. This time we get our printouts telling us that the `Pops` and `Booms` have been removed from memory.

9. Remove both of the `__del__` methods from the classes and resave the file as `ExplosionClasses_02.py`.

What just happened?

It's a good thing we checked the `Explosion` classes, since they weren't cleaning up properly. With the number of them that get created over the course of the game, that could have been a serious memory bug. Imagine hundreds of instances of those classes clogging up the computer's memory!

Time for action – collecting garbage from the Gun classes

Let's move right along to our `Gun` classes. These are created and destroyed with the cycles, so we need to make sure they are getting garbage collected properly.

1. Open the `GunClasses_00.py` file from the `Chapter12` folder. Update the imports section to use `ExplosionClasses_02.py`.

2. Testing comes first, so put the following method at the bottom of the `MachineGun` class:

   ```
   def __del__(self):
       print("Machine Gun Removed")
   ```

3. Then, put this method at the bottom of the `Cannon` class:

   ```
   def __del__(self):
       print("Cannon Removed")
   ```

4. This time, resave the file as `GunClasses_01.py`. Open `CycleClass_00.py` and update the import to use `Gunclasses_01.py`, then resave the file with *Ctrl+S* and run the game. Click the **New Game** menu button to destroy some cycles and check our garbage collection on the guns.

5. This time we got it in the first try, as we can see from the printout to the command prompt shown in the following screenshot. Go ahead and remove the `__del__` methods from both Gun classes and resave the file.

What just happened?

As shown in the previous image, all three guns are being removed from each cycle. That's what we like to see, nice and easy. Now, let's move on to the `Cycle` class.

Time for action – collecting garbage from the Cycle class

We're going to cheat a little on this one. We won't test it right away because with the current `destroy` method, garbage collection isn't going to happen.

1. Open the `CycleClass_00.py` file.

2. Our destroy method is missing two things that will prevent the cycles from getting cleaned up. First off, our `Cycle` class inherits from `DirectObject` and is set to accept a message when it collides with another cycle. The Panda3D message system is going to retain a reference to the class instance. To get rid of that, we need to call `ignoreAll`. Add this line of code to the `destroy` method, right before we set `self.cycle` to None:

    ```
    self.ignoreAll()
    ```

3. The other problem is related to `self.shieldCN`. Remember way back to the chapter on collisions when we used `setPythonTag` to attach a reference to the class instance to `self.shieldCN`? Well, that reference is enough to keep the class instance alive. It has to be done away with. Put this line of code right below the line we added in the last step to remove the offending reference:

    ```
    self.shieldCN.clearPythonTag("owner")
    ```

4. Now, let's go ahead and add our `__del__` method to the bottom of the class:

    ```
    def __del__(self):
        print("Cycle Removed")
    ```

5. Save the files as `CycleClass_01.py` and open `RaceClass_00.py`. Update the import, and then resave that file with the same name. Run the game and click the **New Game** menu button to destroy some cycles. Instead of clicking **Yes** when the game asks if you're ready, click **Exit**. We'll see the following printed out to our command prompt. Count the number of times **Cycle Removed** is being printed.

6. If we count the number of printouts in the command prompt, we can see that there are seven of them. There should be eight! When we returned to the demo race, one of our cycles didn't get cleaned up.

7. The destroy method in the `Cycle` class is perfect; the culprit causing this error is actually our HUD class. Remember that we pass a reference of a cycle into the HUD class, and it stores it until we pass in a different one. To fix this, open HUDClass_00.py and add this line of code to the bottom of the `hide` method:

```
self.cycle = None
```

8. Save the file as HUDClass_01.py and update the `World` class' imports to use the new file. Then, run the game and follow the same testing procedure as we did in step 5.

9. Once we've verified that the last cycle is being garbage collected, remove the `__del__` method from the `Cycle` class and resave the file.

What just happened?

All eight cycles are being properly garbage collected now. That covers all but one of our classes that we create and remove instances of during runtime. The last one is the `Track` class, so let's handle that next.

Time for action – collecting garbage from the Track class

Let's test the `destroy` method we've built up for the `Track` class so far.

1. Open `TrackClass_00.py`.

2. Type in our `__del__` method to the bottom of the class:

   ```
   def __del__(self):
       print("Track Removed")
   ```

3. Resave the file with the same name and run the game. Test the clean up by clicking the **New Game** button and checking the command prompt.

4. As shown in the following screenshot, this time our garbage collection is working fine. Remove the `__del__` method from the `Track` class and resave the file again.

```
C:\BGP3D\Chapter12>python worldclass_00.py
DirectStart: Starting the game.
Known pipe types:
  wglGraphicsPipe
(all display modules loaded.)
Track Removed

C:\BGP3D\Chapter12>
```

What just happened?

That does it for our garbage collection! This is one of the most important things to get right in a game; if it isn't working correctly it will cause memory leaks as the game continues to run and eventually result in poor performance or crashing.

Pop quiz – garbage collection

Garbage collection is often complicated, but it's also very important, so let's double check our knowledge.

1. What steps are required to ensure proper garbage collection of a custom class?

2. When cleaning up collision systems, when is it necessary to use `removeCollider` and when is it not?

Creating a preloader

A preloader is a custom class that loads game assets ahead of time, while providing the player with some indication that the game is loading something. They serve to get the loading out of the way so it interferes with game play as little as possible. For our game, we'll make a preloader with a progress bar.

In order to make a preloader with a progress bar in Panda3D, we'll have to force the game to render frames to our window during the loading process. When the game is stuck in a function or method, it won't update the window automatically. To force an update, we can call `base.graphicsEngine.renderFrame()`. This will do two things for us:

1. It will display the last processed frame in the window.
2. It will process the next frame.

Because of this order of operations, we'll have to make the call twice in order to get the results we want.

Time for action – creating a preloader to load models

Let's get a feel for how this works by creating a preloader to load our models before the game starts.

1. Create a blank new file in Notepad++. Save it as `PreloaderClass_01.py`. Then, add these two import lines to the top of the file:

    ```
    from direct.gui.DirectGui import *
    from pandac.PandaModules import *
    ```

2. It would be easy to just have the preloader load the models and be done with it, but that wouldn't be any different than having a black screen when the game loads. We'd accomplish nothing. We need our preloader to show the loading progress, and that means we need to create some GUI elements. Add in the class definition and `__init__` method, and have them look like this:

    ```
    class Preloader:
      def __init__(self, fonts):
        self.createGraphics(fonts)
    ```

3. Next, we'll add in that `createGraphics` method we just made a call to. We're going to do this in one big shot because the method is going to look very similar to the methods we used to create the HUD components. Even so, let's make sure we get everything right.

    ```
    def createGraphics(self, fonts):
      self.modTS = TextureStage("Modulate")
    ```

```
self.modTS.setMode(TextureStage.MModulate)

self.frame = DirectFrame(frameSize = (-.3, .3, -.2, .2),
    frameColor = (1,1,1,0),
    parent = base.aspect2d)
loaderEgg = loader.loadModel("../Models/EnergyBar.egg")
self.loaderBG = loaderEgg.find("**/EnergyBG")
self.loaderBar = loaderEgg.find("**/EnergyBar")
self.loaderFrame = loaderEgg.find("**/EnergyFrame")
self.loaderBG.reparentTo(self.frame)
self.loaderBar.reparentTo(self.loaderBG)
self.loaderFrame.reparentTo(self.loaderBG)
self.loaderBG.setPos(0, 0, -.2)

alpha = loader.loadTexture("../Images/LoaderAlpha.png")
alpha.setFormat(Texture.FAlpha)
alpha.setWrapU(Texture.WMClamp)

self.loaderBar.setTexture(self.modTS, alpha)

self.text = DirectLabel(
    text = "Loading Suicide Jockeys...",
    text_font = fonts["orange"], text_scale = .1,
    text_fg = (1,1,1,1), relief = None,
    text_align = TextNode.ACenter,
    parent = self.frame)
return
```

4. Scroll back up to the __init__ method and add this line to it:
```
self.prepLoadGroup()
```

5. That line will call this new method, which we should add to the bottom of the class:
```
def prepLoadGroup(self):
    self.models = ["../Models/Track.egg",
            "../Models/Planet.egg",
            "../Models/Ground.egg",
            "../Models/LinearPinkSkySphere.bam",

            "../Models/TargetCone.bam",
            "../Models/ShieldBar.egg",
            "../Models/SpeedBar.egg",
            "../Models/EnergyBar.egg",

            "../Models/RedCycle.bam",
            "../Models/RedTurr.bam",
            "../Models/YellowCycle.bam",
            "../Models/YellowTurr.bam",
```

```
            "../Models/GreenCycle.bam",
            "../Models/GreenTurr.bam",
            "../Models/BlueCycle.bam",
            "../Models/BlueTurr.bam",
            "../Models/Disc.bam",

            "../Models/MachineGun.bam",
            "../Models/Cannon.bam",
            "../Models/LaserFlash.bam",
            "../Models/LaserProj.bam",

            "../Models/Explosions/Laserburst1.bam",
            "../Models/Explosions/Laserburst2.bam",
            "../Models/Explosions/Laserburst3.bam"]
    self.totalItems = len(self.models)

    return
```

6. Scroll back up to the __init__ method again; we have a bit more code to add there. Before we start loading anything, we need to set the loading bar to be initially empty, force a new frame to be displayed, and create a variable that will let us count how many things we've loaded so far. Add these lines to the bottom of the __init__ method:

```
    self.loaderBar.setTexOffset(self.modTS, .015, 0)
    base.graphicsEngine.renderFrame()
    base.graphicsEngine.renderFrame()

    self.itemCount = 0
```

7. We're all set to start loading things now. We'll use a `for` loop to iterate over the list of paths to make it happen:

```
    for M in self.models:
      item = loader.loadModel(M)
      self.itemCount += 1
      progress = self.itemCount / float(self.totalItems)
      self.loaderBar.setTexOffset(self.modTS,
        -progress  + .015, 0)
      base.graphicsEngine.renderFrame()
      base.graphicsEngine.renderFrame()
```

8. There's just one more thing to do in the __init__ method. Add this line to the very bottom of the method:

```
    self.destroy()
```

9. And, finally, we need to add in that `destroy` method. Here it is; place it at the bottom of the class:

    ```
    def destroy(self):
        self.loaderBG.removeNode()
        self.text.destroy()
        self.frame.destroy()
    ```

10. Resave the file with the same name and open `WorldClass_00.py`.

11. Add this line to the imports of custom classes:

    ```
    from PreloaderClass_01 import Preloader
    ```

12. Find the spot in the `__init__` method where we load up our fonts. Right after that, add this line:

    ```
    preloader = Preloader(self.fonts)
    ```

13. Resave the file with the name `WorldClass_01.py` and run the game. We'll see something like this as the game loads up:

What just happened?

That wasn't so bad, was it? In practice, a better way to use this sort of loading screen is in between levels. Since we only really have one level in this game, putting the preloader at the beginning of the game worked just fine. Note that in the places where we called `base.graphicsEngine.renderFrame()` we called it twice. That's necessary because of the order of frame display and processing we discussed before the Time For Action. Keep that in mind for every time we need to force an update to the window.

File handling

Many games require the saving and loading of files or other similar uses of data that is impractical to include in the code itself. Python has its own file input/output module, and the makers of Panda3D have included a similar, thread-safe module that we can use for file I/O in Panda3D applications. We can import it with this line:

```
from direct.stdpy.file import *
```

The interface for `direct.stdpy.file` is identical to the Python interface, and since this book is intended for those already familiar with Python, we won't spend a lot of time explaining this interface. We will talk a little bit about it just to illustrate its use in Panda3D.

To open a file, we use the `open` function. We need to give this function the filename and path as its first argument, and the mode to open the file in as the second:

```
File = open("example.txt", "w")
```

The different modes for open are as follows:

- ◆ `w`—This mode is for writing to the file. If the file does not exist, it will be created. If the file does exist, all its contents will be deleted.
- ◆ `a`—This mode is for appending to the file. Any lines written to a file in this mode will be added to the bottom of the file.
- ◆ `r`—This mode is for reading the file, and does not allow the file to be edited.

To work with a file in a binary format, we can append `b` to the end of the mode, so it's `wb`, `ab`, or `rb`.

When we finish with a file, we need to close it with the `close` method:

```
File.close()
```

Once we have an open file, we can use a few different methods to interact with it.

- ◆ `write`—This method will write a text string to the file. To create a newline in the file, put the line break character "\n" in the string being written.
- ◆ `read`—This will return a string that contains the entire contents of the file.
- ◆ `readline`—This will return a string containing a single line from the file. The file system will automatically remember the current position in the file, so repeated calls to this method will return lines in sequential order.
- ◆ `readlines`—This will return a list of the lines in the file. Each line will be its own entry in the list.

Time for action – reading data from a file

To get a look at file handling in action, we're going to replace the `prepLoadGroup` method of our `Preloader` class with a file loading operation.

1. Open `PreloaderClass_01.py`. Scroll down to the `prepLoadGroup` method and copy this line with *Ctrl+C*:

    ```
    self.totalItems = len(self.models)
    ```

2. Once you have that line copied, delete the entire method.

3. Scroll back up to the __init__ method and find the line where we call self. prepLoadGroup. Highlight that line and hit *Ctrl+V* to paste the line we copied over it, replacing it.

4. Right above that line we just pasted, add this code:

```
file = open("models.txt", "r")
self.models = file.readlines()
file.close()
for N in range(len(self.models)):
    self.models[N] = self.models[N].replace("\n", "")
print(self.models)
```

5. Resave the file as PreloaderClass_02.py. Open WorldClass_01.py, update its import to use PreloaderClass_02, and then save it as WorldClass_02.py. Run it and watch the command prompt for the print statement we put in.

6. Once you've seen the output of that print statement, go ahead and remove the print from the __init__ method of the Preloader class and resave the file.

```
C:\BGP3D\Chapter12>python worldclass_02.py
DirectStart: Starting the game.
Known pipe types:
  wglGraphicsPipe
(all display modules loaded.)
['../Models/Track.egg', '../Models/Planet.egg', '../Models/Ground.egg', '../Mode
ls/LinearPinkSkySphere.bam', '../Models/TargetCone.bam', '../Models/ShieldBar.eg
g', '../Models/SpeedBar.egg', '../Models/EnergyBar.egg', '../Models/RedCycle.bam
', '../Models/RedTurr.bam', '../Models/YellowCycle.bam', '../Models/YellowTurr.b
am', '../Models/GreenCycle.bam', '../Models/GreenTurr.bam', '../Models/BlueCycle
.bam', '../Models/BlueTurr.bam', '../Models/Disc.bam', '../Models/MachineGun.bam
', '../Models/Cannon.bam', '../Models/LaserFlash.bam', '../Models/LaserProj.bam'
, '../Models/Explosions/Laserburst1.bam', '../Models/Explosions/Laserburst2.bam'
, '../Models/Explosions/Laserburst3.bam']
```

What just happened?

That's all there is to it. File handling in Panda3D is pretty simple and easy. The only downside is that the files are text files, and therefore are human readable. We'd have to build an encryption system to fix that, which is beyond the scope of this book.

Customizing the mouse cursor

Replacing the mouse cursor with a custom image with a game-appropriate one is a common practice. A practice we should know how to do as well.

Time for action – customizing the mouse cursor

In this case, it will be easier to let the process explain itself, so let's dive right in.

1. Open `WorldClass_02.py`.

2. Add this line of code to our imports. While we're here, let's update our imports to use `RaceClass_01.py` instead of `RaceClass_00.py`.

```
from pandac.PandaModules import *
```

3. Scroll down to the `__init__` method and add this block of code right at the top of the method:

```
cursor = loader.loadModel("../Models/Cursor.egg")
    cursor.reparentTo(render2d)
    cursor.setBin("gui-popup", 100)
    cursor.hide()

    props = WindowProperties()
    props.setCursorHidden(True)
    base.win.requestProperties(props)
    base.mouseWatcherNode.setGeometry(cursor.node())
    self.totalItems = len(self.models)
```

4. Next, scroll down to the line where we instantiate an instance of our `Race` class. Change that line to include a new argument:

```
self.race = Race(self.inputManager, hud, cursor)
```

5. Resave the file as `WorldClass_03.py` and open `RaceClass_00.py`.

6. Rewrite the definition for the `__init__` method to accept a new argument:

```
def __init__(self, inputManager, hud, cursor):
```

7. Add this line of code to the `__init__` method, right after the line that stores a reference to the HUD:

```
self.cursor = cursor
```

8. This line goes in the `createDemoRace` method. It doesn't really matter where, so just put it at the very top of the method:

```
self.cursor.show()
```

9. Scroll down to the `startRace` method and add this line to it:

```
self.cursor.hide()
```

10. Resave the file as RaceClass_01.py and then run WorldClass_03.py.

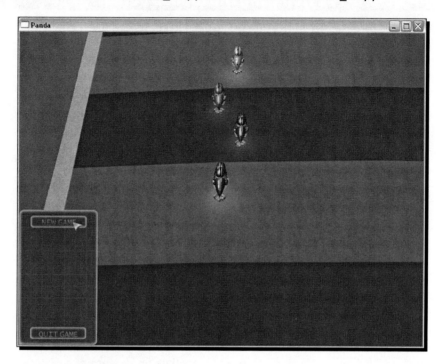

What just happened?

Now, our mouse cursor is customized, and it vanishes while we're playing. Note that if you move the mouse out of the window and then back into it, the cursor will reappear, but since this game will be a full-screen game, we don't need to worry about that.

After we loaded our cursor we attached it to `render2d` rather than `base.aspect2d`. This is an important consideration because `base.aspect2d` is a child of `render2d`, which automatically compensates for the non-square nature of the window. If we had used `aspect2d` our cursor wouldn't reach all the way to the left and right edges of the window.

Remember back to when we added the sky sphere to the `Track` class. That was the first time we used `setBin`, and here we're using it again. The purpose of `setBin` is to control render order, and we're taking advantage of that to ensure that our mouse cursor is always on top of the menus we create. We achieve this effect by setting the bin to **"gui-popup"**. The second number we pass to `setBin` is the sort order, with lower numbers being rendered first, but since the mouse cursor is the only thing we've put in the bin **"gui-popup"**, it doesn't really matter.

Take a look at these three lines of code:

```
props = WindowProperties()
props.setCursorHidden(True)
base.win.requestProperties(props)
```

The first line creates an instance of the `WindowProperties` class. This is why we needed to import `pandac.PandaModules` for our `World` class; the `WindowProperties` class is found in those modules. `WindowProperties` stores a wide variety of settings for the game windows of Panda3D. We change one of those properties, whether or not the default Windows cursor is displayed, with `setCursorHidden`. We then call `requestPropterties` on `base.win` with our new properties as the argument to change the properties of our default window so that the default Windows mouse cursor is no longer displayed.

The last new line of code we put into `World` class attached our new mouse cursor to the mouse position in the window:

```
base.mouseWatcherNode.setGeometry(cursor.node())
```

The call to `base.mouseWatcherNode.setGeometry` requires the actual geometry itself, not the `NodePath` that links to it, so we supplied `cursor.node()` instead of cursor.

 Note that with this method, the mouse cursor will be tied to the frame rate of the game. If the frame rate of the game falls, the mouse cursor won't move the way we expect. We could use the alternative method that replaces the mouse cursor at the operating system level, `WindowProperties.setCursorFilename("myCurscor.ico")`, but this method has its own complications depending on the operating system of the computer.

Have a Go Hero – the end of the race

At this point we've covered every aspect of Panda3D that's needed to create a video game, other than packing it into an installer for the customer. That doesn't mean the game is quite finished, but we have the skills we need to finalize it. Take the time to do that now. Add a system that counts the number of laps that each cycle has made and ends the race. It should also display the positions at the end, and give a menu choice so the player can race again or return to the main menu.

 Here's a hint: in the lists of track markers, the first entry, index 0, is at the finish line. A simple way to count laps is to increment a counter when the cycle passes that marker.

Pop quiz – using a custom mouse cursor

Be sure to answer these questions before moving on:

1. When replacing the mouse cursor with custom geometry, what is the purpose of the `setBin` method?

2. What method do we use to attach custom geometry to the mouse cursor?

Creating an Installer

Once the game is ready to go, we just need to pack it up and get it ready to ship to the customer. For this, we'll use a command-line utility called packpanda. This utility will compress the game and all of Panda3D into a convenient Windows installer that our customers can use to install the game on their own computers. The customer won't need to install Panda3D to run the game; they won't even need to know that the game runs on Panda3D.

For the packpanda utility to work correctly, we'll have to adjust our file structure a little bit. We'll need to move all the game components into a single folder (it can have subfolders). We'll call this folder `SuicideJockeys` (any name is fine, but that's the one we'll use). In that new folder, we'll need to create a file called `main.py` that launches the game. For packpanda to work, the launch file must be called `main.py`, and it must be located in the `SuicideJockeys` folder, not in any subfolders. We can also put three optional files in the `SuicideJockeys` folder: `installer.bmp`, `icon.ico`, and `license.txt`. Here's the breakdown of these four files and what they're for.

- `main.py`—this is a Python file that imports DirectStart and starts our game. Once the game is installed on a customer's computer, there will be a shortcut located in the customer's start menu that runs this Python file.

- `installer.bmp`—this is a bitmap file that is exactly 164x314 pixels. This image will be displayed in the installer window while the game is being installed.

- `icon.ico`—this is the icon that will be used for the game's shortcut in the start menu. If it is not supplied, the Panda3D icon will be used.

- `license.txt`—this is a plain ASCII text file that contains the license agreement for the game that the customer will have to agree to in order to install the game. Of course, the license only covers the code for the game, not Panda3D, which is covered by its own license.

Time for action – packing a Panda3D game

We'll be using one of the very convenient features of Notepad++, Find and Replace, to fix some of the file paths in our files.

1. Create a new folder on the `C:` drive and name it `SuicideJockeys`.

2. Copy the most up-to-date versions of all of our Python files into the new folder.

3. Remove the underscores and numbers from the ends of the files that have them.

4. Close any and all open files in Notepad++. Then open, all of the files in the `SuicideJockeys` folder in Notepad++.

5. Press *Ctrl+F* on the keyboard to open the **Find** window. Select the **Replace** tab. In the box labeled **Find what:** type **../Models**, and in the box labeled **Replace with:** type **Models**. Then, click the **Replace All in All Opened Documents** button. This will change all of the paths for loading models in all of the files.

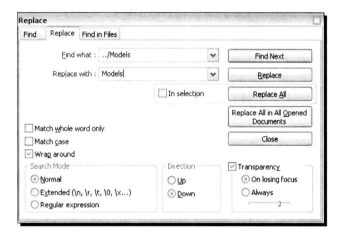

6. Repeat step 5 to change all the paths to the `Fonts`, `Images`, and `Sound` folders.

7. Go through the open files one-by-one and remove all underscores and numbers from the import lines, because we removed them from our files.

8. In `WorldClass.py` remove the line that imports `DirectStart`.

9. Save and close all of the open files.

10. Notepad++ should open a new blank document once all the files are closed. If not, create a new blank document.

11. Type this code into the new document, which will serve as the launcher for our game:

```
import direct.directbase.DirectStart
from WorldClass import *
w = World()
run()
```

12. Save the new file in the `SuicideJockeys` folder with the name `main.py`.

13. Copy the `Images`, `Fonts`, `Models`, and `Sound` folders from the `BGP3D` folder to the `SuicideJockeys` folder.

14. From the `BGP3D/Extras` folder copy `installer.bmp` and `icon.ico` to the `SuicideJockeys` folder.

15. Navigate to the folder `C:\Panda3D-1.6.2\etc` and open the file `config.prc`. Look for a line with the word fullscreen, and change that line to look like this. That will cause the game to load in fullscreen mode by default.

```
fullscreen 1
```

16. Open a Windows command prompt and navigate to the folder `C:\Panda3D-1.6.2\bin`. Type this line into the command prompt and hit enter.

 Note that the hyphens in front of `dir` and `name` are double hyphens.

```
Packpanda.exe --dir C:\SuicideJockeys --name "Suicide Jockeys"
```

```
Command Prompt                                              _ □ ×

C:\Panda3D-1.6.2\bin>packpanda.exe --dir C:\SuicideJockeys --name "Suicide Jocke
ys"
PANDA located at C:\Panda3D-1.6.2
Dir             : C:\SuicideJockeys
Name            : Suicide Jockeys
Start Menu      : Suicide Jockeys
Main            : C:\SuicideJockeys\main.py
Icon            : C:\SuicideJockeys\icon.ico
Bitmap          : C:\SuicideJockeys\installer.bmp
License         : C:\SuicideJockeys\license.txt (MISSING)
Output          : C:\Panda3D-1.6.2\bin\SuicideJockeys.exe
Install Dir     : C:\SuicideJockeys
```

What just happened?

The packpanda utility will take a bit of time to create the installer for the game. When it's finished, it can be found in the same folder as the packpanda utility itself, `C:\Panda3D-1.6.2\bin`. Go ahead and install the game to see the fruits of our labor.

The `--dir` flag we supplied to `packpanda.exe` told the utility where to find our game. The files `main.py`, `installer.bmp`, `icon.ico`, and `license.txt` must be located in the folder that we specify with `--dir`, not in any subfolders, or `packpanda.exe` won't be able to find them. The `--name` flag allows us to tell `packpanda.exe` what the name of the game is. If we don't specify it, the name of the folder is used. The installer window will use the name of the game, and the name of the game will also be used as the default installation directory. There are other flags that can be used with `packpanda.exe` to automate certain tasks related to packing the game, but typically it's a better idea to handle those things manually so we can be sure they're done properly and double check the results.

Have a Go Hero – improving load times

To improve the loading times in the game, it would be a good idea to ship with `.pyc` and `.bam` files instead of `.py` and `.egg` files. To create `.pyc` files, simply run the game in the folder that will be packed up with `packpanda.exe` and Python will automatically create them for you. Then, just remove the `.py` files. We talked about creating `.bam` files using the `writeBamFile` method earlier, so use that to create `.bam` files to replace all of the `.egg` files. Use Notepad++'s **Find and Replace** window to change all of the model files in our code to use the `.bam` files. There is one `.egg` that shouldn't be changed, however. `Markers.egg` is loaded as raw egg data, so it should be left in the `.egg` format. Once all that is done, repack the game into a new installer.

Pop quiz – building an installer

It's time now for our last Pop Quiz. Answer these questions to make sure we have a handle on how to use `packpanda.exe`:

1. What file absolutely must be present for `packpanda.exe` to run, and where must it be found?

2. What optional files can we place alongside the file from question 1, and what are the restrictions on those files?

Summary

That's it! Our game is finished and ready to go to the customer, though there isn't much of it at this point. That's okay, though; all we would need to do is add more content, like extra levels. We've covered every piece of vital knowledge for creating a game with Panda3D. It was a long road, but a rewarding one. Let's take a minute to pat ourselves on the back, and then go over what we covered in this last chapter.

We talked about several finishing touches to apply to the game, including garbage collection, building and using preloaders, how to interact with files, and more. Our last bit of business was to pack our game up into an installer to make it ready for the customer.

Creating a Sky Sphere with Spacescape

This appendix is all about creating sky spheres to use as backdrops in Panda3D games.

We'll hit these topics:

- ◆ Learning Spacescape basics
- ◆ Blending layers
- ◆ Using point stars and billboard stars
- ◆ Creating a sky sphere from a skybox made with Spacescape

Learning Spacescape basics

Spacescape creates skyboxes full of nebulas and stars. A **skybox** is a set of six images that, when arranged properly and folded into a cube, will seamlessly blend together along the edges of the cube.

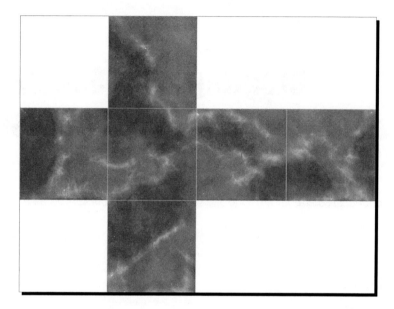

Skyboxes see extensive use in 3D video games where they serve as the backdrop that encapsulates the world. The real trouble with skyboxes is getting them; they're difficult to paint by hand, they take fancy camera work and compositing to create from real world scenery, and it's hard to find quality skyboxes for free on the Internet.

Thankfully, Spacescape allows us to create our own skyboxes, though it does specialize in night time or outer space views. With it, we can create complex, intricate, and beautiful backdrops for use in our games.

Spacescape uses a system of layers to work its magic. We create layers, adjust their settings, and stack them on top of each other until we get a rich, complex tapestry of stars and nebulas.

There are three kinds of layers in Spacescape: noise, point stars, and billboard stars. Noise layers create cloud-like patterns that vary between two colors, and are used to create the colored nebulas and also to create masks that limit the visibility of other layers. Point star layers create distributions of simple points and are used for basic stars. Billboard star layers are similar to point star layers, except instead of just creating a simple point of color they place an image. Both point star and billboard star layers can be given their own masks, which only affect that layer, to limit where they appear.

Time for action – getting started with Spacescape

To get a basic understanding of how to use Spacescape, let's create a simple nebula with some stars in it.

1. Double-click the `Spacescape.exe` file in the `Spacescape` folder to start the program. When the program starts, a screen similar to the following screenshot comes up:

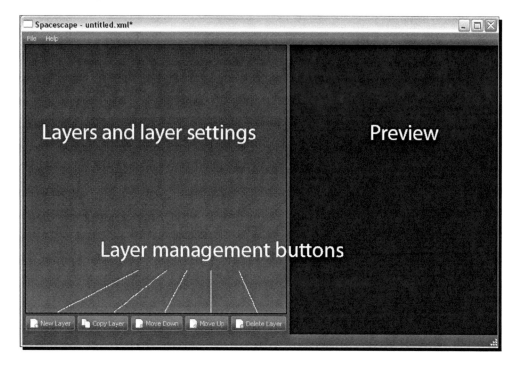

2. Click on the **New Layer** button to introduce a new layer to the scene, and then click on the plus icon to the left of the new layer. This will open the settings for that layer. The second item on the list, **Layer Type**, is currently set to **points**. Click on the word **points** to get a drop-down box of options and then select the **noise** option.

3. This changes the available settings for the layer, and instead of seeing white dots in our preview we now see a gray cloud. Without worrying about what they all mean exactly, we're going to edit some of the values for this layer.

4. Click on the values to the right of the **Inner Colour** setting and a button with an ellipses(. . .) on it will appear on the right-hand side of those values. Click on that button to open the color picker, and choose the purple color at the bottom-left of the **Basic Colours** section.

5. Next, change the **Lacunarity** from **2.000** to **2.200**.

6. Change the **Octaves** to **6**.

7. Change the **Power** to **1.200**.

8. Change the **Threshold** to **.450**.

9. Now, we have a dark purple cloud with a bit of graininess to it that looks sort of like a nebula. Let's go ahead and throw in some stars as well. Click on the **New Layer** button again.

10. Click on the plus icon next to the new layer to open its options. Click on the values for the **Near Colour** and open the color picker again. Choose the same purple, but adjust the **Sat** down to **180** and then click on the **OK** button.

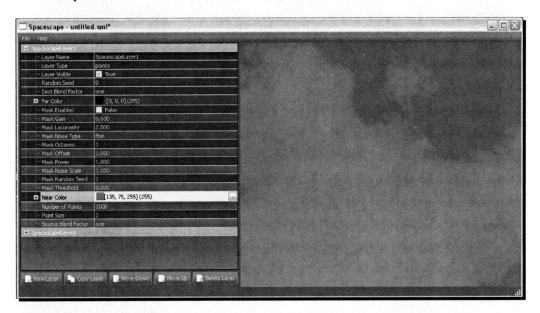

What just happened?

We've got a decent start going there, and we've seen the basic premise behind Spacescape: layers of noise and stars. Before we start getting more complicated, though, we should talk about the noise layers and their controls.

The noise layers are generated by adding a series of noise functions together. These noise functions use wave-forms to produce a value between 0 and 1 for each pixel, and that value determines the mix of the inner and outer color for the pixel. A value of 0 means pure outer color, and a value of 1 means pure inner color. A value of .5 would be halfway in between the two.

There are two types of noises to choose from: fbm and ridged. Fbm noise creates a smoother, more cloud noise. Ridged noise contains ridges that resemble tendrils or electricity.

There are three settings that control the basic wave-form: octaves, gain, and lacunarity.

- ◆ Lacunarity: Controls the size of the "major" regions in the noise. Higher values produce smaller, more numerous regions. Typically, this value is kept fairly close to 2.

- ◆ Gain: Controls the grittiness, or roughness, of the "major" regions. Higher values will produce rougher regions. This value is usually set between 0 and 1.

- ◆ Octaves: Controls the number of additive noise functions that are used. This value effectively multiplies the lacunarity and gain. Usually 4 to 8 octaves are used. If this value is less than 2, gain and lacunarity will have no effect.

We have two settings that let us control the distribution of the noise value after it has been generated by the wave-form: power and threshold.

- ◆ Threshold: This setting creates a lower limit for the noise value. Essentially, the noise value in each pixel is reduced by the threshold. This value needs to remain between 0 and 1.

- ◆ Power: This setting is an amplifier for the noise value, and it is applied after the threshold. Essentially, a higher power will push the noise values that remain toward 1, the inner color. Noise values of 0 are not affected by power.

There are three remaining settings for noise that we haven't talked about yet. They are noise scale, noise offset, and random seed.

- ◆ Noise scale: Adjusts the initial coordinates for the noise. It's difficult to predict exactly how this will affect the result, but that doesn't mean it's useless. We'll use noise scale to produce variation in noise layers we've copied.

- ◆ Noise offset: This setting is only used by ridged noise. It controls the contrast of the ridges. A value of .5 results in a flat mix of the inner and outer colors, and a value of 1 allows the ridges to reach the pure inner color. Overdriving this value beyond 1 will force more of the ridges to the pure inner color, which can look pretty ugly. Values between .5 and 1 are recommended.

♦ Random Seed: It's impossible for a computer to generate a truly random number, but by performing operations on a seed number a pseudo-random number can be generated. Spacescape uses pseudo-random numbers when generating noise, and random seed is the seed number used. The same seed number will always produce the same result, so two layers that have the same settings and the same random seed will be the same. Different random seeds will produce different layers of the same style.

Blending layers

Controlling how the layers in Spacescape blend together is both the most important aspect of creating a skybox and also the most complicated. All of the layers have controls for blending that work similarly to the blending methods available in image editors, such as Photoshop or GIMP, but unlike those programs there aren't any control presets like "Multiply" or "Lighten". Instead, we get direct access to the equation those presets use.

Before we get into the equation itself, we need to define some things the equation uses. First off, let's talk about the destination and the source. These refer to the two things that are being blended. The source is the layer whose blending controls we're working with. The destination is the combination of all the layers beneath the layer we're working with. In other words, the source is the layer itself, and the destination is all the layers beneath it.

Here's an example with four layers named **Red Point Stars**, **Nebula Mask**, **Blue Nebula**, and **Green Nebula**. The source and destination of the **Nebula Mask** layer are labelled.

Spacescape v0.2, the most up-to-date version at the time of this writing, uses values ranging from 0 to 255 for color, but to understand the math in the blending equation we have to think of the colors as ranging from 0 to 1, like they do in Panda3D. That's because multiplying colors together makes them get darker, rather than lighter, and that only makes sense when we're using decimal numbers, rather than numbers greater than 1.

Keeping these things in mind, let's take a look at the following equation:

```
( Source * sourceFactor ) + ( Destinaton * destinationFactor )
```

The equation is composed of four parts. Two of those parts are the source and destination. The other two parts are multipliers that alter the source and destination. These multipliers, called the `sourceFactor` and `destinationFactor`, are the items we get to change. The addition and multiplication operations are performed on the red, green, blue, and alpha channels separately. This means that for each pixel in the image, the equation is calculated four times, once for each channel.

```
( srceR * srceFactorR ) + ( destR * destFactorR ) = outR
( srceG * srceFactorG ) + ( destG * destFactorG ) = outG
( srceB * srceFactorB ) + ( destB * destFactorB ) = outB
( srceA * srceFactorA ) + ( destA * destFactorA ) = outA
```

To control blending of layers, we change the `sourceFactor` and `destinationFactor`. We have a bunch of options, all of which can be used for either the `sourceFactor` or the `destinationFactor`. Here's the list of options:

Option	Description
One	This gives a value of 1 for every pixel.
Zero	This gives a value of 0 for every pixel.
Dest_colour	This option inputs the color values of the destination.
Src_colour	This option inputs the color values of the source.
One_minus_dest_colour	This option inputs 1—value for each of the destination color channels. For example, a dark blue (.1,.1,.3) would be input as an orange-white (.9,.9,.7).
One_minus_src_colour	This is the same as one_minus_dest_colour, but it uses the source color channels instead.
Dest_alpha	This option uses the destination alpha values. In v0.2 of Spacescape, the color alpha values are not used. Instead, the noise value is used for alpha blending. The outer color shows through where the noise value is lower, and the inner color shows through where the noise value is higher.
Src_alpha	This option is the same as dest_alpha, but it uses the noise value from the source instead of the destination.
One_minus_dest_alpha	This uses the inverse of the noise value from the destination. If the noise value is .3, for example, a .7 will be used.
One_minus_src_alpha	This is the same as one_minus_dest_alpha, but it uses the source noise value instead of the destination noise value.

The default option for both `sourceFactor` and `destinationFactor` is one, which uses a value of 1 for every channel of every pixel. Since multiplying a value by 1 will cause it to stay the same, the default settings simply add the source and destination together. If the `destinationFactor` was changed to `zero`, which uses a value of 0 for every channel of every pixel, the destination would get thrown out entirely and only the source would show.

A **Multiply** layer in an image editor multiplies the source by the destination. To achieve the same effect in Spacescape, we could set the `sourceFactor` to `dest_colour` and the `destinationFactor` to `zero`.

To create a mask that hides a part of the destination, but allows some of it to show through, we could set the `sourceFactor` to `zero` (so the mask layer doesn't affect the color of the result at all) and set the `destinationFactor` to `src_alpha` or `one_minus_src_alpha` (so the noise value of the source controls the alpha of the destination).

Time for action – blending layers to create nebulas

Blending layers together will allow us to produce nebulas that are richer and more complicated.

1. In Spacescape, go to **File | New**.

2. Click on the **New Layer** button and open the settings for the new layer. Change the **Layer Name** to **Purple Nebula**.

3. Change the **Layer Type** to **noise**.

4. Click on the little plus icon next to **Inner Colour** to open the list of channels. Input the following values for the color channels, and leave **Alpha** at **255**:

   ```
   Red: 0
   Green: 0
   Blue: 255
   ```

5. Click on the little plus icon next to **Outer Colour** to open the list of channels. Input the following values:

   ```
   Red: 255
   Green: 0
   Blue: 0
   ```

6. Set the **Gain** to **0.700**. Set the **Lacunarity** to **2.2000**. Set the **Octaves** to **6**. Set the **Random Seed** to **3587**.

7. Click on the **New Layer** button again. Change the name for this layer to **Purple Nebula Smooth Mask**, and then change the **Layer Type** to **noise**.

8. Set the **Random Seed** to **9216**, set the **Octaves** to **6**, and change the **Threshold** to **0.200**.

9. Change the **Dest Blend Factor** to **src_alpha** and the **Source Blend Factor** to **zero**.

10. Add another new layer. Name this one **Purple Nebula Ridged Mask** and change the **Layer Type** to **noise**.

11. Change the **Noise Type** to **ridged**.

12. Enter the following settings:

```
Random Seed: 4981
Dest Blend Factor: one_minus_src_alpha
Gain: 0.700
Lacunarity: 2.700
Octaves: 7
Power: 0.500
Source Blend Factor: zero
```

13. Create another new layer and give it these settings:

```
Layer Name: Light Pink Nebula
Layer Type: noise
Noise Type: ridged
Random Seed: 1154
Gain: 0.450
Lacunarity: 2.250
Octaves: 5
Power: 0.150
Threshold: 0.700
```

14. Click on the small plus icon beside **Inner Colour** and change the three color channel values.

```
Red: 127
Green: 32
Blue: 63
```

15. Use the **Copy Layer** button to create a duplicate of the **Light Pink Nebula** layer. Change its settings to match the following values:

```
Layer Name: Light Purple Nebula
Gain: 0.600
Lacunarity: 2.100
Noise Scale: 1.025
```

16. Naturally, we need to change the color of this layer to be light purple instead of pink:

```
Red: 127
Green: 32
Blue: 127
```

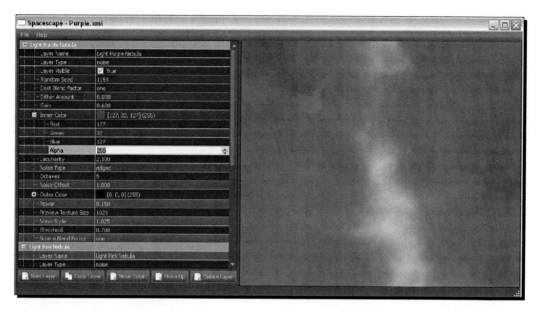

What just happened?

That should do it for our nebulas. The layer blending options we picked for the two masks are the real stars of the show here. We set the **Source Blend Factor** to `zero` to turn off the layer's color completely. We only need the noise values.

For the smooth mask we set the **Dest Blend Factor** to `src_alpha` to tell the layers underneath, in our case just **Purple Nebula**, to use the noise values of **Purple Nebula Smooth Mask** for its alpha. This darkened it because the background in Spacescape is black and we're letting more of the background show through. The important part is that we based it on the mask's noise values, which means parts of it darkened more than others, creating additional variation.

The second mask, **Purple Nebula Ridged Mask**, adds some grit and detail to the background nebula. We used `one_minus_src_alpha` for the **Dest Blend Factor** on that layer because we wanted the higher noise values, the peaks of the ridges, to be the darkest parts of our nebula. In effect, by using `one_minus_src_alpha` instead of `src_alpha`, we turned the peaks of the ridges into canyons that cut into Purple Nebula.

Using point stars and billboard stars

The last step to completing our skybox will be adding stars. To get good results with stars, the most important things to remember are blending and variety. We want the stars to meld into the night sky in a natural way, so we have to blend them nicely with the elements already in place. We also want to hide the fact that they are computer generated, and most of them are just colored pixels. To do that, we introduce a lot of variety in them so that the eye is less likely to notice the similarity that gives away those weaknesses.

When using point and billboard star layers, we rely on masking to control their placement. We have two masking strategies to choose from. Our first option is to use the built-in masking available to us in the point and billboard star layers themselves. This option allows the most accurate control over positioning and color. The second method is to use masking noise layers, like we did for our dark background nebula. The second method is great for making background stars to populate our background nebula, because we don't have to create a new mask, we can use the **Purple Nebula Ridged Mask** we've already made.

There's one other note to mention about using stars. The size input for billboard stars is relative to the size of the eventual texture output. The size input for point stars isn't. What that means to us is that the size of billboard stars will be the same, relative to the nebulas, no matter what resolution we choose to export at. The same is not true for point stars; their size is an absolute number of pixels. If we set a particular size for our point stars and export both a 512x512 image and a 4096x4096 image, we'll see a huge difference in the point stars between the two. That's why, when checking to see if point stars look the way we want, we always have to export an image at the final desired resolution. That's the only way to see how the point stars are actually going to look.

Time for action – populating the sky with stars

There's no better teacher than experience, so let's get some stars in that sky. To get the variety we want, we'll be using nine-point star layers and five billboard star layers. Once we finish with all the layers, we'll do an export to make sure they look how we want them to.

1. Starting from where we left off, click on the **New Layer** button to create a new point star layer.

2. Select the new layer and click on the **Move Down** button to move the layer down in the stack. We want it to be between the **Purple Nebula Ridged Mask** and the Purple Nebula Smooth Mask layers.

3. Change the settings on the new layer to the following:
```
Layer Name: Dark Purple Stars
Near Colour: 96, 0, 96
Number of Points: 10000
Point Size: 2
```

4. Set the **Random Seed** for **Dark Purple Stars** to **2573**. Make sure to set the **Random Seed**, NOT the **Mask Random Seed**. **Random Seed** applies to the stars; **Mask Random Seed** applies to the mask that controls star placement. That mask is turned off right now, so **Mask Random Seed** won't affect anything.

5. With the `Dark Purple Stars` layer highlighted, click on the **Copy Layer** button. This will put a duplicate layer above it. We're going to use this duplicate layer to create some brighter stars in the background layer. Change its settings to the following values:

```
Layer Name: Bright Purple Stars
Random Seed: 6413
Near Colour: 255, 64, 255
Number of Points: 1000
Point Size: 1
```

6. Just because we're using point stars doesn't mean we can't give the bright ones a subtle halo. To do that, we'll use a second layer of darker, larger point stars with the same **Random Seed** so that the stars will stack on top of each other. Use the **Copy Layer** button to create a copy of the `Bright Purple Stars` layer then select the new copy and click on the **Move Down** button to put it right beneath the `Bright Purple Stars` layer.

7. Change the settings of the copied layer as follows:

```
Layer Name: Bright Purple Stars Backing
Near Colour: 160, 0, 160
Point Size: 2
```

8. We have two more layers to add beneath `Purple Nebula Ridged Mask`. This time, though, we'll be using billboard layers. Click on the **New Layer** button and then use the **Move Down** button to move the new layer just underneath `Purple Nebula Ridged Mask`.

9. Give the new layer these settings:

```
Layer Name: Dark Blue Billboard Stars
Layer Type: billboards
Random Seed: 6457
Far Colour: 127, 127, 127
Max Billboard Size: 0.050
Min Billboard Size: 0.010
Near Colour: 255, 255, 255
Number of Billboards: 75
Billboard Texture: flare-blue-purple1.png
```

10. **Billboard Texture** must be set to the exact string `flare-blue-purple1.png` or it won't be able to find the file. Spacescape looks in the folder `Spacescape\media\materials\textures` for the images to use on billboards. There's a decent number of images there that we can use.

11. Use the **Copy Layer** button to duplicate the `Dark Blue Billboard Stars` layer then give the copy these settings:

```
Layer Name: Dark Red Billboard Stars
Random Seed: 4153
Billboard Texture: flare-red1.png
```

12. Next, we're going to create some stars that will coincide with small, bright nebulas. We'll make sure the stars stick to the nebulas by turning on the masks in the star layers and setting the mask settings to match the nebula. Create another new layer with the **New Layer** button. Leave it on the top of the stack this time. These are the settings for it. Note that the mask settings are the same as the settings for the `Light Purple Nebula`, with the exception of the **Threshold**.

```
Layer Name: Bright Light Purple Stars
Random Seed: 2837
Mask Enabled: True (check the box)
Mask Noise Type: ridged
Mask Gain: 0.600
Mask Lacunarity: 2.100
Mask Octaves: 5
Mask Power: 0.150
Mask Noise Scale: 1.025
Mask Random Seed: 1154
Mask Threshold: 0.650
Near Colour: 255, 84, 255
Number of Points: 2500
```

13. Use the **Copy Layer** button to duplicate the `Bright Light Purple Stars` layer we just made. Change the settings on the new copy as follows:

```
Layer Name: Extra Bright Light Purple Stars Backing
Random Seed: 3571
Near Colour: 127, 64, 127
Number of Points: 500
Point Size: 2
```

14. Copy `Extra Bright Light Purple Stars Backing` as well. Change the new copy to these settings:

```
Layer Name: Extra Bright Light Purple Stars
Near Colour: 255, 84, 255
Point Size: 1
```

15. Unfortunately, we can't use the layer copying feature to keep the same mask settings for a billboard star layer. Changing the **Layer Type** to **billboards** will remove the mask settings. We'll just create a new layer instead, and put in these settings for it:

```
Layer Name: Bright Blue Billboard Stars
Layer Type: billboards
Random Seed: 2311
Far Colour: 127, 127, 127
Mask Enabled: True
Mask Noise Type: ridged
Mask Gain: 0.600
Mask Lacunarity: 2.100
Mask Octaves: 5
Mask Power: 0.150
Mask Noise Scale: 1.025
Mask Random Seed: 1154
Mask Threshold: 0.700
Max Billboard Size: 0.040
Min Billboard Size: 0.015
Near Colour: 255, 255, 255
Number of Billboards: 25
Billboard Texture: flare-blue-spikey1.png
```

16. That's it for the stars that will mimic the `Light Purple Nebula` layer. Next, we'll use the same techniques to add stars to the `Light Pink Nebula`. Click on the **New Layer** button and open the settings for the new layer. Change these values:

```
Layer Name: Bright Light Pink Stars
Random Seed: 9164
Mask Enabled: True
Mask Noise Type: ridged
Mask Gain: 0.450
Mask Lacunarity: 2.250
Mask Octaves: 5
Mask Power: 0.150
Mask Random Seed: 1154
Mask Threshold: 0.650
Near Colour: 255, 114, 114
Number of Points: 2500
```

17. Make a copy of the `Bright Light Pink Stars` layer we just made and change these settings in the copy:

```
Layer Name: Extra Bright Light Pink Stars Backing
Random Seed: 3654
Near Colour: 127, 64, 64
Number of Points: 500
Point Size: 2
```

18. Make a copy of the `Extra Bright Light Pink Stars Backing` layer we just finished and change the following settings to the new values provided:
```
Layer Name: Extra Bright Light Pink Stars
Near Colour: 255, 114, 114
Point Size: 1
```

19. That's all of our point star layers. We just need two more billboard star layers, and our night sky will be finished. Make a copy of the `Bright Blue Billboard Stars` layer and use the **Move Up** button to move the copy up to the top of the layer stack. Then, change the following settings in that layer:
```
Layer Name: Bright Pink Billboard Stars
Random Seed: 7388
Mask Gain: .0450
Mask Lacunarity: 2.250
Near Colour: 255, 180, 180
Billboard Texture: flare-red-yellow1.png
```

20. For our last layer, copy the `Bright Pink Billboard Stars` layer we just made and make the following changes to it:
```
Layer Name: Bright Purple Billboard Stars
Random Seed: 8414
Mask Gain: 0.500
Mask Lacunarity: 2.150
Near Colour: 255, 170, 255
Billboard Texture: flare-blue-purple2.png
```

21. Next, click on the **File** menu at the top of the window and select **Save**. **Save** the `.xml` file. We can load this file later if we want to edit the sky we've created.

22. Once the work we've done is safely saved, go to **File | Export Skybox** to bring up the export dialog box. At the very bottom, change the **Image Size** from **512** to **1024**. Navigate to `BGP3D/Images` then type in `Purple` for the filename and click on the **Save** button.

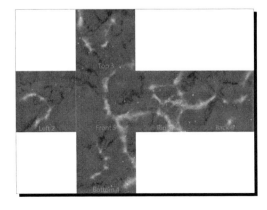

What just happened?

The preceding image shows all six of the pictures that Spacescape has output for us, and that brings us to the end of our work with Spacescape. The next step is to take those output images and turn them into a usable sky sphere for Panda3D.

Creating a sky sphere from a skybox made with Spacescape

To utilize our skybox images in Panda3D, we'll need to create a cubemap. A cubemap is a special kind of 3D texture in Panda3D that will take our six images, make them into a cube, and shrink wrap them onto an object. This process can create distortions on complex objects, but on a simple object like a sphere it works beautifully. Once we have the cubemap, we'll need to create 3D texture coordinates on the sphere so that we can use it. After that, we'll apply the cubemap to the sphere, set some render attributes on the NodePath, and then save it out into a bam file.

Time for action – populating the sky with stars

Before we start writing some Panda3D code to make all this happen, we have to change the names on our skybox image files. Panda3D and Spacescape use different naming conventions and we have to switch over to the Panda3D naming methods in order to use the images.

1. Navigate Windows Explorer to BGP3D/Images and locate the skybox images we saved. All of their names will start with Purple_.

2. Remove the top, bottom, left, right, front, and back words from the filenames so the files are named Purple_1.png, Purple_2.png, and so on.

3. Reduce all the numbers in the filenames by 1. 1 becomes 0, 2 becomes 1, and so on. We should have Purple_0.png through Purple_5.png when finished.

4. Rename Purple_2.png to Purple_3temp.png.

5. Rename Purple_3.png to Purple_2.png.

6. Rename Purple_3temp.png to Purple_3.png.

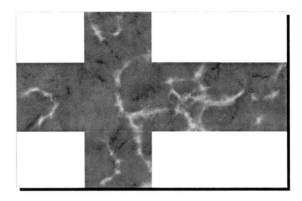

What just happened?

The preceding diagram shows the new numbers for each of the images to double check against.

Time for action – creating the sky sphere in Panda3D

Next, we'll create a sky sphere writing tool that we can use to create sky sphere bam files.

1. Open a new file in Notepad++. Type the following two lines at the top:

```
import direct.directbase.DirectStart
from pandac.PandaModules import *
```

2. Next, we'll define a new class and its __init__ method:

```
class SkySphereWriter:
  def __init__(self):
```

3. After that, we'll load the skybox as a cubemap and also load the inverted sphere, which is a normal 1 unit sphere, except that the faces point inward instead of outward. The # sign in the first line is replaced with the numbers 0 through 5 when Panda3D loads the cubemap.

```
self.texture = loader.loadCubeMap("../Images/Purple_#.png")
self.sphere = loader.loadModel("InvertedSphere.egg")
```

4. Now, we need to create 3D texture coordinates for the sphere. To do that, we need to make two calls on the sphere: setTexGen() and setTexProjector().

```
self.sphere.setTexGen(TextureStage.getDefault(),
  TexGenAttrib.MWorldPosition)
self.sphere.setTexProjector(TextureStage.getDefault(),
  render, self.sphere)
```

5. The sphere is ready to have the texture applied, so we'll do that next:

```
self.sphere.setTexture(self.texture)
```

6. We can also put in some `NodePath` settings here so that they'll be saved in the bam file:

```
self.sphere.setLightOff()
self.sphere.setScale(1500)
```

7. Now, we just need to write out the file, and reparent the sphere to render so that we can preview it:

```
self.sphere.writeBamFile("PurpleSkySphere.bam")
self.sphere.reparentTo(render)
```

8. To finish up the file, we need to instantiate our class and call the `run()` method:

```
SSW = SkySphereWriter()
run()
```

9. Save the file in `BGP3D/Models` as `SkySphereWriter.py` and run it.

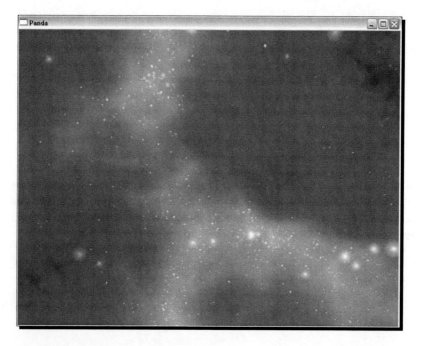

What just happened?

That does it, we now have a sky sphere ready for use. We can even reuse our sky sphere writer just by changing the filenames.

Summary

In this appendix, we went over the process of creating a sky sphere for use in Panda3D with Spacescape.

We talked about the basics of using Spacescape, blending layers, and the two different types of stars available to us. When we finished that, we quickly covered a simple method for turning the output of Spacescape into a sky sphere for use in Panda3D.

With this knowledge in hand, we can freely produce our own seamless, fully enclosing backdrops for our games.

B
Using Egg-Texture-Cards and ExploTexGen

In this appendix we'll look at how to create explosions with ExploTexGen, how to convert those explosions into usable bam files for Panda3D, and we'll talk about other uses for Panda3D's egg-texture-cards utility.

These are the specific topics we'll discuss:

- ◆ Using ExploTexGen and its output
- ◆ Creating flipbook animations with egg-texture-cards
- ◆ Additional egg-texture-cards options

Using ExploTexGen

ExploTexGen is a simple but effective utility created by Sascha Willems to produce 2D animated explosions with alpha channels. The final output of the utility is a single image with all of the frames of the animated explosion laid out in a grid, as seen in the following screenshot. One of the key features of the program is that the output is in the PNG format with alpha built in, so we won't have to put in much effort to make parts of the image that aren't covered by the explosion invisible. In fact, in Panda3D we don't have to put in any effort at all.

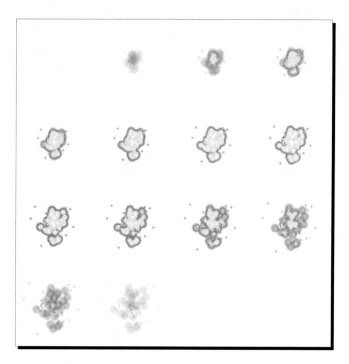

ExploTexGen works its magic by using two particle images, which can be in the PNG format and should have their own alphas already built into them. It places multiple copies of each image at the centre of the explosion and animates them moving outward and spinning. When the particles overlap they use additive mixing, so the colors brighten and approach white. As the explosion reaches the end of its life, the particles are faded out.

Time for action – reading the ExploTexGen documentation

ExploTexGen comes with excellent documentation that explains all of the available settings in clear, brief descriptions, so rather than restating all that information here, we'll just take a quick look at that.

1. Double-click the `ExploTexGen.exe` file in the `ExploTexGen` folder to start the program. Once it starts, click the **About** button on the upper-left of the screen and it will open the default web browser to view the HTML documentation.

2. The license information is available at the beginning of the documentation. It states that the images produced by ExploTexGen may be used for any purpose, commercial or not, and that ExploTexGen is freeware and should not be sold.

3. The rest of the documentation explains the usage of ExploTexGen, including descriptions on the seven settings that are used to control the look of the explosion. Take the time to read these short descriptions.

4. When finished, click the **Generate Explosion** button at the bottom-left of the screen to get a preview in the right section of the program. It will look something like the following:

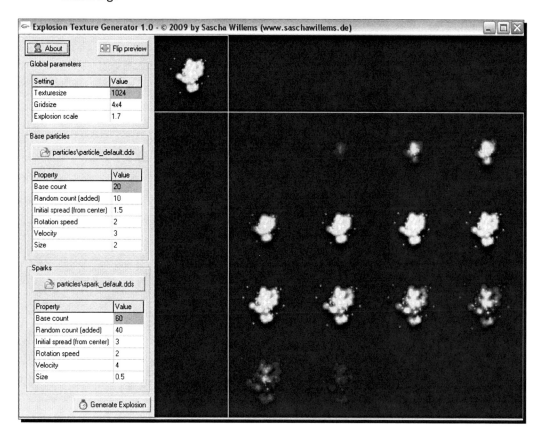

What just happened?

The preview feature of ExploTexGen presents the explosion that has been generated. The texture file itself can be found in the `ExploTexGen/output` folder. Note that in order to get a preview, an output texture has to be generated. Fortunately, output textures aren't overwritten.

Time for action – designing an explosion

Let's dive right in by creating a sci-fi explosion for some type of energy weapon.

1. In ExploTexGen, click the button that says **particles\particle_default.dds** in the **Base Particles** section to open a file dialogue box.

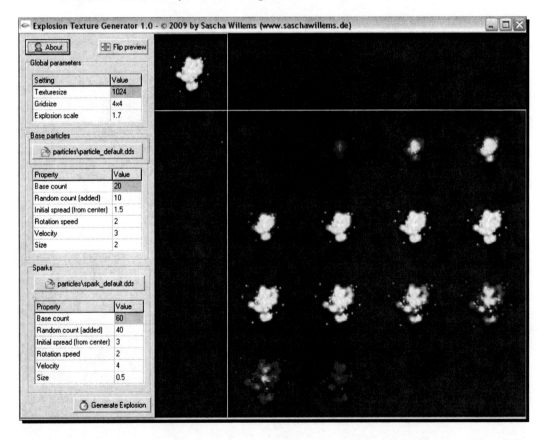

2. Navigate the dialog box that appears to the `BGP3D/Misc` folder. If no files appear, change the **File of Type** drop-down box at the bottom to **Portable Network Graphic**. Select the `StarParticleTeal.png` file.

3. Click the button in the **Sparks** section to change that particle as well. This time, select the `RingParticleBlue.png` file.

4. In the **Global Parameters** section, set these values:

   ```
   Texture Size: 1024
   Grid Size: 4x4
   Explosion Scale: 2
   ```

5. Enter these values in the **Base Particles** section:

   ```
   Initial Count: 50
   Random Count: 25
   Initial Spread: 1
   Rotation Speed: 5
   Velocity: 6
   Size: 1
   ```

6. For the **Sparks** section, type in these values:

   ```
   Initial Count: 30
   Random Count: 15
   Initial Spread: 1.5
   Rotation Speed: 2
   Velocity: 6
   Size: 2
   ```

7. Click the **Generate Explosion** button until you get a satisfying explosion. Make sure that none of the particles reach the edge of the preview. It should look something like this:

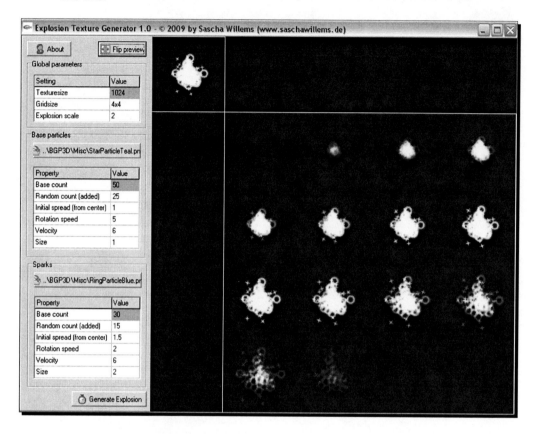

What just happened?

That's all it takes to make a nice-looking blast in ExploTexGen. The reason we put the smaller teal particles in the **Base Particles** section is because the **Sparks** section particles don't actually rotate, despite having a **Rotation Speed** setting.

There's one last thing to do before we use egg-texture-cards to create an egg file of the explosion. We need to take the output of ExploTexGen into an image editing program and cut it apart. Instead of one large texture, we want 16 small ones: one for each frame of the animation.

Creating flipbook animations with egg-texture-cards

Egg-texture-cards is a command-line utility provided with Panda3D. It takes an image and creates a single rectangular polygon with the image set as its texture. The output is an egg file that contains the polygon and the texture information for it. We can also supply multiple images to egg-texture-cards and it will create a polygon for each of them, all in one egg.

The options for egg-texture-cards are accessed by using flags. Each flag is a combination of a hyphen and a letter, or set of letters, and should be followed by the setting for that option. Here are a few examples:

- `-o`—specifies an output filename.
- `-fps`—tells egg-texture-cards the frame rate for the animation.

An example usage of egg-texture-cards could be:

```
Egg-texture-cards.exe -o output.egg input.png
```

By default, the polygons created by egg-texture-cards are automatically placed in a sequence node that we can use to animate them like a flipbook. Of course, we don't have to.

The output egg will have relative filepaths to the images it was created with. It's best to create the egg file in the folder that it will be loaded from, or the filepaths will have to be edited by hand later.

Time for action – using egg-texture-cards

The two flags mentioned earlier are the two we're going to use to create our flipbook animation.

1. We can find `egg-texture-cards.exe` in the `Panda3D-1.6.2/bin` folder. Copy it and paste it into the `BGP3D/Misc` folder.

2. Open a Windows Command Prompt and navigate it to the `BGP3D/Misc` folder.

3. Type the following in and press enter:

```
egg-texture-cards.exe -fps 16 -o EBoom.egg EBoom_00.png EBoom_01.
png EBoom_02.png EBoom_03.png EBoom_04.png EBoom_05.png EBoom_06.
png EBoom_07.png EBoom_08.png EBoom_09.png EBoom_10.png EBoom_11.
png EBoom_12.png EBoom_13.png EBoom_14.png EBoom_15.png
```

```
Command Prompt                                               _ □ ✕

C:\BGP3D\Misc>egg-texture-cards.exe -fps 16 -o EBoom.egg EBoom_00.png EBoom_01.p
ng EBoom_02.png EBoom_03.png EBoom_04.png EBoom_05.png EBoom_06.png EBoom_07.png
 EBoom_08.png EBoom_09.png EBoom_10.png EBoom_11.png EBoom_12.png EBoom_13.png E
Boom_14.png EBoom_15.png

Writing EBoom.egg

C:\BGP3D\Misc>_
```

What just happened?

We've just made an egg file that contains a flipbook animation of our 16 images. Go ahead and open the egg file to take a look.

 It's important to note that the polygons created with egg-texture-cards don't receive lighting terribly well when placed in the 3D scene graph.

We can turn off lighting for them by calling on setLightOff() on the NodePath to solve that problem. That's why the explosions we used in this book were in bam files instead of egg files. They were prepped by being loaded and having setLightOff() called on them. Then, they were saved into bam files to retain that NodePath attribute.

Additional egg-texture-card options

There are three more flags for egg-texture-cards that we'll talk about here. The first is the flag -g, which is used to set the dimensions for the polygon that's created. It takes the left, right, bottom, and top values as inputs. The origin for the card is always at 0. For example, if we wanted these dimensions:

```
Left: -0.25
Right: 1.25
Bottom: -0.4
Top: 0.8
```

We would use the flag like this:

```
egg-texture-cards.exe -g -0.25,1.25,-0.4,0.8
```

If the -g flag isn't supplied, the default dimensions are -0.5, 0.5, -0.5, 0.5, or a one unit square centered on its origin.

The next flag worth mentioning is -p. This flag tells egg-texture-cards the pixel size of an image that exactly fits the polygon described by the dimensions of the -g flag. If both of these flags are used when multiple images are supplied, egg-texture-cards will resize each polygon for each image. That way, images that have different dimensions will get different sized polygons. This method was used to create the egg file that stores the menu backgrounds used in our game.

The last flag is -h, and it's probably the most important. Using the -h flag will make egg-texture-cards print out a help screen that describes every flag we can use. When using -h, we don't have to supply an input or output file. We can just use the flag, like this:

```
egg-texture-cards.exe -h
```

Summary

This short appendix described how to use ExploTexGen with Panda3D. We discussed the usage of ExploTexGen itself and then we went over how we can use egg-texture-cards. exe to convert the output from ExploTexGen into a flipbook animation for Panda3D.

Now, we can easily create beautiful and efficient two-dimensional explosions for all our games.

C
Pop quiz Answers

The answers to the pop quizzes from each chapter are provided here for your reference. How did you score?

Chapter 2: Creating the Universe: Loading Terrain

Starting Panda3D and loading models

Question number	Answer
1	`import direct.directbase.DirectStart`
2	All methods in Panda3D are passed as a reference to the class instance they are called on. We call this reference `self` so we know that it points to the class instance that owns the method.
3	By giving it the keyword name `__init__` we ensured that the method would be called when an instance of the class is created.
4	`import direct.directbase.DirectStart` created the `loader` object.
5	It searched along the path we gave it, starting from the folder where the Python file we ran was located.
6	Bam and Egg files store information on art assets such as models, textures, and animations.
7	Egg files are designed to be human readable and editable with text editing programs. Bam files are built to load quickly and efficiently and are not human readable or editable.

Using NodePath and understanding scene graph inheritance

Question number	Answer
1	A node is one of many types of objects in Panda3D that inherit from the `PandaNode` superclass. A `NodePath` is a handler that points to a node and aids in interacting with that node.
2	They were created automatically by the call to `loader.loadModel()`.
3	It changes the position of a `NodePath` in the scene graph.
4	Model B will also move to a new position in the world, keeping the same relative position to model A.
5	Nothing at all.

Chapter 3: Managing Tasks Over Time

The task manager

Question number	Answer
1	The task manager, called `taskMgr`.
2	`taskMgr.add()` executes the task immediately. `taskMgr.doMethodLater()` gives the task a delay.
3	We can see a list of the tasks in the command prompt by printing the task manager with `print(taskMgr)`.

Delta time

Question number	Answer
1	Delta Time is "change in time" or the amount of time that has passed since the last frame.
2	We use Delta Time to make changes in our game time-based instead of frame-based, so that the change rates are constant regardless of frame rate.

Task return options

Question number	Answer
1	`task.cont`, `task.again`, and `task.done`.
2	`task.done`
3	`task.again`

Chapter 4: Taking Control: Events and User Input

Working with events

Question number	Answer
1	This allowed us to use the `accept()` method to register event responses.
2	The `accept()` method registers an event response. It tells the Panda3D event system what event we want to respond to and what method we want to call when that event is triggered.

Using keyboard input

Question number	Answer
1	A dictionary.
2	`shift-alt-q`

Utilizing mouse input

Question number	Answer
1	This will cause an error that will cause the program to abort and return the user to the desktop.
2	To determine if the mouse is inside the Panda3D window to prevent the error described in the answer to question one.

Chapter 5: Handling Large Programs with Custom Classes

Importing custom classes

Question number	Answer
1	It looks where we tell it to using `from`.
2	We can use the * wildcard, like so: `from file import *`

Accessing custom classes from other classes

Question number	Answer
1	By storing a reference to the second class in a variable in the first class.
2	This creates additional references that will have to be deleted to properly clean up the class instance later on.

Chapter 6: The World in Action: Handling Collisions

Regarding basic collision detection

Question number	Answer
1	A collision solid is a shape used to define a mass for collision purposes.
2	`CollisionNodes` store many variables that determine collision behavior, including collision solids.
3	A `CollisionTraverser` is an object that does the actual work of checking to see if collisions happen.
4	The traverse method is passed as `NodePath`, and the `NodePath` matters because only that `NodePath` and its children will be checked for collisions; the rest of the scene graph won't.

Understanding handlers that generate events

Question number	Answer
1	They generate events based on collisions, according to the patterns that we define for them.
2	A collision entry object.
3	`%fn` and `%in`, which are replaced by the names of the From and Into `CollisionNodes`, respectively.

Understanding BitMasks

Question number	Answer
1	A BitMask is a series of 32 bits that can either be 0 or 1.
2	To limit the amount of possible collisions to the bare minimum to increase the overall performance of the game.
3	Using the setFromCollideMask and setIntoCollideMask methods.
4	A From mask limits what an object can cause a collision with; an Into mask limits what can collide with the masked object.
5	Yes, because bit 5 on both masks is set to 1.

Using Python tags

Question number	Answer
1	Using the setPythonTag() method.
2	Any Python object we want.
3	Using the getPythonTag() method.
4	A PythonTag will retain a reference to whatever is put in it, so we have to be careful to remove these references if we want that object to be removed from memory later.

Complex collision detection

Question number	Answer
1	With the sortEntries() method.
2	To get the CollisionNodes we use the getFromNodePath(), and getIntoNodePath() methods. To get the solids themselves, we use the getFrom() and getInto() methods.
3	Since we had two CollisionRays pointing down from the cycle, we checked to make sure that both of them collided with the track. if either of them didn't, then the cycle went off the track.
4	We used the getSurfacePoint() method of the collision entry object to which we passed render in order to make sure we got the point in the coordinate of the render system. We could pass in a different NodePath to get the point in a different coordinate system.
5	We checked the height of the points where our CollisionRays collided with the track and compared them to determine the slope our cycle was on, and changed our pitch to match it. We did this by placing a reference NodePath at one collision point and telling it to look at the other, which forced the reference NodePath to have the pitch our cycle should have.

Chapter 7: Making it Fancy: Lighting, Textures, Filters, and Shaders

Using lights

Question number	Answer
1	The position and rotation of the NodePath.
2	AmbientLight, DirectionalLight, PointLight, SpotLight
3	It allows per-pixel lighting.

Understanding textures and TextureStages

Question number	Answer
1	A TextureStage is a container for textures that can be applied to objects.
2	To set up the options and variables for how a texture is displayed on an object.
3	Modulate, Add, Replace, Decal, Blend, Gloss, Glow, Normal, ModulateGloss, and ModulateGlow.
4	It writes a NodePath, and all its children, into a bam file that contains all of the options that have been applied to those NodePaths.

Setting up a sky sphere

Question number	Answer
1	background, to ensure that it renders before, and therefore behind, everything else.
2	It scales the Alpha channel of the NodePath. We used it to set the Alpha channel of the skysphere to 0 so that the bloom filter wouldn't affect it.

Chapter 8: GUI Goodness: All About the Graphic User Interface

Understanding DirectGUI

Question number	Answer
1	A set of tools for constructing a graphical user interface.
2	Because they contain a large quantity of optional arguments.
3	The root `NodePath` of a special 2D scene graph that adjusts its contents to compensate for non-square windows.

Creating a Heads Up Display

Question number	Answer
1	We are using it to simulate the movement of the bars.
2	We give it a `TextureStage` to tell it that we want to adjust that `TextureStage`.

Chapter 9: Animating in Panda3D

Animation basics

Question number	Answer
1	An `Actor` is a model that is prepped for animation. `Actors` are loaded using the `Actor` constructor, instead of a method of the `loader` object.
2	They are loaded when the `Actor` is loaded.
3	Egg and bam files, just like models.

Advanced animation

Question number	Answer
1	A specific frame number or numbers.
2	Animation blending, via `myActor.enableBlend()`.
3	Using the `setControlEffect()` method.
4	We need to create and use subparts to play the different animations on.

Chapter 10: Creating Weaponry: Using Mouse Picking and Intervals

Mouse picking

Question number	Answer
1	We used the `setFromLens()` method. This method takes a camera node, an X-coordinate, and a Y-coordinate. The intended coordinates are the mouse coordinates from `base.mouseWatcher.getMouse`. The method places the `CollisionRay` at the position of the camera and points it through the mouse coordinates out into space.
2	We used `getSurfacePoint()` to find the exact location of the collision.

Intervals

Question number	Answer
1	An `Interval` has a defined duration, or start and stop values. An `Interval` also can be controlled in a similar fashion to animations. Neither of these is true for tasks.
2	A `Sequence` is a collection of `Intervals` that will be played one after another. A `Parallel` is a collection of `Intervals` that will all be played at the same time. Only `Intervals` may be put in either.
3	`Func` and `Wait` are used for creating scripts with `Sequences` and `Parallels`. The `Func Interval` simply calls a function or method. `Wait` does nothing, for a set amount of time.
4	`isPlaying()` and `isStopped()`. `isPlaying()` will return `True` if the Interval is paused; `isStopped` will return `False` in that case.
5	We use the `getDuration()` method.
6	We use the `getT()` method.

Chapter 11: What's that Noise? Using Sound

Making music

Question number	Answer
1	A grouping object for sounds that allow multiple sounds to be controlled at once.
2	A list of sound effects `AudioManagers` with one `AudioManager` in the list and a music `AudioManager`. We can conveniently control these `AudioManagers` with methods of `base`.
3	`getSound()`.
4	Using the `setLoop()` method like so: `mySound.setLoop(True)`.

Sounding off

Question number	Answer
1	A wrapper for an `AudioManager` that causes the sound to emit from a specific location within the Panda3D world.
2	We must use the `loadSfx()` method.

Chapter 12: Finishing Touches: Getting the Game Ready for the Customer

Garbage collection

Question number	Answer
1	◆ Call `removeNode()` on all `NodePaths` in the scene graph ◆ Clean out collision systems ◆ Call `delete()` on all `Actors` ◆ Call `destroy()` on all `DirectGui` objects ◆ Set all `Intervals`, `Sequences`, and `Parallels` equal to `None` ◆ Detach all 3D sounds connected to class `NodePaths` ◆ End all tasks running in the class ◆ If the custom class inherits from `DirectObject`, call `self.ignoreAll()` ◆ Remove all direct references to the custom class instance
2	`removeCollider` is only necessary when the `CollisionTraverser` and/or `CollisionHandler` aren't being removed.

Using a custom mouse cursor

Question number	Answer
1	We use `setBin()` to ensure that the mouse cursor geometry will be rendered on top of any menus or other 2D elements.
2	`base.mouseWatcherNode.setGeometry`.

Building an installer

Question number	Answer
1	`main.py`, and it must be found directly in the folder supplied to `packpanda.exe`, not any subfolders.
2	`installer.bmp` is a 164x314 bitmap image. `icon.ico` is a Windows icon file. `license.txt` is an ASCII text file.

Index

Thank you for buying
Panda3D 1.6 Game Engine Beginner's Guide

About Packt Publishing

Packt, pronounced 'packed', published its first book "*Mastering phpMyAdmin for Effective MySQL Management*" in April 2004 and subsequently continued to specialize in publishing highly focused books on specific technologies and solutions.

Our books and publications share the experiences of your fellow IT professionals in adapting and customizing today's systems, applications, and frameworks. Our solution based books give you the knowledge and power to customize the software and technologies you're using to get the job done. Packt books are more specific and less general than the IT books you have seen in the past. Our unique business model allows us to bring you more focused information, giving you more of what you need to know, and less of what you don't.

Packt is a modern, yet unique publishing company, which focuses on producing quality, cutting-edge books for communities of developers, administrators, and newbies alike. For more information, please visit our website: www.packtpub.com.

About Packt Open Source

In 2010, Packt launched two new brands, Packt Open Source and Packt Enterprise, in order to continue its focus on specialization. This book is part of the Packt Open Source brand, home to books published on software built around Open Source licences, and offering information to anybody from advanced developers to budding web designers. The Open Source brand also runs Packt's Open Source Royalty Scheme, by which Packt gives a royalty to each Open Source project about whose software a book is sold.

Writing for Packt

We welcome all inquiries from people who are interested in authoring. Book proposals should be sent to author@packtpub.com. If your book idea is still at an early stage and you would like to discuss it first before writing a formal book proposal, contact us; one of our commissioning editors will get in touch with you.

We're not just looking for published authors; if you have strong technical skills but no writing experience, our experienced editors can help you develop a writing career, or simply get some additional reward for your expertise.

3D Game Development with Microsoft Silverlight 3: Beginner's Guide

ISBN: 978-1-847198-92-1   Paperback: 454 pages

A practical guide to creating real-time responsive online 3D games in Silverlight 3 using C#, XBAP WPF, XAML, Balder, and Farseer Physics Engine.

1. Develop online interactive 3D games and scenes in Microsoft Silverlight 3 and XBAP WPF

2. Integrate Balder 3D engine 1.0, Farseer Physics Engine 2.1, and advanced object-oriented techniques to simplify the game development process

3. Enhance development with animated 3D characters, sounds, music, physics, stages, gauges, and backgrounds

Flash Multiplayer Virtual Worlds

ISBN: 978-1-849690-36-2   Paperback: 412 pages

Build immersive, full-featured interactive worlds for games, online communities, and more

1. Build virtual worlds in Flash and enhance them with avatars, non player characters, quests, and by adding social network community

2. Design, present, and integrate the quests to the virtual worlds

3. Create a whiteboard that every connected user can draw on

Please check **www.PacktPub.com** for information on our titles

Irrlicht 1.7.1 Realtime 3D Engine Beginner's Guide: RAW

ISBN: 978-1-849513-98-2   Paperback: 300 pages

Create complete 2D and 3D applications with this cross-platform, high performance engine

1. A comprehensive guide for C++ programmers to learn Irrlicht from scratch

2. Learn to add, manipulate, and animate meshes

3. Manage scenes, nodes, and cameras

4. Use particle systems, shaders, and lights for enhancement

Cocos2d for iPhone 0.99 Beginner's Guide

ISBN: 978-1-849513-16-6   Paperback: 368 pages

Make mind-blowing 2D games for iPhone with this fast, flexible, and easy-to-use framework!

1. A cool guide to learning cocos2d with iPhone to get you into the iPhone game industry quickly

2. Learn all the aspects of cocos2d while building three different games

3. Learn all the aspects of cocos2d while building three different games

Please check **www.PacktPub.com** for information on our titles

Panda3D 1.7 Game Developer's Cookbook

ISBN: 978-1-849512-92-3   Paperback: 344 pages

Over 80 recipes for developing 3D games with Panda3D, a full-scale 3D game engine

1. Dive into the advanced features of the Panda3D engine

2. Take control of the renderer and use shaders to create stunning graphics

3. Give your games a professional look using special effects and post-processing filters

3D Graphics with XNA Game Studio 4.0

ISBN: 978-1-849690-04-1   Paperback: 292 pages

A step-by-step guide to adding the 3D graphics effects used by professionals to your XNA games.

1. Improve the appearance of your games by implementing the same techniques used by professionals in the game industry

2. Learn the fundamentals of 3D graphics, including common 3D math and the graphics pipeline

3. Create an extensible system to draw 3D models and other effects, and learn the skills to create your own effects and animate them

Please check **www.PacktPub.com** for information on our titles

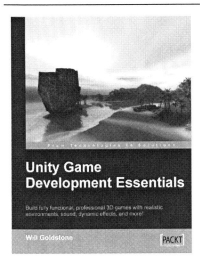

CPSIA information can be obtained at www.ICGtesting.com
Printed in the USA
BVOW071447071011

273078BV00004B/19/P